Karen Harvey is a devoted mother of two children and six fur babies. She had a happy childhood growing up and has always worked in a healthcare setting, first animal, then human.

She loves to write, having written poetry in her twenties, some of them published, but her real passion was to always write a book. She never imagined that it would be one written on her true-life experience of being entangled with a narcissist.

On life, Karen believes that everything happens for a reason, and this has led to her writing this book and sharing her experience now.

To all the victims and survivors of all types of domestic abuse. Stay strong, keep moving forward and never look back. You got this! For all those still struggling to leave, you ARE brave, you ARE strong, and YOU have got this too!

Karen Harvey

'I PROMISE I'LL MAKE YOU HAPPY'

AUSTIN MACAULEY PUBLISHERS™

LONDON • CAMBRIDGE • NEW YORK • SHARJAH

A CIP catalogue record for this title is available from the British Library.

ISBN 9781398433168 (Paperback)
ISBN 9781398433175 (ePub e-book)

www.austinmacauley.com

First Published 2022
Austin Macauley Publishers Ltd®
1 Canada Square
Canary Wharf
London
E14 5AA

It goes without saying that it is only fitting and correct that I give thanks to the authors of all the books and articles that I have read along the way, which inspired me to write this book. Without my journey into narcissism and without the help and knowledge that I achieved from reading these, this book would not have been possible.

Massive thank you, especially to HG Tudor and Maria Consiglio whose knowledge and material has proved invaluable to me in the production of this book. I have the greatest respect for their knowledge and insights into narcissism.

Also, to all the online web pages, support sites and forums whose quotes I have so gratefully used throughout the book. I hope the use of these quotes will inspire the readers just in the same way that they have inspired me.

I want to also thank my family and friends, without their constant love and support, and without their unwavering confidence in me to write this book and get my story down on print, it may never have been finished. Thank you also for being my proof-readers when the book was finished and for critiquing it for me. Thank you for always believing in me, for supporting me over the years and for providing me with constant and invaluable advice along the way.

Most of all, I want to thank my two beautiful, wonderful children, Adam and Megan, for ALWAYS being there for me. Thank you for your endless support, for your patience, for your advice, but most of all for your unconditional love, trust and belief in me, not only as a mother but also as a person. I love you both to the moon and back!

A special thank you as well to an extremely talented young man by the name of Craig Cumberton who helped design and create my book cover. The graphics and finished product were all his hard work too. You can find him on Instagram under the name cumbertoons where he brings to life animation that has been created, drawn and designed entirely by him. His talent is truly endless.

Table of Contents

Introduction

Quite a catchy book title, don't you think?

I can promise you that it was not thought up in a nostalgic cheesy moment, nor was it done with any sentimental meaning or thought behind it.

It was a sentence that my narcissistic ex-husband (Nex) once said to me at the very beginning of our relationship when I was packing up my entire life, and that of my two children's so that I could move across the country to embark on a new life with him.

I never forgot it. Why?

Because I went on to spend so many times after that moment muttering the comment to myself sarcastically while following it rapidly with my own muttered comment of, 'But instead I've spent more time crying!' This was a fact that I had genuinely spent more time crying in our fourteen years together then I had in my entire life up to the point that I met him at the age of forty-one. My Nex did not even know how to make himself happy, let alone anyone else.

So, the next thing you are probably wondering is what led me to write this book? Well, I have always said that I wanted to write a book and that it would probably be when I was old and grey (not quite there yet!) and I always thought that it would be a nice romantic fiction novel or something like that. They say that 'Everyone has a book inside of them' and I guess when the right moment presents itself, you just know. For me, this was and is the right moment. Though it was not to be some nice fictional love story, rather instead, it is an informative and true account of narcissism and narcissists and my own true-life story of being in an abusive relationship with one and living with them.

I guess that after reading so very many books and articles on narcissism and narcissists, I came to realise that they were all just a little bit too 'clinical'. Too much description with science-based facts but without any true-life stories attached to them. Yes, there were references of the author experiencing an instance of say 'love-bombing' or 'devaluation' but not often with an account of what they really experienced or went through. I realised that I wanted to read a book that was an account of someone's real life with a narcissist with the 'clinical' details and terminology littered throughout so that I could clearly see what love-bombing meant or looked like, or what a devaluation actually was. I could compare my experiences when reading those books, but it was not quite the same thing as reading about one on the page, 'seeing' it come to life, and I needed to be really sure that this was what I had experienced. As I have already stated, I have longed to write a book my entire life and have always thought that maybe I would get round to it when I retired (another point my ex-narcissistic husband belittled me about, which I will tell you about later) but the longing to get my story down on paper was so overwhelming that I just had to start writing it and once I started writing, I decided that I would turn it into a book. My hope was that it would be a cathartic experience for me coupled with an account of events that other people could acknowledge and relate to, draw comfort from and even recognise themselves in it and have the courage to leave an abusive relationship if still in one.

Most of the books I have read and came across delivered fact after fact to me as to what a narcissist was, what made them tick, why they were one, how they viewed the world, etc, and why you had finally ended up in that awful moment of realisation that just maybe this was what was wrong with your relationship, and why you had always known that it was not a normal relationship. Which, do not get me wrong, was an absolute life saver for me, both physically and mentally, but I still felt something was missing.

I could not get enough of scouring Amazon for more books to download to my Kindle and read or search the narcissist support group sites on Facebook and Instagram for articles on narcissists. After deciding that I would turn my experience into a book, I spent more than six months extensively researching and reading about narcissists and narcissism. This was when I then experienced my biggest lightbulb moment. Do not get me wrong, there were plenty of those moments over the period of intense reading I can tell you. Some were like so many flashbulbs exploding in my face all at once, but the one big defining moment, the one almighty thunderclap flash of the lightening lightbulb moment came when I was on holiday with my daughter in September 2019, more than fourteen months since day one... Day one: I hear you mutter rather confused? Well let me enlighten you. Day one for me is the first day of the rest of my life, the day that my relationship with my narcissist was finally over. The day that I knew I would no longer have to walk on eggshells throughout my life anymore. The day I would no longer have to think about how to say something so it would not be taken the wrong way but still inadvertently would be no matter how much thought I had put into it. The day of no more devaluation, invalidation, gaslighting, projection, blame-shifting, stonewalling, lies, silent treatment (Yay!) and so on. The day I finally knew that I had 'escaped' and now had the rest of my life to look forward to, narcissist free. Except of course it was not quite like that as I went on to face the mother of all nightmares post-split!

So, back to my holiday. The only books I had downloaded onto my kindle were of course about narcissistic relationships and narcissism. No 'Fifty Shades of Grey' for me this time! One book was written by someone who had encountered narcissists from as early on as their childhood and who narcissists were particularly drawn to. She pretty much said a lot of what all the other books had, just with a different slant to it. But the one massive, humongous lightbulb moment for me was when she wrote that to move forward you had to accept that your narcissist had never actually loved you. Never! Not ever! Great big fat zilch where love was concerned!

Wow! What a concept to try and get your head around. What a thought to mull over. For me, that meant denying what I thought had been real for fourteen years of my life! Accepting that those fourteen years had all been based on a lie. An illusion, a façade, fake.

Trust me when I say that the first time you read this fact, digest it and let it sink in is not a moment to be trivialised, that is for sure. To recognise this fact and realise and accept that the one feeling you thought was real in your relationship and had been real, was not real at all. That one feeling that you used as an excuse for their behaviour towards you, the one feeling that stopped you from ever leaving them before, this is a massive definite 'stop you in your tracks' kind of moment. Just like you have been punched in the face. Which I guess in a way you have. To realise that your partner, your husband, had never actually loved you, is one where you will beat yourself up over until you realise that it is not because they chose not to love you but rather because they are actually incapable of feeling love towards another human being. A narcissist is devoid of how it feels, they can mimic love and mirror it and know how to say it and make it look like they do love you but deep down they just do not

13

feel it. What they are doing is mimicking and mirroring your actual feelings for them. This is something that they have learnt how to do over time to achieve their goals and ultimately ensnare a victim – their partner.

A narcissist is devoid of so many emotions that you or I would just take for granted. Yes, they feel anger, jealousy, superiority, hate, rage and entitlement, but they do not feel love, compassion or empathy. The emotions that they do feel we will look at further on in this book. We will also look at why they do not feel love, compassion or empathy.

Most importantly, I am hoping that this book will help anyone caught up with a narcissist – present or past, and personally – to understand what they went through or are currently going through, recognise what has happened to them and why, and then how to move forward, physically and emotionally, from their entanglement with a narcissist. This book is designed and written with intimate relationships in mind rather than family, professional or child narcissists.

We will look at what is a narcissist? We will look at the sub-divisions of one, their make-up, the different traits involved, how they operate, how they ensnare you, how they prevent you from leaving, what exactly drives them and most importantly how they will never change and why. Also, we will look at the 'red flags' that they display to help your avoidance of their kind. Hopefully by achieving all of these aims it will help you to establish and understand what kind of narcissist exactly you are dealing with, or dealt with, so going forward you will be able to make informed decisions and choices but most importantly will know what to look out for in future so you will never be a victim of one again.

As I said at the start, I will be using my own personal examples and accounts throughout in the hope that you will recognise some of this behaviour, identify with it and most importantly understand it and maybe even recognise a reflection of your own life?

I will also be making references in my book to certain professionals and quotes that I have come across but especially with one individual in mind whose articles and books I have found to be so invaluable in my understanding, acceptance and recovery phases and during the writing of this book. Ironically, he himself is a narcissist, a 'greater' to be precise. So, who better to accurately dissect and ruminate the makeup of a narcissist? This person goes by the pseudonym of HG Tudor. His articles, available online, are found under the title 'Knowing the Narcissist'. He also has a website called Narcsite.com. His description of a narcissist and narcissism, the attention to detail, the honest and sometimes brutal descriptions and explanations really are second to none. Real eye openers and quite literally, lifesavers.

Normally a narcissist will not acknowledge what they are, and in fact they will go to great lengths to deny it vehemently and of course, to mask it. This narcissist, HG Tudor, through therapy, has acknowledged and accepted what he is. This does not mean though that he accepts blame of any kind. Oh no, rather as you read his articles and books you might be forgiven in thinking that his acknowledgement of being a narcissist and the subsequent therapy that he is receiving will 'cure' him of his narcissism. Which will allow him to see a perspective from his victim's point of view. But of course, it will not. The Therapy has purely helped him to understand his behaviour and subsequently write about it.

When psychotherapists talk about narcissists never being able to change, and why they cannot change, you can be forgiven for thinking that 'surely some can'. The answer is still no. No, they cannot change. If they are low down on the spectrum then there may be a chance to get them to look at their behaviour and maybe even accept blame and adjust, but not if they are a full-blown narcissist. They simply will not and cannot change.

What HG Tudor does with his brilliant insightful writing, is make you realise and understand why this finding is completely true and that it really is a fact. Once a narc, always a narc. What makes reading his material even more compelling and interesting is again the very fact that he goes into such great detail as to exactly what he receives from his narcissistic behaviour and how and why he devours the narcissists' life force, which is classed as either fuel or narcissistic supply. Quite simply, you begin to understand why a narcissist behaves the way that they do, and you start to have an understanding into narcissism.

To help you understand the terminology involved with narcissism and narcissists, I have created an Index at the start of this book, before the first chapter, because I found that while I was reading books and articles on the subject, I was constantly pausing and 'googling' what a particular term of phrase was or what it actually meant so I could then understand that phrase, description or terminology. I found this to be time consuming and frustrating, especially if at that precise moment, the internet was not accessible. Therefore, it is at the start of the book for you to keep referring to if you need to as you make your way through it.

I can certainly promise you that I have not written this book to 'score points' or avenge any wounded pride. Rather, it was written as a cathartic exercise. To understand, acknowledge and accept what I had experienced. But most of all, for closure. Closure is of course something your narcissist will never give you, so I found the best way for me to achieve it was to understand what I had been through and to seek it myself. Do not get me wrong, at times things were 'great' with the narcissist in my life, in fact he could even make me laugh sometimes, but what you have to realise is that during these 'idealisation phases' (we look at this later), everything in the narcissists world was and is rosy, and you are at that moment painted white instead of black because you are supplying him with what he craves, and that is the only reason why you were, and are given a brief respite, and a slighting glimpse of what happiness could look like. But the fact of the matter is that these idealisation moments were and are nothing more than fake.

I have also come to realise that my journey through life so far has been littered with narcissists, especially in my working life; I just never knew it. I just always knew that there was something wrong with a particular certain individual, be it a work colleague or even a friend, but I just shook it off and simply put it down to a negative experience in my life.

For the purpose of this book, I will refer throughout to my narcissist as the NEX (Nex), quite simply translated as narcissistic ex. I have of course much stronger terminology that I use with family and friends but for the purpose of this book I will keep it clean.

I will also at times shorten their title to just narc which of course is short for narcissist.

Lastly, you will also discover littered throughout the book, phrases and quotes that I have come across on my journey of enlightenment that I found to be brutally true, useful, informative, soothing, and at times healing. I hope my use of them will also be of some use and comfort to you too.

Never admits to being wrong

Avoids emotions and accountability

Rages if anyone challenges them

Childish when they do not get their own way

Instils doubt in their victims

Stonewalls during conflicts
Smears and slanders you
In denial and gaslights, you
Subjects you to the silent treatment
Triangulates you and tears you down
'Shahida Arabi'

Index of Terminology

Overt Narcissist: This is a very typical narcissist who cannot hide their feelings of superiority or grandiosity. Their emotional displays are played out for all to see, and their arrogance and sense of entitlement is in full view.

Covert Narcissist: This is a narcissist who can hide his narcissism and feelings of superiority and entitlement. They will come across to the general public as nice, charming, amiable and compliant whilst saving their vitriol of narcissistic behaviour for you, their victim. They are probably one of the worst kinds of narcissists because their behaviour towards you is insidious, and is delivered slowly, so as not to alert you as to what they are. Therefore, you can be in a relationship with a covert narcissist for many years without connecting all the dots and not understanding why your relationship is not normal.

Malignant Narcissist: As well as the necessary fuel supply, these types gain actual pleasure from hurting others. You will generally see aggressiveness, deceit and no remorse from one of these.

Love Bombing/Idealisation: This is displayed at the start of the relationship but will also be used as part of a cycle throughout the relationship. It is used to impress and ensnare you at the beginning and latterly to retain you and throw you off guard. You are showered with overtly displays of warmth, attention and flattery. Constant praise is given, gifts, promises of undying love, soulmates, promises of a future together and ultimately a quick commitment.

Devaluation: This phase starts when the narcissist is bored of you, or their rose-coloured glasses of you have fallen off, or when you have stopped supplying them with their beloved fuel. Or if they have suffered a perceived 'injury' by you – real or not. This is when you will encounter verbal abuse, mind games, gaslighting, blame-shifting, projection, 'one-upmanships', provocation of arguments and fights and even smear campaigns. Also, for some victims, violence. This phase has no set timetable to it at all.

Dosing: These are 'drip fed' moments of normality or positive attention from the narcissist and can consist of moments of love-bombing or idealisation. Usually initiated when devaluation is taking place simply to keep their victim on their toes and to string them along and allow them to believe all is okay.

Discard: This is the phase where the narcissist will discard you. It could be an ultimate final one or it could be a 'virtual' discard coming many times over as part of the Idealize-Devalue-Discard cycle that is commonly deployed by the Narcissist. These can and will go on for months and years, especially with a covert narcissist.

Fuel: Otherwise known as 'narcissistic supply'. This is the narcissist's life-force. It is what he or she lives for, breathes for, exists for and craves. Without it they simply cannot function. The fuel comes via one of three ways. Positive, negative or challenge. It also comes from many 'supply' sources, such as family, friends and work, but the main constant source is obviously from the intimate partner (you). Every aspect and moment of your relationship with the narcissist is spent with them seeking and acquiring this fuel from you.

Supply: This is anyone or anything that provides the narcissist with their fuel to enhance his/her self-esteem. It consists of adoration, attention, respect, love, and if negative supply then fear, sorrow, anguish, despair and even hate. A narcissist requires a continuous constant supply of fuel to be able to function.

Blame-Shifting: This is the narcissist blaming their entire actions on you. It is your fault that they acted the way they did, however bad. You caused it. If not you directly, then they will blame stress, work, alcohol or some other factor as long as it is not them.

Mirroring: This is where the narcissist becomes just like you. They will copy your mannerisms, your likes and dislikes, even your behaviour. This is normally part of the love-bombing phase.

Projection: Here the narcissist will project his or her flaws and bad behaviour on to you. They simply will not allow any accountability for their actions, instead placing this blame directly and entirely on to you.

Gaslighting: Taken from the 1944 movie title 'Gaslight' it means that the narcissist will make you believe that you are going crazy. They achieve this through manipulation. They provide you with conflicting information, even if the facts are staring you in the face. They will lie outright and deny any wrongdoing, even if they have been caught in the act, they will attempt to make you think you are paranoid or delusional even when they are presented with the facts. You end up questioning yourself and your own perception of reality and even possibly your feelings of sanity. It is classed as a form of psychological and emotional abuse.

Word Salad: This is disorganised and confusing speech by the narcissist. Normally made up of lies, denial and confabulation to avoid being wrong or blamed for something. Interestingly, the formal name for this is 'schizophasia'.

Triangulation: This is where the narcissist will involve a third party to try and generate jealousy from you. This is done purely to boost their ego. It has also been described in psychology as meaning controlling and manipulating communication between two parties. It is related to gossiping, smearing and slandering also, when the narcissist is spreading false information and lies about you. It can also involve another love interest.

Stonewalling: This is a refusal to communicate or cooperate with you. It is used by the narcissist to manipulate and control you. It has been described as using a tactic by a bully to control a situation and to isolate, humiliate and frustrate their victim when the victim is trying to resolve a conflict through reasonable discussion.

Silent Treatment: This is one of the narcissists' favourite weapons. It is exactly as it says, they will ignore you completely, even if you live with them. It can last hours, days or even weeks. It is deployed by the narcissist as a form of punishment and to exert power and control over you. It is recognised as a form of emotional abuse.

Ghosting: This is a common tactic used by a narcissist when they discard you. They will suddenly disappear without a trace, and usually without any warning whatsoever. They will ignore your every attempt to communicate with them, going so far as to change their phone number and block you on social media.

Hoovering: Exactly as in a vacuum cleaner. An attempt by the narcissist to suck you back into the relationship with declarations of love and false apologies. This can also be a negative or 'Malign Hoover' attempt by the narcissist purely to obtain and suck in fuel. It will come in the form of verbal or written abuse in the hope you will respond and then engage with them. It is usually deployed when a relationship has ended, either by them or by you.

Flying Monkeys: Taken from the book 'The Wizard of Oz' this simply applies to the group of people that the narcissist has engaged or enrolled to enact their evil on the narcissist's victim. They are usually enticed by lies about the victim. They will always side with the narcissist and believe what they say.

Smear Campaign: This will be deployed by the narcissist against you either before discard, during it or after it. It is used to discredit you and gain support for themselves. If you are the one who has left the narcissist, this campaign against you will be vicious and extreme because your 'discard' of them will be perceived as a 'narcissistic injury' to them. If you have dared to call them on what they really are, then the smear campaign will be used to protect their false image.

Narcissistic Injury: This is what a narcissist feels when you have threatened or criticized them, whether for real or in their warped opinion. They will take this as a direct insult, a disagreement against them or even an ultimate act of rejection and it will wound them severely and deeply. Their need for revenge will be intense.

Red flags: These are indicators and warning signs that the narcissist will display that will warn you that your relationship is toxic. Recognising them can be invaluable to you.

Grey Rock: If you do have to communicate with the narcissist then this is you being unemotional, neutral, boring and uninteresting to them. The aim of this is to simply not provide them with what they seek the most, which is their fuel.

No Contact: This is establishing a set of self-imposed rules of absolutely no contact with the narcissist. This means no phone calls, texts, emails and social media interaction. You are placing an invisible wall between you and them. This is seen to be an invaluable tool for all victims to adopt and will benefit them greatly in moving on and more importantly preventing the narcissist from attempting a 'Hoover' manoeuvre.

Invalidation: This is used by a narcissist to make you believe that your opinions and thoughts are not correct or valid, or that your thoughts and feelings are not important and do not matter. That you are a nobody.

Narcissistic Rage: A direct reaction to the 'injury' that they perceive to have received. This will manifest by way of a 'temper tantrum', aggressive behaviour, violent behaviour, rows or even 'ghosting', 'stonewalling' and 'the silent treatment'. Maybe even a 'discard'.

Trauma Bonding: This is where a narcissist's victim becomes emotionally attached to them to the point where they cannot leave the narcissist. The victim remains loyal to them at all costs. The narcissist programmes you to accept their bad behaviour with the use of slow and insidious abuse. You are made to feel unworthy, invalidated and unimportant. Then you are suddenly subjected to slithers of niceness and hope. Then back to the abuse. The bond is strengthened by this inconsistent positive reinforcement. A more formal definition is that 'trauma bonding' is a strong and emotional attachment between an abused person and their abuser, formed as a result of the cycle of abuse.

Splitting: A narcissists' view of you. Basically, you are good, or you are bad, you are black, or you are white. With a narcissist, there is no grey. This viewpoint of theirs is what can cause the dramatic swings you will encounter. One minute all is fine and the very next minute you are subjected to a violent outburst of rage or even the silent treatment and you are left wondering what the hell has happened or caused it.

Baiting: This is when the narcissist will deliberately goad you into a row or a fight with them. It is a deliberate act of provocation by them purely to obtain their precious fuel from you by invoking an emotional response. This can also be enacted if the narcissist is angry with you, but you are unaware of this.

Coercive Control: This can be Overt or Covert. The narcissist will attempt to control every aspect of your life from what you wear, to what friends you see, your career and even your finances. It can be covered by a pretence that it is born out of love or concern. The start can be very subtle or even hidden, so by the time you realise anything is amiss you may have already been isolated from your family or friends. It can also be of an insidious nature where the narcissist will make such comments, so they appear to be made from love and care, but they are not.

Double Standards: A narcissist really lives by the motto 'Do as I say and not as I do'. He/she will often have two sets of rules. One that he/she will follow and one that is for everyone else to follow. This is usually born out of their sense of entitlement and feelings of superiority. They will expect everyone to follow their rules for them in their entirety all the while ignoring the rules totally themselves as they will simply not apply to them at all.

Futureproofing or Faking: These are generally events that the narcissist says will happen, but they never will. They are used to keep their victim interested, confused, attached or even close to the narcissist. If the victim has suffered a period of 'devaluation and/or discard', this part will come during the 'idealisation' phase to throw the victim off balance and to cover up what abuse they have just encountered.

Reactive Abuse: The narcissist will deliberately antagonise you to generate a reaction. You end up shouting at them and then they will point the finger of blame at you and accuse you of being the abusive one. This can happen so often that you start to doubt yourself as to who is the abuser and who is not. A narcissist will do this to make you think that you are the problem and not them. That you are the crazy and abusive one and not them. You are purely reacting to their abuse.

Chapter One
What Is a Narcissist?

I must confess to having never really paid any attention to the turn of phrase 'Narcissist' before. Oh, for sure I had read the word in news articles and heard it mentioned occasionally on the TV and the Radio in the past, but I never really had any cause to pay particular attention to it. It never piqued my interest enough to 'google' its meaning, or research what it meant or find out what one was. After all, a narcissist is extremely good at hiding behind their false mask so why would I. I did not know that I had one living right under my very nose!

This though all changed for me in the spring of 2018 towards the very end of my marriage to my Nex. I cannot pinpoint exactly when it occurred, but a friend and colleague mentioned the word narcissist and pointedly asked me if I had ever considered the fact that my husband could be one. Of course, this did then pique my interest so I finally 'googled' the word narcissist and up popped article after article and I was suddenly consumed with an overwhelming desire to find out as much as I could on the topic of narcissism and narcissists. It was when we had finally split up only a few weeks later that I guess what I had set out to do initially was to prove to myself that he was not one, that the man I had married and lived with for almost fourteen years and more importantly had loved, could not possibly be a narcissist, but I could not ignore it any longer. I mean how could he be a narcissist? To even begin to believe or accept this meant that I had to face the fact that my life as I had known it had not been real, was not real. That it was a total lie and had always been a total lie, that what I had believed was true, was not. But I could not deny it any longer. The evidence was completely over-whelming, and I became obsessed with the topic. I think that deep down I was trying to find a rational reason for his behaviour, just one small point that would jump out and show me that he was not one. I really wanted to prove to myself that I had got it so wrong, and that my husband could never be labelled as a narcissist. But I could not. All it did instead with my newfound knowledge was prove more and more that my husband was in fact a narcissist, and I do not mean that he just displayed traits of one either. I mean that he was a full-blown bona fide narcissist!

So, where does the phrase narcissism and narcissist originate from?

Narcissus was a mythical Greek god who fell in love with his own image, so much so that he died next to a pool of water, so self-obsessed that he would not leave his own reflection.

The phrases, Narcissus-like, narcissism and narcissistic personality disorder, followed in 1898, 1899, 1911, 1914 and finally later on in the nineteenth century.

Interestingly, narcissus is also the name of a flower that looks like a daffodil.

Hashtag, narcissisticabusesurvivor have a quote that describes narcissism in a nutshell:

'You're tricked into thinking that you've found your soulmate, when actually you've met the person who will be the cause of some of the lowest moments in your life.'

So, just a little bit of history as to what brought me to this very point of writing my book; When the Nex and I did finally split at the end of June 2018, I still did not know what a 'discard' was. For me, I had experienced so many 'end of relationship' scenarios with the Nex that it was not uncommon or unusual. This particular day was a completely innocent day, with him having gone to price a job (self-employed builder) while I went to view a house. Ours was on the market and had been since the previous October. I had forgotten about the viewing so had also forgot to mention it to him, but I went along anyway with the intention of filling him in about it later and whether it rated a second viewing. I was bowled over with the property, namely because of the fantastic workshop that went with it. It was perfect for my Nex's business requirements. He had previously been turned down for planning permission on our current property, so this was an essential requirement of where we bought next. I made the fatal mistake of calling him while I was at the property to see if he were free to come and join me as I could clearly see that the property had a lot to offer. He moaned at me for not telling him about the viewing sooner and would not accept my explanation that I had simply forgot. He still refused to come, and I ended the call. I arrived home about half an hour later to find he had gone out. When I asked my daughter where he was, she was surprised that he was not in as he had been only moments earlier nor had he said that he was going out and nor had he said goodbye to her. She informed me that I had been on loudspeaker when I had called him so when the call had ended she had asked him why he did not go to view the house with me. It was an innocent enough question. She went on to say to him what was the point in viewings if he was not going to view the properties with me. He then informed her that he did not want to move at all and that he wanted to remain living where we were (this was news to me!). He then went AWOL for almost five hours. He ghosted me and did not answer his phone or respond to any text messages that I sent. When he finally returned home he, disappeared straight upstairs so I went up to speak to him and to find out where he had been, and he said that he had been thinking about what my daughter had said and he thought she was right, 'What was the point?'. The big major difference here was the fact that my daughter had simply referred to what was the point in viewing any properties unless we viewed them together. My Nex on the other hand took this to mean what was the point of 'us', what was the point of 'our' relationship. He stated that it had made him think that she was right, what was the point of our relationship. He would not accept that he had read it wrong, even when my daughter tried to say she had not meant it like that. Well of course he would not accept that he was wrong, knowing what I now know about narcissism.

Now this was not the first time that the Nex had 'threatened' me with the end of our relationship either. It was often dished out on a regular basis after an argument/disagreement/sulk regardless as to whether everything had been fine just prior to that exact moment. Almost all our arguments or disagreements usually came out of nowhere and were instigated by the Nex and would usually be over the most stupid trivial thing or perceived slight that he had felt. In the beginning it did alarm me, but I gradually learnt that he never meant it and that it was used as a way for him to not only 'win' but also to control me. I never once knew the meaning behind the end of the relationship threat or that they were 'virtual' discards until later that year once I had started to read so much about narcissism. I just knew at the time that it was not normal behaviour. Once I did learn about narcissists though, I did learn that a discard or end of the relationship scenario were used as a form of control and manipulation. And that it was a favourite method meted out by a narcissist.

Most telling of all though that this was merely yet another virtual discard by the Nex was the fact that he had sent me a text message only a matter of a few weeks earlier telling me that he 'loved me', (a brief idealisation moment).

So, back to that end of that June in 2018 and I just assumed at this point that this was simply another one of his usual tricks. I then experienced his most favourite trait of all which was the 'silent treatment'. Again, even though I knew that is what it was I never knew it was a specific emotionally abusive form of control and punishment used by a narcissist. As I was going away for work that Sunday evening in preparation for a work course the next day, I informed the Nex that he needed to think about what he wanted and whether he had meant it or not. On the Tuesday, two days later, I texted him as I was due home the next day and was concerned with what I would be walking into. I asked him if he had meant what he had said and unsurprisingly I received no response. I still did not know at this point if this was for real or not as he had played 'The boy who cried wolf' and instigated virtual discards so many times in the past. I returned home on the Wednesday and asked him again if he had meant what he had said, and he said yes he did. Again, nothing unusual going on past events so I still did not know for sure whether to believe him or not and he then resorted back to a further bout of the Silent Treatment against me, again nothing unusual as I had experienced so many of them over the years. I simply slept in the spare bedroom on my return.

Roll on to the following Saturday and Sunday at the start of July, and I remember clearly that it was a hot two days as my daughter, and I were sunbathing outside. On the Sunday evening, we were travelling to Wales as I was working away for a few days and my daughter and boyfriend were travelling down with me. While my daughter and I were laying outside, the Nex came out and stated that I could file for the divorce (I now know this to be called Baiting), and I simply agreed with him and said that I would. He then said that he would see if he could buy me out of the house, again to which I simply replied in agreement with him (yet another Baiting attempt by him). I knew then at this point that he was spoiling for a fight, and I was determined that he was not going to get one. If he had meant what he had said that we were over, then I was more than okay with it. To be honest it had been a long time coming as I had started to accept that his unpredictable unreasonable cold behaviour towards me was not normal and would never change, and the love that I had once felt for him had been slowly chipped away from years of abuse by him. I do not want to go into too much detail on the abuse at this point as it is more relevant throughout the book as examples of what I am going to explain as narcissistic behaviour and abuse.

So, I then went into the utility room to sort out the washing I had just brought in and the Nex followed me into the room repeating the same things as he had said outside in relation to a divorce and house purchase. I just continued to agree with everything he said as I knew how volatile he could get. But unfortunately I was 'damned if I did and damned if I didn't' because as I had not reacted the way he wanted me too which was (a) begged him not to end the relationship, or (b) started arguing with him which again was the other alternative of what he was wanting so he could unleash his anger on me, he subsequently unleashed it anyway because he was so angry and enraged that he was not getting the response that he had hoped for. In other words, I was not providing him with his narcissistic supply, or fuel, so that he could feel better. He squared up to me and screamed at me in my face that I was a 'fucking ugly bitch'. He was shouting so loud that it brought my daughter running downstairs as she was so concerned for my safety. She hovered in the kitchen and when the Nex realised she was there he walked away into the dining area off the kitchen. My daughter closed the door to him (it slammed in the wind), and he flew into the kitchen and got right up into her face too, screaming at her, waving his fist and threatening to punch her lights out. My daughter was already upset that he had meted out the silent treatment to her as well the previous week while she had been away, and she told him as much. By this point, I had grabbed my phone to call the police and positioned myself between her and the Nex to which his immediate response was, 'Oh look at this, the two of you ganging up against me'. My daughter then ran upstairs crying and shouted an obscenity to him as she was halfway up the stairs, and he again ran after her making threats of violence towards her. I was so upset and angry, but I had passed the point of boiling rage to where I just felt such a calm ice-cold fury at how he had just treated my daughter. I walked over to him shaking as he was sat on the sofa, bent down so my face was just inches from his and said through gritted teeth that if he ever threatened my daughter again, I would call the police. He just stared at me in shock, I think that this was because I had finally had enough of his behaviour, and he could see this. I had finally stood up to him. It was one thing me living with the abuse but not when it then involved my daughter. After a short while, he went up to my daughter's room where he proceeded to turn on the crocodile tears and 'apologise' for what he had done but he was quick to follow this up with comments that it was all her mum's (me) fault because I had wound him up. I now know this to be a typical narcissistic reaction and response called blame-shifting. He was also attempting to hoover my daughter, another typical narcissistic trick. So, fast forward and we left for Wales that evening, still in complete shock from what had just happened earlier. On Monday, he sent my daughter a grovelling apology again to which she did not feel ready to respond to and then on the Tuesday evening he sent me a text saying that now he'd had a drink (alcohol) and calmed down he accepted that maybe he was to blame for some of it, but of course the large majority of it was my fault blah, blah, blah. Again, this was a narcissistic trait called a 'positive hoover' attempt, just as was the text message that he had sent to my daughter the previous day. I did not respond to it. I returned home on the Thursday, still in the spare bedroom with the 'silent treatment' prevailing by him once again and on the Saturday I asked him again if he wanted us to be over. You become so conditioned over time to accept all levels of behaviour from the narcissist (Trauma Bonding) that in the end you question your own beliefs and even your own sanity and whether you really want the relationship to end or not. Deep down I knew that I did, especially after the way he had just treated my daughter, but I also wanted him to acknowledge for sure that we were over.

A short while later on that same day came the pivotal moment for me when he came downstairs and asked me if I was prepared to compromise and be friends again with a couple who I had refused to have anything to do with since the previous March of 2017 (this will be explained later on in the book) and I suddenly realised, and trust me when I say that this was an 'Oh my God' kind of moment for me which I did proceed to exclaim out loud to the Nex, that he had deliberately created 'The end of the relationship' routine just to coerce and manipulate me into being friends with them again. I told him as much. To say I was shocked was an understatement. That he would stoop to such a low level to try and manipulate and control me into doing what he wanted. I knew in that exact instant that there was no going back. As I have already said, I had really struggled with the decision of going back anyway after he had treated my daughter the way that he had but this just sealed it for me. You can call it the 'Final nail in the coffin' or the 'Straw that broke the camel's back'. I realised with a sense of horror that I had been silently punished by him for the past seventeen months. So much of his behaviour over that period suddenly became so clear to me. This was a devaluation phase that had lasted for seventeen months.

I won't go into any more detail on what happened after this point just yet as I want to explain in more depth further on in the book when we look at different terminology and examples, and also, it is more relevant in further chapters.

So back to what exactly is a narcissist.

According to the Mayo clinic, a narcissist is a person who has what is called Narcissistic Personality Disorder (NPD). It is classed as a mental condition where a person has an inflated sense of their own importance, coupled with an obsessive need for constant attention and admiration. They commonly have troubled relationships and a distinct lack of empathy for others. They wear a false mask of confidence to hide a fragile self-esteem that is extremely vulnerable to the slightest criticism.

Maria Consiglio shores up this belief by stating that 'narcissism is a personality disorder; it is not a mental illness. It is a set of characteristics that together make up this personality'.

You will find a Narcissist in all walks of life. It could be a parent, a sibling, a partner, a work colleague, a boss, a friend and even a son or a daughter.

Some scientists believe that a narcissist can be predisposed to it through genetics or neurobiology. Other researchers believe it is caused by certain parenting styles in that a parent can be overprotective, placing the child on a pedestal and idolising them and giving in to their every demand so the child then develops a sense of superiority and entitlement. Coupled with not setting boundaries and allowing the child to develop such a sense of self-importance. On the flip side though is the abusive parent, who neglects the child, puts them down constantly and verbally abuses them. It is found that often in this scenario the parent in question is also a Narcissist themselves, so the child learns the pattern of behaviour directly from the parent. This does not mean though that every child of a narcissist will automatically develop the same disorder themselves.

Now comes the interesting factor and this is that narcissism is a spectrum that all people are on to some degree. This is explained by 'melody wilding' who is a professor of human behaviour who states that narcissism is a personality trait that every person possesses to some degree. For most of us, this is seen to be a healthy trait to possess as a certain amount of self-centredness can contribute to possessing confidence and ambition, not to mention self-preservation. Also, it is healthy to look after ourselves, and feel important, but it is a problem if taken too far. Throughout our life this level of narcissism can fluctuate, depending on what is going on and how we feel at the time.

Wilding states that if a person possesses an excessive high amount of narcissism then they will have what is referred to as Narcissistic Personality Disorder (NPD) which is a diagnosable mental illness. With someone who has NPD, their entire personality is built on a fake persona that is detached from their emotions. This explains why they lack empathy.

To be able to diagnose someone formally with NPD they must meet certain criteria;

- An excessive need for admiration and adoration
- A sense of entitlement
- An inability to recognise the feelings and needs of others = Empathy
- Vast fluctuations in mood
- Superficial relationships
- Manipulation and Gaslighting
- Aggression and Antisocial behaviour

Other acts of behaviour to look out for with a Narcissist is: projection, blame shifting, pity play, stonewalling, ghosting, silent treatment, mirroring, triangulating, baiting, futureproofing, faking, invalidating, using coercive control, using 'word salad' and consistent double standards. The meaning of all of these have been described earlier on in the index.

If you are experiencing any or all the above plus going through the cycle of idealisation, devaluation and discard then you are most definitely witnessing and experiencing the actions of a narcissist.

We will look at the three phases above in more detail in the next chapters where you will be given my own personal examples and experiences of them.

So back to the narcissist. Hopefully, you will now be able so start to recognise what one is and what examples of their behaviour you need to look out for.

Basically, the narcissist has two selves. In other words, they have a dual personality. One is their false self, and the other is their true inner self. The false self is the defence mechanism that was enacted from when they were a child, typically from abuse or neglect, or from being overvalued which then made them feel entitled. The true inner self consists of self-loathing and insecurity that never leaves the narcissist but is hidden in their subconscious mind where there is a constant battle going on to project their false self out to the world, thus giving them a feeling of superiority and grandiosity, and of course, entitlement. However, because we are ruled by our subconscious mind, the narcissist is constantly left with a void, a great big black hole that is devoid of love and empathy.

Interestingly, HG Tudor claims that not all narcissists have grandiosity. He states that some are aggressive, some are passive-aggressive, some even haughty, and others can be just needy.

Therefore, the narcissist must constantly supress their true self and instead present their false self to the world. This is to ensure that they do not feel worthless but instead feel superior. Their ultimate goal is to ensure that the world does not get to see that wounded inner child of theirs. They will literally stop at nothing to ensure that their self-image is preserved, while hurting and damaging other people along the way. The narcissist will lie, cheat, project, deflect, gaslight, blame-shift, smear, and use any other of their arsenal against another person to ensure that a narcissistic Injury does not occur, or worse still, exposure of what and who they really are. To ensure that the world does not see them for who and what they really are. Only those closest to the narcissist (usually their intimate partner) will witness their true self. Therefore, it is so hard for a Narcissist's victim to be believed. The narcissist will go to whatever length they have to go to, to prevent the outside world from seeing their true, vile, evil real self.

Now this is where it gets a little bit more complicated. Why?

Because according to HG Tudor, you are not just dealing with one specific type, rather the narcissist is divided into three distinct levels.

- The Lesser
- The Mid-Range
- The Greater

To simplify this for you, quite simply the lesser is the one who will usually react with violence and does not know what he is and will deny it vehemently and not even know what one is if you ever suggested he was a narcissist, probably followed with a punch to your face. If you are in an abusive relationship that is often violent then the chances are your partner is a lesser narcissist.

The mid-range narcissist favours the silent treatment, though they all do use it to some degree but nowhere near as much as the mid-ranger. The mid-ranger does not tend to be violent like the lesser but can be known to kick, spit, push and even punch if greatly provoked. He does not know what he is either and will deny it vehemently if you suggested he was a narcissist. In fact, the mid-ranger would retaliate by mirroring, projecting, deflecting and blame-shifting and calling you the narcissist instead. This is exactly what my Nex did when I called him out and told him in the July of 2018 following our split at the end of June, that I thought he was a narcissist. He was quick to retaliate with projecting this back at me and calling me the narcissist instead, even though he did not have a clue what one was!

The greater narcissist tends to be highly intellectual and does have a knowledge of what he is doing to some degree. If he seeks therapy he may even accept what he is being told, unlike the other two, but his sense of grandiosity will still leave him to believe that he is always in the right and everyone else is still at fault, just like HG Tudor. Whereas, with the other two their reactions against you are predominantly knee-jerk ones but again with the greater, he will acknowledge what he is doing and not only revel in the effects of it but know that he is revelling and why.

So, we can delve even deeper now into further sub-divisions of a narcissist like whether they are an overt or overt narcissist or maybe an exhibitionist narcissist or worse still, the malignant narcissist. Again, we have touched on these descriptions in the Index earlier. Further types as documented are, the toxic narcissist, the seducer narcissist, the bullying narcissist, commonly found in the workplace, and finally the psychopathic narcissist who is obviously violent by nature and it has been said that serial killers largely make up this type of narcissist. This one is also likely to be a malignant narcissist too.

Then we have further sub-titles we can adorn them with like the victim narcissist. This is exactly what it says, where they believe that they are always the victim, that they are the ones being abused by you. After all that I have learnt and read and more importantly what I have experienced, I have confidently 'diagnosed' my Nex to be a victim covert mid-range narcissist. I also believe that he does have sociopathic tendencies too.

Once you yourself learn the meanings behind all the jargon and start to recognise signs and examples that you can relate to you will be able to reach an informed decision as to what type of narcissist you are dealing with too, just like I did. This could be invaluable information for you if you are still in the relationship with the narcissist and for whatever reason are unable to leave. Likewise, if the narcissist in your life is a parent, sibling, child, friend or co-worker, identifying firstly that they are a narcissist then more specifically what type exactly they are, could help you going forward in learning how you manage that relationship with them.

The biggest realisation that you need to recognise and learn is that 'there is no cure' for someone with NPD. Therapy can help to some degree, but it all depends on what type of narcissist you are dealing with and how far up the spectrum they are. The consensus is, if you are in a relationship with a full-blown narcissist then get the hell out of there because they will 'never' change. If you cannot get out, then there are support groups and networks out there to help you cope. Furthermore, there are techniques that you can adopt to help defuse situations with a narcissist like using the grey rock technique, and if you have managed to leave, then going completely no contact with them.

There are support groups on social media too, like Instagram and Facebook. I have found these to be so helpful, whether it is from seeking advice myself, or just reading about someone else's experience with a narcissist and how they dealt with it. I have even commented on some sites with advice using my own experiences.

The biggest thing I have discovered though is the emotional and psychological damage that being involved with a narcissist does to you. The scars run far deeper than any physical ones. This is of course not to trivialise domestic violence by any means. This not only leaves physical scars, but also psychological and emotional ones too. In an emotionally abusive relationship, like one with a narcissist, the scars are not generally seen on the outside, but rather they are internal, deeply emotional and psychological scars, and because of this the victims do not usually tend to speak out as they have nothing tangible to show. If they tried to explain what they have been through they may not be believed, or it may be that the listener just assumes that it is not as bad as what is being told. Like the local police force who stated that I was 'seeing more into it then what it was'. If the narcissist is seen as a 'Pillar of Society' then the doubt in others is stronger. Or the Narc has successfully fooled the outside world as to 'What a nice person they are'. But a victim should speak up, and speak out, because it does go on, day after day, week after week and year after year, and in far more many homes and relationships then we would ever care to imagine. Today's society needs to really wake up to what is a far more common issue than is generally known. Schools should educate their pupils on what narcissism is, what a narcissist is, then if someone ever does find themselves involved with a narcissist they can go on and make an informed choice and decision on whether to proceed, especially if it is a potential relationship. A potential victim will have a clear understanding on what they are potentially getting involved with. It is not uncommon for a victim of narcissistic abuse to go on to develop PTSD due to the mind games that they have endured, the gaslighting, and the control when in the relationship. This is just how damaging a relationship with a narcissist can be.

Shelea Daily at hashtag, 'narcissisticabusesurvivor' states:

'When a narcissist is gaslighting you, they are ripping apart your thoughts then reorganising them in a way that feeds their own agenda. That's why you're confused.'

For me, there are most definitely psychological and emotional scars. Finding out that you have lived in a lie for fourteen years of your life is a real game changer. You resent the narcissist at first for the loss of all those years. I am quite 'lucky' really when you read some people's stories who have been in a toxic relationship with their narcissist for twenty years or more, and even one poor woman was with hers for forty years! Oh boy, can you imagine how they must feel. The long-term damage that they have ultimately suffered. The wasted years of their life. Something that they can never ever get back.

It certainly makes you very wary going forward too. You are not going to jump into another relationship anytime soon that is for sure. The only positive you can glean from what you have learnt and experienced from being in a relationship with a narcissist and your subsequent recovery process is that if and when you do dip your toe in the relationship pool again, you will be informed enough to know what signs to look out for and you will hopefully recognise the red flags at the start and therefore, give any future narcissist you may encounter a very wide birth!

Statistically, more men than women are narcissists. This has been found to be as high as almost forty percent more likely. Yet no one can say exactly why. There are assumptions surrounding this, like most leaders are men and most leaders have narcissistic traits. Or it could just be that less men have come forward with their stories of abuse. In fact, Sam Vaknin, the author of *Malignant Self Love* states that most narcissists are male, as high as seventy five percent, with very few gender differences. She goes on to state that the primary role of the narcissist is to use everything around them for their narcissistic supply.

If you contact the National Domestic Abuse hotline, it cites that abuse can take many forms.

For instance, manipulation, monitoring, spying, control, invasion of privacy, insults, passive-aggressiveness, isolation, unfaithfulness/adultery, threats to you or themselves, withholding love or bargaining with love and affection, unfounded blame and accusations, lies, mistruths and misdirection.

Every single one of these can and do describe a narcissist.

A narcissist cares very much about how they are perceived and viewed, and they have been known to go to great lengths to convince others that they are in fact a good person. This is a well-known trait of a mid-range narcissist, and a covert one. Both of which my Nex is. HG Tudor also states that a mid-range narcissist does genuinely believe that he or she is a good person, a decent person, an empathic person. It is the other people who are horrible, abusive narcissists, not them. HG Tudor goes further to state, 'A mid-range does not know what he is doing, all he knows is how he is expected to behave so he can con his victims. He also knows that reactions he gets makes him feel better (fuel)'. Post-split I heard my Nex state to his latest victim that when someone says something he does not like, he retaliates by shouting at them and insulting them to hurt them because this then makes him feel better. I was quite literally WTF?! Good old HG Tudor sure does know his stuff! But best of all I had quite literally heard my Nex 'admit' albeit subconsciously to being a narcissist! It is after all, instinct that rules the behaviours and responses of the narcissist, as demonstrated by my Nex. HG Tudor knows that a victim will question this and ask that surely they must know what they are doing is wrong? That their behaviour is wrong? That it is deliberate to upset and hurt their victim. But HG Tudor states no this is not the case. That their narcissism is designed to blind them to that to make it effective. He says, 'Their narcissism works in a way as a self defence mechanism to enable them to function and be effective because they have not developed other coping mechanisms like a normal person would.'

In relation to the use of the silent treatment, HG Tudor states further, 'Dishing out a silent treatment is instinctive because that is the optimum response and consequence of him having been wounded. His narcissism operates to make him issue a silent treatment. This then draws fuel and asserts his perceived superiority over you. But he has not decided to give you a silent treatment, he just does it. He knows that he is not speaking to you, but he does not understand the full reasons why'. HG Tudor describes it as a manipulative response to being wounded. What the narcissist does know though is the fact that his use of the silent treatment does hurt their victim, but they feel no remorse or guilt whatsoever as they feel that their actions are justified.

By using the silent treatment against you, the narcissist is sending out a loud clear message to you. They are telling you how much of a complete lack of respect they have for you and your feelings, how inferior you are, and how they could not care less about you.

A narcissist presents a false image and façade to the outside world all the while showing you, their victim, their real true colours behind closed doors. But if you do not know what a narcissist is and do not know about narcissism you do not realise this or recognise that this is what you are experiencing, you just know that your relationship is not and cannot possibly be normal.

If the narcissist is covert in their behaviour then this can be soul destroying for their victim, as the Narc will project what they see as their 'truth' only. Yet the victim is living with a completely different version of someone that the outside world does not get to see. They are master manipulators, they have already convinced themselves that they are fabulous, kind and an all-round nice, good human being. This description fits my Nex perfectly.

At the start they know how to make you feel extremely special, giving you their undivided attention. This is what is termed as the idealisation phase. This is where they will love-bomb you. A narcissist will use this idealisation/love-bombing phase intermittently throughout your entire relationship with them to keep you ensnared, throw you off balance and to generally make you crave more. This is known as intermittent enforcement. They will play on your emotions by being affectionate, attentive and loving. Then just as suddenly it will all be withdrawn completely, leaving you confused, bewildered, insecure but mostly wanting more of the love-bombing treatment. A return to the nice period. We will look more closely at this phenomenon in more detail in the next chapter.

A narcissist's sole intention is to manipulate and control you purely to meet their own needs. Once they have captivated you, hooked you entirely, their job of manipulation becomes so much easier and more accessible for them.

They can present as confident, charismatic individuals and will have placed a whole lot of effort into their appearance. Deep down they are an insecure and fickle individual who is constantly fighting an inner battle. They believe that the more attractive they are, the more confident they are and even more successful that they appear then their insecurities will be sufficiently masked. At the start of my relationship with the Nex, he claimed he ran a successful building business, he drove a car which he thought was special (lost on me as it was just a car) and had the latest expensive model of mobile phone. Later, in the relationship, the Nex used to brag about what we/he had. He often used to say 'I/we have done really well haven't I/we, big house, good lifestyle, holidays, nice cars,' etc. But it was not said in a 'Aren't we really lucky or fortunate kind of way', rather it was a boastful 'Look at me' kind of way that often left me feeling uncomfortable. I on the other hand used to think yes we are blessed, and we are extremely lucky for what we have.

With a narcissist, you must envisage that they live in a world that is all about them. All about their wants and their needs. They are totally self-absorbed, and they think that the entire universe revolves around them. A narcissist will 'always' put their needs first. This is a really hard thing to stomach when you think of a narcissistic parent behaving like this. Especially if you are a parent yourself, like me, because quite honestly you would give your life for your child.

So, what ultimately drives a narcissist? Well, a narc's ultimate biggest craving and need is the one for what is called narcissistic supply, or fuel. This is what they need to exist, to live, to survive and to ultimately stop their true insecurities and demons from surfacing. We will look at this in more detail later. For now, just think of a car and its engine and the petrol (fuel) it needs to work. The fuel that a narcissist needs so they can function and maintain their false image, is supplied via all your emotions, happy, sad, angry and so on. The more unhappy you are, the 'happier' the narcissist is. The more praise, adoration and admiration the narcissist receives, the better they feel.

A narcissist behaves in such a way in a relationship that they use the three cycles associated with narcissism. This is idealisation, devaluation and discard. This cycle is meted out intermittently and is a very potent tactic of manipulation. It will leave you chasing them nine times out of ten and they know this and that is why they do it so they can obtain their precious fuel from you. So, the cycle goes on and on and round and round. This cycle will also be displayed in other non-intimate relationships that the narcissist has.

Quite frankly, a narcissist is also a con artist. They will con you into loving them and believing in them, they will also con you out of your money, your home, your way of life and just about anything else that they can. They will also use the method of gaslighting against you to obtain their fuel and to leave you thinking that you are going crazy. As I have stated earlier, the one thing that you must keep at the forethought of your mind while reading this book is that 'everything' a narcissist does leads to the very one precious thing that they crave, what they need to survive, which will prevent their inner vile self being exposed, and this is their narcissistic supply, or fuel. To them it is a drug, a necessity for their very existence. Once you realise and recognise this you will start to learn their methods of obtaining it. Without their fuel, a narcissist will implode, and the true inner self could be and would be revealed to the world and this must not ever happen to a narcissist.

So, let us look at their obsession with their appearance. It is true that not all narcissists are, but for those that are, not only are they obsessed with their own appearance, but they are also obsessed with yours too. They want you to look good so that they will look good too. They will target an insecurity of yours, or imperfection, for example your weight, and they will make comments about it. These will be insidious in nature by a covert narcissist, for example, 'Hey, chubster, your bums getting rounded, but I still love you'. For an overt narcissist, he will simply not hold back the nasty comment, striking you exactly where it hurts the most. The underlying message that both types of narcissists is sending you is that you are not good enough for them, that they are disappointed in you. It is designed to hurt you and in doing so they are again obtaining their precious fuel. Remember what I said earlier that you must always keep this at the forefront of your mind because the fuel a narc can obtain from you is what drives them completely. These comments and insults will obviously be coming during the devaluation phase and will be made so that the narcissist can and will draw this fuel from you.

I just gave you an example above of what my Nex used to do with me. He made comments about my bum on a regular basis. Bear in mind that when I met him I was around eight stone in weight and at five foot and five inches tall, I was always considered to be underweight and skinny. I still am that weight now. Granted that at times I would put on a few pounds like around Christmas or an all-inclusive holiday, but I never went above nine stone which was the ideal weight for someone of my build. Nevertheless, my Nex would often tell me that I had a fat arse! Or would comment if I did gain a pound or two. Oh, the irony of this because when I met him he was almost fourteen stone in weight and what would be described as stocky, but he gained weight in our first year of living together, and for the majority of the rest of the fourteen years that we were together he was touching sixteen stone and had a 'Santa Clause' belly and chubby legs that rubbed together! He would go on to tell people post-split that his weight gain was my fault because I was a 'feeder', but this was so far from the truth. The reality was and is, that the Nex had always been prone to being chubby because he is just greedy and always has been. He would devour an entire six-pack of crisps in one sitting or an entire cheesecake, as well as just graze on food all day long.

He also used to call one of my best friends chubster too and like me she has never been overweight. Another favourite comment of the Nex's in the early days was to comment on one of my upper side teeth that slightly crossed over another tooth. It had never bothered me, nor had I ever really noticed it until he did. And boy did he often comment about it then! At the start, it was subtle, saying things like 'Have you ever thought about a brace for that tooth?' I just used to brush it off because I really did not care but then he started to say things like 'Do you know you would have a lovely smile if that tooth didn't stick out'. Obviously, I was offended but I just tried to ignore it and not let it bother me and I would just think that he was being tactless. This comment of his is a perfect example of passive-aggressive behaviour, another firm narcissistic trait. I had absolutely no idea though of what it was and that it was a classic trait of a narcissist during a devaluation phase and that he was deliberately trying to hurt me in order to obtain fuel. The notion of tactfulness was for sure missing in my Nex! The amount of people he offended because he had and still has absolutely no filter whatsoever. I never could understand it before, how someone could not give a shit if they said something that would hurt another person's feelings, but the Nex used to just say, 'I just say it as it is'. Now I know about narcissism and their lack of empathy, I now know why.

You must also keep at the forefront of your mind whilst reading this book the very fact that to a narcissist they are never wrong, and by that I really mean 'never ever!' To admit fault is to admit a weakness and to admit weakness would destroy their false image and allow their true inner self to surface and that must never ever happen. A narcissist honestly believes that their lies are their truth. There is absolutely no point in trying to convince them otherwise. Or waste your time and emotion in trying to show them that they are wrong or at fault even if you have overwhelming tangible evidence to place in front of them. They will simply blame-shift, project, deflect and gaslight you into doubting your own truth. I will reiterate this point over and over throughout this book because once you do realise this and accept it you will begin to recognise examples of this behaviour and avoid them if you are still unfortunately living with your narc. This is because when a narcissist gaslights you they are hell bent on weakening your spirit and gaining complete and total power and control over you.

The best description I have read to describe it is the proverbial 'Frog in the pan' scenario. A narcissist will increase their abuse against you so slowly and insidiously that you will not even realise what is happening to you. They will up their ante of abuse and effectively 'Turn up the heat' so slowly that you will not recognise or realise that you are being psychologically and emotionally boiled alive.

As part of the cycle, the flip between the two phases of idealisation and then devaluation will have this effect on you, they will know that it will confuse you and in turn this will make you more vulnerable. They will convince you that you are losing your mind and that you are crazy and even that you, the victim, are in fact the abuser. The Nex did exactly that to me.

A narcissist behaves like this for two reasons.

1. To maintain their mask, their façade
2. To gain fuel

The kind of things a narcissist will not do is,

1. Encourage you

2. Trust you
3. Allow you to express an opinion if it does not sit with what they believe
4. Support you, especially if they do not agree with you
5. Emotional intimacy

For me, the Nex never actively encouraged me in anything whatsoever. In fact, he would do the exact opposite. For instance, I mentioned at the start that I have always wanted to write a book and when I used to say this to him in conversation he would instantly belittle me and say that I was a sayer and not a doer and so I would never write one. This became his favourite expression in the first few years once he had realised that it would upset me. Of course, at the time I did not know about narcissism and fuel, but clearly now with hindsight this is what I was inadvertently providing him with in abundance. Hence his use of this turn of phrase over and over. The irony though was the very fact that I had done the very biggest 'Do' of all time by packing up my entire life to move down and be with him and start all over again, but this was completely lost on him when I would state it as an example. He simply could not see it or refused to see it which again now with knowledge was probably exactly what it was because he would have had to admit then that he was wrong, and this was something completely unacceptable to him. Furthermore, he would have lost one of his weapons that he used against me. The fact of the matter is that a narcissist is always very much the sayer, as in they say and never do, which ties in with their narcissistic trait of futureproofing.

Trust, I was often accused with having affairs, especially towards the end of the relationship. But I do not think this just applies to this kind of trust, I really think it applies to any kind of trust. For instance, I was not even allowed to knock a picture hook in the wall, despite having done it for the previous thirty years of my life! He said I would probably hit a wire or something. Again, I think not only was this to gain a reaction and subsequent fuel from me by effectively putting me down, but also because I really do think that he did not trust me to do it properly. I guess you could also say that it is demonstrative of control and power that he was covertly doing too. Another example came not long after I had moved down to be with him and when the idealisation phase was still in play. Two of my dearest friends came down to visit me in my new home and new city and I had bought some blackout material for the children's bedrooms. This was only ever going to be a temporary fix until the rooms were decorated and I spread the material out on the floor and measured up the sizes and started cutting out the first one. The Nex immediately passed a comment to the effect that I was not doing it properly and if I did it a way he suggested it would be better and one of my friends said in the nicest possible way that I was doing just fine and that I knew what I was doing and had in fact done it before, which was true. To quote Julia Roberts and the movie scene in 'Pretty Woman' this was a big mistake, huge, huge mistake! He fell silent but what I had not realised at the time and did not until I learnt about narcissism was that her comments had caused him a narcissistic injury.

He never said anything to her or to me until they had gone back home. Then he started passing snidey comments about my friend and stating that he did not know why she had to say that to him. That he was only trying to help me. Such was his narcissistic injury that he made it clear to me that she was not welcome again and this lasted for over ten years before he accepted her coming to visit me again, even though we had moved to a new house six years prior to her finally being allowed to visit! He used to say it was because she had questioned him on his motives when we had first met, and he also did not like the influence she had on me, but I now know these were just excuses. She had inadvertently challenged him. When I say, a narcissist can hold a grudge for a lifetime I really do mean a lifetime!

Express an opinion. Oh boy, where do I start?! The only opinions were the ones that would sit with him, agree with his and believe in his. You learn as I did, not to question the narcissist or freely offer your thoughts and opinions on something because if you did or do, you are and were shot down, belittled. The irony of this is the fact that belittle was my Nex's favourite term of phrase to use against me in the early days of our relationship! He became like a broken record 'Stop belittling me,' said over and over. I used to say to him that he should look up what it meant but it fell on deaf ears. Now I believe it was once said against him from one of his previous victims, so he purely mirrored and projected this on to me.

Support me. That will be a no then. And I mean not in anything. Not when I was diagnosed with a degenerative Auto Immune Disease in 2012. In fact, he went on to totally ignore the diagnosis over the years and would only mention it in a derogatory way if I happened to say I was tired or something and he would instantly say 'Oh stop blaming your illness' even if it was my illness that 'was' the cause! A lack of sleep and stress were and are the two biggest causes of relapses of my illness, but I could never tell him when I was symptomatic or how ill I felt at times because no support was ever forthcoming. So, instead I learnt to just shut up and put up and suffer in silence and just ride the storm that the symptoms brought and just get on with things until it had passed. Other than the odd derogatory comment about my illness, it was as if I was never diagnosed. He still expected me to work all hours, cook, clean, shop and keep house. Even if he had days or weeks off work, I would work a 12-hour day then still have to go and do a supermarket shop at 9 pm at night while he had spent the day idling at home. He probably only came shopping with me a handful of times over the span of fourteen years and his excuse not to come would always be because 'it wasn't his job'. This is another classic trait of a narcissist. They will not help you around the house, no housework for them, no childcare, etc. because of their sense of entitlement. They feel entitled to have you waiting on them hand and foot, to keep the house clean and so on. Once when we were on holiday, and I was suddenly struck down with vertigo it took him five hours to finally pitch up back to our room and even then it was not to see where I was and how I was but rather for him to have a snooze! I found it so strange at the time and so hurtful. For all he knew, I could have been lying dead but with a total lack of empathy I now knew why he had acted this way.

No support not even when my friend and I fulfilled a life-long dream and opened a restaurant. Do not get me wrong, credit where credit is due, he did the shop fitting for us and made it look fabulous, but once we were open and under way he would constantly tell me that the business would fail. My friends' husband recently told me that at the onset of our business opening the Nex had stated to him that he was never going to put any of his money into the business, and that if we ever needed financial help with it he would not be giving it to us. I am so glad that I never learnt this at the time. The Nex also never once came to help us when we were short staffed but did regularly come in on the Saturday for free food. Any success or achievement we had was met with a negative comment. I felt at the time as if he purposely wanted us to fail but simply could not understand why until now and knowing what I do know now about narcissism. Throughout my friend and I's two-year court battle over the restaurant (we had to close due to a dodgy building), he would constantly tell me that we would lose the case and that I was not to ask him for any help financially whatsoever when we did lose. He was so negative about it, constantly. Funnily enough, he gave evidence at the trial and was so aggrieved when the landlord tried to say that he had done a bad job fitting a floor, he did not let that one drop for weeks. Now I know why. We did go on to win our case though, and of course the Nex benefitted from our win with the luxury holiday I then took him on! But of course, if we had have lost I was not to have expected any help from him financially. This is a prime example of the double standards you live by with a narcissist. A narcissist also hates to see you succeed in anything because this is taking attention away from them and because they see themselves as far more superior than you. I do also now believe that he only helped with the shop fitting in order to obtain the praise and adoration that it would bring him. You must remember that a narcissist will 'never' do anything unless there is something in it for them.

Emotional intimacy. I was not quite sure what this meant exactly so I must admit that I did 'google' it. It is described as able to communicate your feelings to show how much you care. Wikipedia states that it relies primarily on trust. That it can be expressed verbally and non-verbally through communication. It goes on further to state that 'Emotional intimacy is a psychological event that happens when trust levels and communication between two people are such that it fosters the mutual sharing of one another's deepest selves'. Are you starting to see why this is impossible to achieve with a narcissist and why it simply does not fit the bill of a narcissist!

Why does a narcissist marry? Well, marriage for a narcissist serves all their needs in that they have a constant steady supply of fuel on tap. But it is a parasitic relationship that gradually and imperceptibly drains the life and soul out of the non-narcissist partner. Marriage provides the narc with a cover. I cannot reiterate enough that a narcissist simply cannot live without their fuel. You will see me referring to its importance throughout this book over and over, such is its importance. They cannot be alone, they cannot live without the fuel that constant praise, adoration and validation brings them and that they require. Ironically, the narcissist will spend the duration of the marriage invalidating you, their victim! Neither can they live without the negative fuel that a devaluation phase brings them. Marriage or another form of a long-term relationship will provide all types of this supply of fuel for them on tap. Let us remember that we must think of their fuel supply in all its glorious forms:

positive, negative and even challenge fuel. All these types will be found here and obtained here in abundance. Their ever-flowing narcissistic supply.

A narcissist is also known to quickly move on in relationships. That was certainly the case with my Nex. Just weeks after our split at the end of June 2018 he was already on date sites actively searching out his next victim. In fact, for all I know he could have been on the sites for the entirety of our relationship, gaining fuel from virtual interactions. When I look back over snippets of conversations we'd had in the past about his previous relationships, and believe me when I say they were snippets as he did not like talking about them at all and would say 'I don't remember her/it/that'… Or 'Sharon' who?' Again, I have come to learn that this is a classic narcissistic trait of just dismissing the past and pretending that it did not happen. It demonstrates why they have this ability to just 'switch off' and move on quickly.

This highlights one comment that the Nex used to use on a regular basis in the beginning of our relationship and probably the early years. He used to say, 'Do you know if we ever split up I will just switch off from you.' I found it the most bizarre and disturbing comment to make when he used to say it but simply passed it off as not really being true and that he could not and did not really mean it and that rather it must just be a bravado kind of thing for him to say. I mean, how could it even be possible to switch off feelings of love for someone? Well, not now. Now I believe that he meant every single word of it and that for him he was simply stating a fact. He was subconsciously speaking like the narcissist he was and is. I remember asking him how he could say such a thing when you cannot just switch your feelings for someone off, but he would merely reaffirm it. Now I know that it is a classic narcissistic trait and what I did not recognise and realise at the time was that this was one great big almighty red flag that he was waving at me, right in my face! When a relationship is over for the narcissist, they will quite literally just switch off from it and the person they were involved with. You must think about what I said earlier and that a narcissist does not and cannot ever really 'love' someone. Hence why they truly can just switch off from you. They will only attempt a 'come-back' if they are not getting their fuel supply from a new source. What I missed completely yet again is the fact that this was another major red-flag waving at me in my face. I would go as so far as to say it was probably the biggest one.

A quote by hashtag/narcissisticabusesurvivor goes,

'A normal person can't turn their feelings OFF… but a narcissist can turn it off just as easily as they can turn it on because showing feelings is a tool they use to con people'.

The main point I really want to get across to everyone and cannot stress enough is the fact that even if the relationship is fine ninety percent of the time and the remaining ten percent is abusive, full of lies, insults, gaslighting, blame-shifting etc., you should leave the relationship. Trust me when I say that it will only get worse. It will become twenty percent then thirty percent then forty percent and so on as the months and years go by. I am speaking from experience. At first, I probably had two maybe three massive outbursts a year from him followed by the usual end of the relationship routine and subsequent silent treatment meted out against me. I remember that I was so sure he meant it each time that on one particular occasion I packed the car up with as much of my belongings as I could and with the kids in the car texted him to say I was going. I think we had only been there a few months at this point and of course I had never experienced anything like this before, so I genuinely believed him that he meant it when he said the relationship was over. He immediately called me and said that if I were not there when he got back then we would be over. I mean WTF?! How is that for a double whammy of mind games and gaslighting! I remember he came in and there was absolutely no resolution or discussion of what had caused the row, no closure at all but rather him just saying 'We're okay, aren't we?' I was just so relieved that it was over, and that the silent treatment had ended I said yes. I now know that the use of the silent treatment is frequently used by a narcissist for punishment and control. That it is a form of psychological and emotional abuse. I think that I can remember this incident so well because I was so shocked by it all and little did I know that it was the first of so very many times that this would happen again, over and over. Each time it did happen in those first few years I was so convinced every single time that this really was the last one where the relationship was finally over and that he actually meant it because he was so convincing that it was, so on each occasion I would ask the kids 'hypothetically' where they would want to live if the Nex and I ever split up and would they want to return to our home town or stay where we now were. They were 13 and 11 at this point and I felt that it was only fair that they were included in deciding where they wanted to live, especially as I had already uprooted them once before. Now I know that this reaction and insecure feeling that I had was exactly the feeling and reaction that the Nex wanted me to have. It was his way of maintaining power and control over me. Of course, at the time I did not know this. All I did know was that surely this was not normal behaviour, could not be normal behaviour but you become so conditioned into accepting it that you do accept it and you learn to live with it by walking on eggshells with them. By thinking about what you want to say and how you are going to say it before you say it so as not to cause an argument or put down. Going forward I learnt never to just say what I really wanted to say or what I felt because the fall out that would follow simply was not worth it. I now know that this is psychological and emotional abuse and that this is no way to live your life, having to second guess all the time. Having to live your life walking on eggshells. But at the time you simply do it because it is easier than what would follow. For me, it was the silent treatments that I hated, feared and dreaded the most. I guess what I am trying to say to you is the longer you are in the relationship the higher this percentage will climb, until it is at ninety nine percent, and you are in the devaluation phase for the majority of the relationship. This is all building up to the ultimate final discard. Towards the end of my relationship with the Nex I would say that in the last four years of it the percentage was at eighty then up to ninety-nine percent at the very end. I will talk more in depth about discard in another chapter.

When we look at the use of the silent treatment specifically, as stated earlier in the book, this is a preferred form of abuse that the narcissist uses against their victim. They use it not only because it allows them to exert control, but also because it can be used while still preserving the façade. HG Tudor states that a mid-range narcissist is a sulker, and I can certainly testify to that about my Nex. He could quite literally sulk for England! HG goes on to say, 'He has enough control to sit and say nothing to you and drink up the fuel as you keep badgering him. He can sulk for hours, days if need be, and he can breeze around the house as if you are not there. He revels in the effect of his silent treatment and his dual approach here is providing dividends for him.'

Darius Cikanavicius writing on *Psychology of Self* recently stated, 'The silent treatment, whilst sometimes seemingly harmless when talking about it, can be a highly damaging and effective form of manipulation, coercion, and control used by toxic people. It is common, even though many victims feel alone and like they cannot talk about it because no one will believe them or understand. This is, simply put, the nature of this kind of abuse. It is done in such a way that only the abuser and the abused know what is going on'. He goes on further to say that a victim of the silent treatment is not alone, and they do not deserve to be treated in such a callous and cruel way.

Reading this article further validated my knowledge that the use of the silent treatment by the Nex 'was' abusive, 'was' used to hurt me, to control me and to punish me. Especially when up to 2010, there was no spare bedroom for him to slink off into so instead when I was being punished and treated to a bout of the silent treatment, we still had to share a bed! Wrap your head around how that truly felt! Imagine sharing a bed with someone who completely blanked you, ignored you and acted as though you did not even exist, for days at a time.

In a normal relationship, it is okay to sulk with your partner sometimes if they have upset you or pissed you right off, and you may even fall quiet for a little while. You gather your thoughts, calm down and speak to them once you are ready. What you do not do is completely and utterly blank them and pretend that they are not there and do not exist. You certainly do not then drag this out for days at a time. I can tell you from experience that it is devastating when someone you live with does this to you. To be completely ignored, have them barricade themselves away and not respond or even acknowledge you when you try to talk to them, even when you have apologised and begged and pleaded with them to speak to you, you still get nothing. For me, the silent treatment would last as long as the Nex wanted it to, or until I would finally say, 'Okay, you have made your feelings clear, let's sell the house and go our separate ways.' Then and only then, would the silent treatment come to an end. I am not talking minutes or hours here but instead I am talking days. Can you even begin to imagine how that feels? If you are lucky enough to be in a normal relationship and are reading this book out of curiosity or interest, just imagine your perfectly normal loving husband or wife, or partner, treating you like this. Doling out a silent treatment and making you feel like you do not exist and that you are not worthy of being responded to. Having zero respect shown to you. Not replying when you say good morning, not even looking at you. You both climb into bed at the end of the day, and they immediately turn their back on you, moving out of reach from your attempts to cuddle them, still no words spoken but instead the silence speaking a million words. Picture this lasting for days at a time. You cannot picture it can you. Because you cannot imagine the person you love ever being this cruel to you.

Another important factor to remember and more importantly recognise about a narcissist is that to them this is all done to extract fuel from you. They will thrive on getting under your skin and will deliberately up their abuse if they know that they have succeeded in doing this. My Nex's favourite phrase was 'One up to *****y' or 'I win you lose', and he would literally give me the 'One-up' finger sign while saying it. More importantly you must realise and recognise that you will 'never' win an argument with a narcissist, even when you are in the right because they will 'never' accept that they could be wrong. All you will do is stress yourself out instead. In fact, you may very well demonstrate the very crazy behaviour that they accuse you of, such is your frustration at them. Such is their success at gaslighting you. My Nex was recently heard stating that he always had to win at all costs and that this was why he never left the matrimonial home after we had split up!

When a narcissist issues a silent treatment against you, they are desperately trying to exert their power and control over you, so they do not have to face how inferior they really feel.

You must also be aware that a narcissist feeds off your anger and frustration. These emotions provide them with their precious fuel, albeit it being what is termed as negative fuel. To many narcs this type of fuel is far more potent than the positive fuel. They discover that the positive fuel you are providing them with daily through praise, love, adoration and most importantly attention is dulling their fuel receiving receptors. It no longer gives them the 'High' that it used to. They discover that when they devalue you, they receive a different kind of fuel from you by upsetting you and causing you to cry, shout, and even scream. This is the negative fuel that they are now receiving. They quickly realise that this kind of response from you provides them with a bigger hit. We will touch more on this subject in chapter seven but hopefully you are beginning to understand what a narcissist is and how their fuel supply works.

I cannot keep stressing enough about how important it is to free yourself of a narcissistic individual and go/keep 'no' contact, and if you cannot then you must go 'Grey Rock' with them instead.

My Nex took my birth certificate off me when we first moved down for 'safe-keeping' or so he said. I never saw it again. Fourteen years later and I still do not know where it went, except to now assume that it was merely yet another form of control and power for the Nex to have over me.

So, another perfectly apt name to describe a narcissist that is an easy and understandable name but describes a narc to perfection is a 'Predator'. The formal definition of a predator is,

1. An animal that naturally preys on others
2. A person who ruthlessly exploits others

They literally prey on their victims. They will deliberately seek you out at the start of a relationship and usually always target someone who is naturally Empathic. They will often seek out someone who is successful in life, has a good job, a career, owns their own house and so on. The more you have personally achieved in life the better for the narcissist as your success will reflect off them too. Also, if they can spend your money instead of their own then all the better!

Since the birth of the Internet and online dating, a narcissist is not one who will naturally meet a partner 'off the street'. Oh no, the invention of online dating has been their dream come true for easily finding their next victims. They can sift through someone's profile and photos and find exactly what they are looking for. Not in the way that a normal person would seek out a partner but in a way that their victim can be easily manipulated, easily 'Cast under their spell'. Someone who is not only naturally empathic and successful but who will also offer all that they, the narcissist, desires and wishes that they were. This is called mirroring; another narcissistic trait, but at this stage it is one that the narcissist is doing subconsciously. You are demonstrating all that they wished they were and could in fact be. Their more profound use of mirroring comes at the start of the potential relationship where you will find that 'miraculously' the narcissist happens to like everything that you do. The same taste in music, bands, food, movies, etc. You cannot believe it because to you it appears as if you have found your perfect match, maybe even your 'soulmate'. What you must recognise and realise is the very fact that this is all one big fat con designed to ensnare you. Oh yes, I forgot to mention that did I not? Nope, I did not. A narcissist really is one of the biggest con artists on the planet! So, the narc has literally 'Swept you off your feet' and you honestly believe that they are really 'the' one. What a 'big fat miserable no!' They have further used the art of mirroring to con you into believing that they are your perfect match. They have taken all 'your' interests and likes and pretended that they are theirs too. You love soul music, oh wow, so do they! You love going to live gigs, oh wow, so do they! Are you starting to get the picture? I am not saying this is what everyone is like because there will be genuine, honest folk out there who do genuinely like the same interests as you. But the narcissist will throw up red flags at the onset which you need to be aware of and look out for. Primarily you will be love-bombed and once you learn what this is and how to recognise that this may be happening to you, you will understand what I mean. We look at love-bombing in more depth in the next chapter, and red-flags later in the book. So, me? Oh yes, I was well and truly conned in every sense of the word, I just did not know it!

I met my Nex online, surprise (Not!), We 'talked' online for around two months with promises of meeting up to then sudden silence. Nothing, a big fat zilch. We were meant to have been speaking later that evening so I, being stupidly naïve and gullible, honestly believed that something could have happened to him, so I texted him several times to check if he were okay. I finally sent him an email that was a generic one that simply said it is okay if you do not want to speak with me anymore, but could he just let me know that he was okay. I finally got a response to this email with one back that blabbed on about the distance and how he wanted 'a real relationship' and what with both of us working weekends sometimes we would not see much of each other, blah blah blah. So that was that. I will not lie to you, I was gutted because he had generally gotten 'under my skin' by this point. Anyway, fast forward another month and blow me down out of the blue I got a text message from him saying he had really missed talking to me and would I mind if he gave me a call one night. Stupidly I texted back the next day and said yes. Oh boy, if I knew then what I know now I would most certainly 'not' be writing this book today!

What I have learnt recently though is that this is a narcissist's favourite trick. They will deliberately 'ghost' you then reconnect a short while later to see if you have passed their first test. This is to see how pliable you are. How easily they can manipulate you. If your response after delayed contact is made in a way that questions or challenges them as to why they 'ghosted' you and what have they been doing during that time, then you are history for sure. If you do not make a big deal out of it, you have passed their first test. Yep, unfortunately that was me! I will tell you more about this in the next chapter because of course, I was then love-bombed.

I will keep stressing throughout this book that you must realise with a narcissist, that they will 'ever' change, not one single bit, but instead what they will do is get better at what they do. The only real lesson a narcissist learns from one failed relationship to the next failed relationship is how to hide and conceal what they are, better. How to extract more fuel efficiently. How to avoid being unmasked. It is probably worth pointing out at this stage that these actions of improvement are not done in a conscious manner by the narcissist, by that I mean they do not recognise that they are a narc, or even acknowledge this fact, but rather they now know that some of their previous actions resulted in the loss of that relationship so they will mask it better the next time round.

Again, because of the birth of the Internet and online dating sites, not to mention social media, a narcissist has found that there is an abundance of supply at the very end of their fingertips that now allows them to prey further and ultimately it is so much more easier to replace their lost 'supply', because that is really all you ever were to them, a supply for fuel, and also it is a way for them to gain more supplies all at once.

Looking back on my 'silent' period of the month when the Nex ghosted me I now do strongly believe that not only was it a test but that he had also got other 'supplies' that were on the go and he was working his way through them to find the most pliable one, (guess I drew that short straw there then in the end!), and I can say this with some conviction because we finally met at the start of December and that first Christmas he was getting text messages from another woman wishing him a Merry Xmas and he just passed it off as someone he had casually dated just before me and she was now stalking him. The best part is that I stupidly believed him! But again, I do not want to say too much just yet because this will all come out in the love-bombing chapter.

A reply to a comment on Quora that asked if 'All narcissists are cruel?' was met with a response of yes, all NPD's are evil incarnate. But the reply went on to say that there was a catch. This being that the readers should not be quick to hate the narcissist. Instead, just stay far away from one. The answer went on to say that putting aside their malicious and conscious pain that a narcissist inflicted on their victims we should pretty much just liken them to the gimp character from the movie 'Pulp Fiction'. The gimp was a victim of sadistic sexual, emotional and physical torture. It went on to say that despite all this you should still not release the gimp from his chains because he is still dangerous. You cannot live with the gimp, and you cannot have him around your kids or any other people because he is beyond repair. Simply think of your narcissist as the gimp! I have found it extremely helpful to not view my Nex as a fellow human being but rather I see him as an amoeba – often called an amoeboid – which is a single cell organism that has an ability to change shape. So, my nickname for him is 'One Cell'. I see this 'one cell' as being his narcissistic self that makes up his entire being. This dehumanises him to me and thus helps with my recovery process.

I have mentioned in this chapter about psychiatrists, psychologists and therapists, all 'experts' in the field of narcissism, due to their clinical knowledge and expertise. But I do strongly believe that until you have actually lived a part of your life with a narcissist, until you have experienced first-hand the abuse they mete out against their victim, until you have been in a relationship with a narcissist, no one can ever truly understand what it is actually like, or what it actually feels like. The 'expert' can talk about gaslighting, projecting, triangulation and so on, they can explain what they are, what they entail, but I think that to truly understand the effect these have on you, you have to experience it, know what it feels like, how it makes you feel, what it sounds like, and what it looks like, to live, as the victim, facing this abuse, day after day, month after month, and year after year. Only a victim can honestly say how it affects them, the emotional and psychological damage that it does to them.

I look at the many years I worked in Acute and Critical Care, and the years I worked on an Intensive Care Unit (ICU) in a hospital. I witnessed dying patients and relatives sat helplessly by their bedside. The interaction often moved me to tears, but I never really understood what they were truly feeling or going through. You simply cannot. Not until you find yourself in the same boat as that relative. I finally understood this when my own father spent two days on ICU, dying, after his collapse. Suddenly, I was right there, I 'was' that relative, I was finally in their shoes, experiencing it from the relative's point of view. The feelings of helplessness, the surge of hope quickly followed by the plunge of despair, up and down like a seesaw. The only advantage I had over all those other relatives that I had witnessed over the years was the fact that I had my clinical background and knowledge to fully understand what was happening. To me though, this was a million times worse, because as the saying goes, 'Ignorance is bliss'. So, for me, knowing, recognising and seeing what was happening was just devastating, absolutely devastating, but I could finally understand what it truly felt like to be that relative sat at the side of the bed of a loved one, who was dying. Having to take part in making those God-awful decisions, knowing that in doing so, you were ending the life of your loved one. I lived and experienced that feeling of utter despair, that feeling of drowning, that feeling of helplessness. I was finally that relative at the side of my loved one's bed and I got to fully understand exactly how that relative at the side of that bed felt.

So, likewise, when having been in a relationship with a narcissist, I truly believe that the only real 'experts' on narcissism, is the very victim who has lived through it, experienced it and endured it, and who has gone on to educate themselves on narcissists so they can finally and fully understand everything that they have experienced. For me, I think these victims are the best people to talk to about it, because they can talk about it from the heart, how it really felt and what it was genuinely like being a victim of a narcissist.

So how shall I round off this chapter that has hopefully begun to give you some understanding into what a narcissist is and hopefully the start of a fair description of one for you?

How about a quick summary of what one is and what you can expect in no particular order?

Poison, hate, malice, strife, deceit, shit, bully, deflect, blame, assault, theft, con, attack, mirror, mock, belittle, consume, feed-off, rape, erode, undo, control, take, oppress, strife, shift, err, triangulate, abuse, love-bomb, devalue, discard, erode, gaslight, bait, provoke, fight, argue, rage, insult, malignant, mind-games, ghost, stonewall, silent treatment, smear, one-upmanship, dose, bait, hoover, invalidate, future-proof, zero respect, accusation, isolation, threats, jealousy and devastation.

Are you starting to get the picture?

Am I starting to paint it well for you?

No happy or positive words there at all is there... There are 58 that I count in total above and I can honestly and confidently state that I experienced 51 of them at some point during the fourteen years, many of them over and over.

Welcome to the world involving a narcissist.

Chapter Two
What Is Love-Bombing/Idealisation?

Well, I have certainly ended the last chapter on a negative note that is for sure!

This chapter we will look at the phenomenon that is classed as love-bombing, or the more formal term of idealisation. As I have mentioned previously, this is always at the start of your encounter with a narcissist when in a relationship with one, but it is also played out intermittently during the relationship as well, forming part of the abuse cycle, though it will not be as intense as in the beginning.

If we look at communication and the efforts we make towards organic and or intelligent beings and matter. What is the one thing that transgresses all levels? What is the one thing that most human beings and even some animals respond to?

It is of course 'love'.

I do not doubt for one minute that if you showed or demonstrated love for another being, intelligent or otherwise, that they would not naturally respond to that show of love. It could be another human, or a dog or cat, or another domestic animal, you can guarantee that they all would understand and respond to love.

So, what exactly is it?

I mean what is Love?

If you were asked to describe it, what would your response be?

The official definition is that love is an intense feeling of deep affection, along with a great interest and pleasure in something. It has also been described as having a deep concern for another person. Basically, if you show love, you will show compassion. If you love another person, you are willing to give yourself to that person whole. It goes hand in hand.

If you love your dog or cat you will ensure that they are safe, warm, fed, cuddled and fussed. This is your way of demonstrating your love towards your pet. If you did not love it, yes you may still take care of its basic needs like food and water, but you could not shower it with affection. If you do not feel it, you simply will not demonstrate it and if you did you would be 'faking' it.

This is what a narcissist does.

A narcissist will fake their love for you because they themselves cannot feel the emotion of love towards another person. They learn how to mirror it and how to project it because they know it will give them what they are ultimately seeking, which is of course their narcissistic supply, or fuel.

I-believe-your-abuse state,

'The 'Love' you thought was real doesn't exist. What was going on in the name of 'Love' is this: You were the vehicle to feed the narcissist's 'false self' to avoid his or her internal damage. They never loved you, cared for you, kind to you, supported you…'nothing!' The relationship was never going to be healthy or work.

If you are naturally compassionate, trusting, generous or even vulnerable, and you always seek to see the best in a person then unfortunately you are a picture-perfect match and ultimate target for a narcissist. Some will class this character type as an empath, but I believe that most human beings are naturally compassionate which makes most of us 'empaths'.

Do not get me wrong, please do not credit all narcissists as being emotionally intelligent enough to deliberately seek out this type of person. Rather they have merely learnt how to sense these qualities in another person and are then drawn to them like a magnet. Basically, the more you can offer or give to a narcissist, the more they will be drawn to you and the more they will take.

Another quote I like by narcissist recovery says,

'The 'Narcissist' doesn't want your love. They don't know what love is. They want your admiration and your obedience as a player in their fake make-believe world.'

A Narcissist is extremely skilled at obtaining their target and captivating them by using what is termed love-bombing.

Remember the description of love-bombing in the index at the start of this book?

Well, a narcissist will play on your emotions and will be overly affectionate towards you, often declaring their love for you after a noticeably short period into the relationship. For me, it was just three weeks after we had finally met in person that the Nex told me that he loved me. He told me that I was the love of his life and that he had never felt that way about anyone else before, not ever in his entire life. He stated that he had never felt like this with anyone else and that was what made me so special. What an absolute load of bullshit! I have no doubt whatsoever that going forward he will simply continue to spin this lie to all the future victims that he meets.

Another article I read on Quora states that a narcissist does not bond or have emotional connections with another person. They just need people to fulfil the roles of narcissistic supply (fuel) to keep their ego narratives going. A narcissist will up and leave people very easily if they decide it suits them. This is because they were never really connected to that person. People are nothing more than supply. Supply serves an ego function and an ego purpose. When it no longer serves that function or purpose, they simply discard. They purely aim to treat people like objects. For me, this is one of the best and most simple descriptions of what narcissistic supply (fuel) is, and why they need it.

So, remember what I told you about my first encounter with my Nex, and how we had a month's interlude where he Ghosted me? Well, he got back in touch in the November of 2004 and wanted us to meet up very soon after that. I have to say at this point in my story that such was the huge inexplicable draw that I felt towards the Nex because of his virtual 'love-bombing' that I felt like I had 'known' him for ages.

So, we arranged to meet at a large shopping mall near my hometown. I did offer to meet him halfway, but he said no he would travel up to me. He later went on to retell that story to folk that my halfway was not at all halfway and that he had been left with no choice but to travel all the way up to me! Of course, this was a lie. I simply used to just let it go because it really was not worth the hassle of pointing out the fact to him. Looking back, I am so glad now that I did not have the urge to correct him. I now recognise that it was said his way simply to make him look good and for me to look bad. Anyway, we arranged to meet on the first Saturday in December at this shopping mall in my hometown and I think I got there first. We had arranged to meet inside the complex but outside the doors of one of the shops and after some confusion as to what door it was, we finally met up. One of the first things he said to me after hello was 'You're gorgeous'. Of course, I was flattered, but he had also already seen me on photos and face to face on webcam. We went for a coffee at Starbucks and as we left the coffee shop he asked me if he could hold my hand. It was forward and I knew it was forward but at the time it did not feel odd or wrong. The Nex had spent the previous two weeks on the phone priming me with compliments, tales of fate, etc. When we left the shopping mall, we discovered that our cars were parked almost next to each other. He made such a big thing out of it, like 'We were meant to be' and of course I believed that it must have been fate. What absolute baloney! Now I believe that it was actually done deliberately to get this exact reaction from me, because after all, I had a distinct number plate and as I was parked near to the shop we were meeting at, it was probably orchestrated deliberately by him. In other words, he took a gamble that this was my car and that gamble paid off. This flips me back to what I said in the Introduction that you realise that none of your relationship was ever 'real'. You have so many memories come flashing back through your mind that you start to view them in a completely different way. You cannot help it and you are left never really knowing what was real and what was not real so you cannot help but be left thinking that none of it ever was. That it was all fake. That your entire relationship was fake and made up of fake moments and memories.

A quote by Maria Consiglio sums this up perfectly,

'Imagine coming to the realisation that the person you married, the person you thought you were going to spend the rest of your life with, is neither capable, nor has the desire to love you. Imagine that person has no care or compassion for your difficulties, or trials. Imagine realising your whole relationship was a farce. And the only real thing they feel for you is contempt. That is what it is like for victims, who married a narcissist or sociopath'.

The Nex and I subsequently spent what was left of the rest of that weekend together and on the Sunday as he was leaving he gave me a card. I really cannot remember whether he handed it to me or whether he had left it for me to find when he had gone. This minor detail is not what is important in this instance but rather what is important is what the card contained. It was a Thank You card in which he had written 'I really like you' inside of it. Of course, I was flattered, bowled over and all the other crappy sentimental terminology you can think of but a sensible conscious part of me did find it strange as to how and why someone I had only just met 24 hours earlier could give me a card

59

that he had obviously written 'before' he had even met me the previous day. This was a major Red Flag that with hindsight I should have been alerted to but was not and unless you know about narcissism you would not know this, you really would not. This is how clever and devious a narcissist is at hoodwinking and conning you. More importantly, of how you can be completely blinded during the love-bombing phase.

At the beginning of a new relationship with a narcissist, they absolutely love the way that you are making them feel. They are genuinely not interested in you per se, rather they are only interested in what you can provide to them by way of supply, or fuel, with your praise, admiration, adoration, security and financially. They experience a heady rush of euphoria with dreams of all that you can and will provide to them, but really you are nothing more than their new shiny toy.

So, what can you expect during this love-bombing phase?

I will share more of my examples shortly. In the meantime, here are some signs to look out for that will indicate you are experiencing love-bombing.

The relationship is moving very fast, they love absolutely everything that you do (mirroring), they come across as needing to be rescued (playing the victim), labels you as boyfriend/girlfriend after only two weeks, and they make you feel as though you truly have found your soulmate in them.

The early days are filled with charm, mirroring, feigned affection, lots of calls and texts and wanting to see you all the time. I remember that the following weekend after we had met I had my brother's 40th birthday party on the Saturday evening and I was working during the day so I said I would not be able to see him and so we arranged for me to go to his hometown the following weekend, two weeks later. He rang me the day before my busy Saturday and said he was really missing me, and would I mind if he drove up later that Friday evening to see me even though he knew I would be leaving for work early the next morning (6 am). This is a four-hour round drive that we are talking about here, so a substantial distance just to 'drop by'. I of course, was again flattered and pleased that he was so keen to see me after only one week. Of course, I did not know about love-bombing then and that this was yet another major red-flag. So, he drove up and I remember it was quite late on in the evening because we went to a pub for a meal once he had arrived only to discover that they had stopped serving at 9 pm.

We ended up going back to mine and picking up a Chinese takeaway on the way back. This meant that he had driven for two hours purely to be able to see me for less than ten hours of which the majority would be spent sleeping. Also, later, on that same Saturday evening whilst I was at my brother's birthday party he called me and put me on the phone to a relative of his who he said wanted to say hello to me. Again, a red flag as he knew I was at my brother's party. I have to say though that this relative, is probably the best thing and the only positive thing to come out of the relationship, but more about that later!

What I'm trying to tell you is that at the time it did not feel strange, it did not feel abnormal or over the top behaviour, and that is because the narcissist is very clever at what they do. They have you believe that this intense period spent Love-Bombing you is normal, acceptable, has 'boundaries', that it is to be expected and really what love is all about. Except of course it is not at all. It is all cleverly designed to draw you in and to ensnare you.

A narcissist will target you in such a way that will move your relationship with them on very quickly and which will make the relationship become serious extremely fast. To a narcissist, this is an especially important stage because it will determine just how many boundaries you will allow them to cross. It also gives them an idea of just how much abuse you will tolerate and accept from them.

Rhonda Freeman, PhD, has a particularly good descriptive image of what love-bombing is; it depicts a picture of a man holding a balloon in the shape of a heart and giving it to the woman. It features two captions of 'What you see' and 'What the reality is'.

What you see: 'You're an angel from heaven! I cannot stop thinking about you day and night. I am here for you anytime you need me. I want to take you everywhere, give you the finest things, I love you!'

Reality: 'I am addicted to you because I have a reward system that is hyperactive. It causes me to feel lust and attraction more intensely than others. I am extremely excited with my new thing. This new thing is really fun'.

Maria Consiglio of @understandingthenarc has stated that cult leaders use love-bombing in their pursuit of victims to their cause. She describes love-bombing as 'the excessive use of love and adoration purely for the purpose of manipulating a person and gaining control of them'. A narcissist will love you, make you feel special, wanted and adored until you have let them in then they will criticize you, judge you and put you down. You are no longer good enough. The narcissist now has control of you, a trauma bond is created, the addiction is in place, so the victim will continuously long for the initial love-bombing phase from the narcissist, but most importantly will not leave them. The trauma bond has been created.

She also states that, 'There is no mystery why the love-bombing stage is so powerful. Everyone needs validation. More than anything people want to be seen and heard. During the initial stages of the relationship, narcissists do that in spades. People finally feel special and wanted. That is more powerful than people realise. You could be with a narcissist for ten years and you are still reminiscing about the first few months of the relationship, even though the rest of it was not good.'

During the love-bombing phase, the narcissist will feed you constant praise and attention via text message, Messenger, Facebook, WhatsApp, emails and so on. You will soon have your favourite song, favourite film and pet names for each other. For me, our movie was 'You've got Mail'. I told him it was a favourite of mine and how strange that it was his too! You must remember that we met in the millennium, before Facebook and Instagram, and before smart phones, so emails were a prime source of communication for us. So, can you see where this is going? If you know the movie you will know that it is a love story and the two main characters are played by Tom Hanks and Meg Ryan and yes you guessed it correctly, on email correspondence he fondly referred to me as Meg and himself as Tom! You look back on it now and realise that it really is 'Stick your fingers down your throat' kind of sickness and mentality and you realise just how crazy it really all is but at the time, when you are bang in the middle of it, you simply do not see this, you are so flattered and bowled over, and simply cannot imagine a life without the narcissist. Of course, we had pet names. This is not uncommon in normal life. A parent may have a pet name for their child, a friend for another friend, and of course in an intimate relationship. But when used by a narcissist it takes on a whole new meaning.

My Nex would always call me babe, lovely, sweetheart and so on and I called him hon. This terminology made me feel special, but you learn through your gathering of knowledge on narcissism that a narc does not use your name for a reason. This is not because they want you to feel loved and adored, it is because they do not want to acknowledge you for who you really are which is of course, 'you!' They do not really see you as the person that you are. They purely see you as their supply. To them, by not calling you by your name they are effectively devaluing your identity. You just do not know this. Some will say that this is a red flag to look out for. Likewise, once we were married he often referred to me as 'My wife' but mostly just 'The wife' and in the last couple of years he referred to me as 'Mate'. For example, 'Mate, can you pass me the salt please'. This does not mean that they will never use your name, they will, just not as often as what is normal. The lack of use of your name will not be exclusive to intimate relationships either, friends or family will also be subject to 'pet' names. When I heard the Nex then using the exact same terms of endearment on his latest victim I realised that their use is nothing special at all because the narcissist merely rolls them out for their next victim.

HG Tudor states that the use of a pet name is used to demean, upset and exert control over you. He says that it is done because in their eyes, you are a narcissist's possession. According to HG, the use of a pet name by a narcissist should never be regarded as being a compliment or pleasant.

My friends often called me Kaz, which is short for my name, but the Nex used to take the piss out of this and belittle the use of it. He could not understand why friends liked to call it me and why I did not mind being called it, so much so, that I became embarrassed and uncomfortable when I was called it.

I was effectively placed on a pedestal in the early days and frequently told how wonderful I was and how special I was. My response was always to say that I was really nothing special but rather that I was only normal. Now I can see it for exactly what it was which was a narcissist putting me on that pedestal, way up there, as part of the love-bombing phase.

Love-bombing is designed to break down your defences rapidly. You allow your heart to rule over your head as the chemicals in your brain cause you to become addicted to the intense pleasure that you are feeling. That heady rush. The excessive attention and compliments that you receive fill you up with joy and feed any insecurities that you may have.

To put it more bluntly, when you fall in love with a narcissist you are really falling in love with yourself. I know this sounds weird so let me explain. When you fall for this person, you are really falling for a mask, a false façade, because the person you fell in love with does not really exist. You were simply falling in love with a reflection of what you wanted and what you yourself actually are. This is because the narcissist was reflecting your own wants and qualities right back at you so they could ensnare you. If you saw the real person, the empty shell, their true inner self, that is really the narcissist, the vindictive, cruel, evil and abusive person that they really are, trust me you would run a mile, in fact more like a marathon!

Narc-abuse-is-real state,

'A normal person can't just turn love off, but a narcissist can turn it off just as easily as they turned it on because showing love is a tool they use to con people.'

For a narcissist, the love-bombing phase or idealisation phase is the most important one for them. For it to work, for you to become their next 'victim' they must create such a sense of devotion from you to ensure that you will stick around when the devaluation phases come. Like an addiction, once you are ensnared they know that they can throw whatever crap at you, and you will just keep coming back for more. They know that you will become confused, blame yourself, but more importantly that you will be trying to reclaim the love-bombing phase because you still believe that it was real. Do not get me wrong, you will still encounter periods of love-bombing/idealisation as part of their insidious cycle against you, but all this does is just confuse you more and ultimately prevent you from walking away. HG Tudor refers to these as nothing more than 'respite periods' that come intermittently during devaluation.

From all that I have read, I have formed my own opinion that later in the relationship you do not get the intense love-bombing that you did receive at the start of the relationship. I think this is purely reserved for the initial entrapment. Further down the line when you are on this see-saw of idealise/devalue, what you get from the narcissist is intermittent spurts of kindness. For instance, a bunch of flowers, a meal cooked for you, a night out, a bar of chocolate or futureproofing (pretend nice future things that will of course never happen). These occasions will of course come sporadically. One of the Nex's favourites was a promise of a belated honeymoon on our tenth wedding Anniversary. Why we had to wait till the tenth year I will never know. Ironically, we split six months before our tenth wedding anniversary! Maybe he always knew that this was going to be our 'shelf-life'? At other times he would say 'I'm going to book a nice holiday for us' but of course he never did. If I asked him why he had not booked it, such was his conviction at the time, he would of course blame me and say, 'I can't book one at short notice because you will say that you have to work'.

Another time was when he was diagnosed with a treatable cancer at the start of 2010. Boy was I love-bombed again, then. I received a massive bouquet of flowers (I had not received any for quite some time) shortly after his diagnosis. They were sent to my work too, for full effect. He had 'never' done this before! I then received another massive bouquet of flowers that Valentine's Day which was only about two weeks later. I know this sounds really ungrateful and especially at such a time, but it was so out of character for him that I never forgot it and of course now that I know about love-bombing, I now understand that this is what was happening once again. He was scared that I may have walked away and not care for him during his treatment. I did of course support him totally throughout for the entirety of it, financially, physically and emotionally while still holding down a job and caring for a fifteen-year-old sitting her GCSE's and a seventeen-year-old sitting his A levels, and all the while suffering from my own undiagnosed illness at the time, my best friend's father dying suddenly, my beloved dog dying suddenly and the Nex's mother dying! I cannot stress enough that I am most certainly not after a medal for this because this is part of life, all the shit rolled into one, it is part of being in a relationship and part of a marriage, in sickness and in health, for better or for worse. Most of all, it is part of loving someone. But it will give you a kind of peek into just how particularly difficult and stressful that period was, and just how many curve balls that had been flung along the way, so any 'bad behaviour' by the Nex was excused not only by him completely, but also unwittingly by me.

I will say at this stage that on the day that my dog died in the October of that year and after the Nex was better and had returned to work, there was a family event planned for later that afternoon and it was the last thing that I felt like going to as I was so upset at the loss of my beloved dog. But the Nex had absolutely no empathy for me whatsoever and insisted that I went with him because my presence was expected, and I had to go. I was so hurt by how heartless he was. I cried over the loss of my dog for many weeks and months after that but always in silence when he was not around or late at night in bed when he was asleep. He had made me feel like I could not mourn for the loss of my beloved dog.

At the time of his treatment, you just get on with it, such is life, but I never forgot his constant promise to me that once he had finished his treatment he would take me away for a special weekend. This of course would have been the very first weekend he would have ever taken me away on in our six years together at this point, of which two of them we were married, and I stupidly believed him. I ridiculously clung on to it happening to help me through those dark days. That is what you do as part of the conditioning you go through. You cling on to the morsels that are thrown at you. But the special weekend away never happened. In fact, once he was well and truly back to normal later that year it was never mentioned again. Rather, I was the one who had took him away for a weekend during his treatment and after it, in the August, I had used my redundancy pay to take all the family on a luxurious holiday as part of the recovery process for all of us. For the Nex, the promise of that weekend away was nothing more than another future-proofing exercise.

What I am saying here is the fact that futureproofing will occur not only at the beginning of the relationship when the love-bombing is in full pelt, but it will also carry on throughout the duration of your relationship with your narcissist. Just like the title of this book, 'I promise I'll make you happy', a narcissist will 'promise' to take care of you, that they will look after you, will pay for you and will 'love' you forever. But they will not. This is merely all lies designed to get you hooked, to make you stay. What a narcissist is really wanting is 'you' to make them happy, to take care of them, for you to pay for everything, as was in my case. Do not be surprised if they have told you that you are the love of their life, their soulmate, their everything, the best woman (or man) that they have ever had, and that they cannot wait to marry you. All lies! They are simply telling you everything they think you want to hear. I remember a ludicrous comment that the Nex used to say to me which now that I recall it, is so laughable, and this was that I was the first woman he had ever felt comfortable enough with to fart in front of! Yes, you read that correctly. Prior to me, allegedly, he had never been able to break wind in front of any of his girlfriends, or first wife, before he met me.

By providing you with some examples of what 'love-bombing' looks like, what it feels like, and what idealisation is, I am hoping that you may get to recognise these at the start of any potential relationship with a narcissist, and throughout your relationship when you are in the 'respite' phase (idealise) from the Abuse. Because, you will not know that you have embarked on a relationship with a narcissist that is for sure. What I must stress to you is that you learn the red flags to look out for, to recognise and identify them from what is normal and acceptable behaviour to what is the indication of a narcissist

66

lurking, and this is in the hope that you dodge the nasty curve ball that is a narcissist.

R H Sin states that, 'Love-bombing is an attempt to cover up mistreatment, disrespect and or betrayal by showering a person with forced affection and attention. This can be used to confuse you and manipulate you into providing second chances to people who in fact intended to hurt you. Be careful'.

Post-split, I heard the Nex, during a fall out he had obviously had with his latest victim. He was crying those fake crocodile tears and putting on his pity play act because he did not want her to dump him. He was actively love-bombing her and hoovering her while intermittently blaming her for everything, and to hear it in play rather than experience it myself was amazing. When you yourself are the victim you do not see it, you do not know what it is you are experiencing. He was so damn good that for all of two minutes I felt sorry for him myself! This was despite my knowledge by this stage of what he was and that it was all fake and false. I still actually felt sorry for him! Then I quickly pulled myself together. What was even more tragic was that she had obviously spent a period of Silent Treatment being meted out to her, but clearly did not know that this is what was happening, and during this period the Nex had actually put himself back on the dating sites just in case he did not win her over with the pity party he had lined up for her! How do I know this? Well, it just so happened that an old work colleague of mine was on the same dating site, and she spotted him. This was also around the same time that he had sent me an email telling me that he loved his latest victim more than life itself and that he could not wait to marry her! It just further served as validation for me as to what he was.

A quote by Kathryn Spangler @Kathryn-rising sums up the above paragraph pretty well,

'One of the weirdest aspects of narcissistic abuse is feeling sorry for the person who treats you like complete shit.'

I thought a good way to end this chapter was by citing you a quote that I read recently by @narcissistic-abuse-is-real,

'I'm going to groom you to believe that I am everything you want. But in reality, you're 'all' I'm looking for... I will mirror you and make you believe you have found the love of your life... I will end up with 'everything' I want... And you will lose 'everything' you ever were...'

love-bombing summed up in a quote,

Chapter Three
What Is Devaluation?

Devaluation.

Just as night follows day, this will follow the idealisation (love-bombing) phase of your relationship with the narcissist. There is no escaping from it. No dodging it. Once the narcs rose-coloured glasses of you have fallen off and you are viewed as black, and once he has grown bored of his shiny new toy or more importantly you have pissed him off over something, the devaluation will come. It will come intermittently or continuously, depending on your narcissist's current state of mind.

So, what exactly is devaluation?

The official definition is,

'The reduction or underestimation of the worth or importance of something'.

Personally, I think that this sums it up perfectly.

Why?

Because it describes exactly what the narcissist is going to do to you, is doing to you and has done to you.

A quote by Bree Bonchay at narcissist.sociopath.awareness2 under the heading 'Relationship with a narcissist in a nutshell' states,

'You will go from being the perfect love of their life to nothing you do is ever good enough. You will give your everything & they will take it all & give you less & less in return. You will end up depleted emotionally, mentally, spiritually & probably financially, & then you'll get blamed for it'.

So, the next question is, why does it come?

Well, for starters it is because the narcissist has gotten comfortable with you, gotten secure. Found that you are easy to manipulate. It will then happen because of a perceived slight or upset that you have caused the narcissist. I say perceived because ninety nine percent of the time you really will not have done anything wrong whatsoever. The narcissist may have deliberately manufactured the issue or problem so that they can unleash their period of devaluation on you. Or you have 'injured' them innocently. This can be for any reason. Maybe you have not paid them enough attention, maybe they are getting low on their precious fuel, maybe you simply did not take out the garbage! Or you have said something that the narcissist has simply taken offence to. There is never any true justification for it. You never know when it is going to come, how it will come and what will come. All I do know and can tell you is that it will blindside you when it does come, like a bolt out of the blue.

If it is the remaining one percent of the above scale and by that I mean you did genuinely do something to upset the narcissist it will not be resolved like it would be in a normal relationship. It will not be discussed, debated and resolved. Instead, you will be blamed for 'all' of it, you will face deflection, projection, blame-shifting, and you will then be ghosted, stone-walled, and ultimately may face what will be the first of many silent treatments from the narcissist. If the Narc is of the lesser brigade, then unfortunately you will no doubt also suffer from an act of violence towards you as well.

The devaluation comes in the form of abuse: emotional, verbal and even physical, covertly, overtly, silently and insidiously.

This abuse 'will' start slowly.

So, what forms of abuse are we talking about?

EVERY SINGLE ONE!

Verbal and Emotional Abuse: Screaming at you, calling you names, insulting you verbally, criticizing you, making threats of violence towards you, body shaming you, putting you down, parroting you and what you are saying, gaslighting you, controlling you.

Oh boy, where do I start with examples of my treatment at the hands of my narcissist? I guess I have to say that I was quite fortunate considering what I have since learnt from the Women's Aid meetings that I attended. Most of the Nex's abuse towards me was verbal and emotional followed quickly by the silent treatment! But this does not mean that absolutely none of it was not physical. Nor does it lessen its damaging effects on me psychologically or emotionally.

Over the years during many of my Nex's tirades towards me, I was called 'Crazy bitch' and 'Ugly bitch', or worse still the dreaded 'C' word, often with a prefix of the 'F' word in front for good measure! These were not one offs, but rather during 'every' single tirade I would have these names slung at me. A very memorable occasion of emotional abuse towards me was when I had my graduation in January 2009. We had only been married a few weeks and I had passed my course five months prior to that. So, my graduation arrived, we had stayed at my parent's house the night before because my graduation was in my hometown, and nothing had been mentioned about the context of my graduation at all or what would take place. The Nex had asked me absolutely nothing about it. Well, in the morning as I was donning my gown, the Nex turned around and casually asked me what name my degree was going to be presented in. I replied my previous name. I still innocently did not know what was coming next at this point. He then started questioning me about why it was not in my new married name (his) and I explained that I had passed my degree before we had married but that I had missed the October graduation which I should have attended so I was being presented with my degree in that January instead. A straightforward and simple explanation that anyone normal would have simply accepted. Well, the Nex did not do normal, ever! He went ballistic at me. How did I think he would feel having to stand there and watch me receive my certificate in a name that was not his? How cruel was I. How thoughtless was I. How dare I treat him that way. How dare I belittle him. Now remember I told you that this was one of his favourite words, doled out on a regular basis where you got to the point of thinking 'change the record!' I was so upset and devastated that I could not speak for fear of crying. When we went downstairs, he pretended that all was okay in front of my parent's, but I was still quiet, still in shock and reeling from the onslaught I had just received from him. So, once in the car on the way to the ceremony he had the nerve to ask me what was wrong! Unbelievable! He went one step further and said that if I did not paint a smile on my face and if I continued to 'sulk' with him he would get out of the car and go home. So, I had to paint a strained false smile on my face while inside I felt like I was dying. I do not remember my graduation with happy memories or proud thoughts at all. Instead, I just remember his treatment of me on that day and how what should have been such a proud and happy occasion for me was spoilt, marred, and ruined beyond salvation. I now know through what I have learnt about narcissists that this is a normal behaviour pattern of theirs. That they will deliberately spoil a happy event, a special event, or a birthday or a Christmas because they cannot stand the thought that the attention is not on them and that the occasion is not all about them. They totally resent any attention being on their partner, or anyone else for that matter instead. This was certainly not the last time I witnessed this kind of behaviour from the Nex that is for sure. I will give you more examples later in the book. Of course, on this occasion my graduation and any nice or happy memories I should have had of it were irreversibly and utterly destroyed.

More examples of verbal and/or emotional abuse are alienating you from your friends and family. Humiliating you in front of others. Comparing partners. In the latter days of our relationship, I was compared unfavourably to his ex-wife. Accusing you of cheating. That will be a yes for me too. Insulting and derogatory comments towards you. Another yes there then for me. Orders and demands being barked at you. That one is a yes too, examples of all of these are to follow later in the book. Cancelling events at short notice. Another yes. Not long after I had moved down to be with him we were invited to an RSPCA ball in my hometown with a friend and her partner and I had gotten tickets for the Nex and I. I had of course asked him earlier if he had wanted to go and he had said yes. On the morning of the event, I was getting ready, and he turned around to me and casually said, 'I've been thinking, it's not really my kind of thing so I'm not coming'. And that was that. No further comment or discussion. It was shut down. He did not come! So, I ended up going alone.

One of my good friends recently pointed out that in the beginning the most obvious and easiest option open to us was for the Nex to move up to my hometown, rather than I move to his. He was self-employed and could literally work anywhere, he had no children and already lived a half an hour away from his family. But no, in the Nex's opinion this was not an option, I was the one who had to give up her job, her home, her family and her friends and my entire life as I knew it while my children also had to give up their school, their friends and their life as they knew it too. To him, this was the only option available. He was not prepared to see any aspect of his life changed or altered in any way whatsoever. He had therefore successfully managed to isolate me from my family and friends. With hindsight, I now see this as another red flag that I missed, as this is common behaviour with a narcissist. It is easier for them to manipulate and control you without an audience.

Stonewalling and using the silent treatment are also forms of emotional abuse. So is hacking your phone, social media and emails. The Nex did all of this too, but it was after discard, so I will explain all about it and give examples of what he did and how he did it during that chapter.

Another form of abuse is for them to use cognitive dissonance against you. This basically means that the narcissist is portraying a conflicting attitude towards you. For example, a Narc might say to you 'I can take you or leave you'. As I have said earlier, my Nex's favourite term of phrase that best describes this was, 'If you ever leave me I will just switch off'. He portrayed that he loved me but if I ever left him he would just 'switch' that 'love' off like a light switch. Of course, now I know that he really meant this statement because he could not feel Love, thus switching off for him was no big deal as he did not feel it in the first place. For me, this turn of phrase was alien and confusing because it conflicted with what he was telling me when he said, 'I Love you'. I knew that you just could not switch such an intense feeling like love on and off, unless of course you are a narcissist and do not ever really feel it.

Cognitive Dissonance is used to cause you discomfort, confusion and tension.

Physical Abuse: pushing, biting, slapping, punching, grabbing you, physically stopping you from leaving, tickling you when you have told him to stop and throwing objects at you. I can testify to all of these being used bar the biting.

For a lot of women this form of abuse can escalate, to the point that it can become dangerous for the woman to remain in the home. Statistics show that almost one in three women aged 16–59 will experience domestic abuse or better termed, domestic violence in her lifetime. Two women a week are killed by a current or former partner in England and Wales alone. Or from another perspective, a violent partner will kill a woman every three days.

That is a scary statistic because just how many of those do we hear about in the press?

Very few!

In 2018, 173 women were killed as a result of domestic violence in the UK, and it is at its highest level in five years. The police reported that there had been an increase of 32 deaths since 2017. That is a five-fold increase in just a year, twelve months. The lack of publicity demonstrates that perversely we are becoming accustomed and acclimatised to these murders. Just like we have with the consistent rise in knife crime in the UK. It is important to note that domestic abuse and domestic violence is orchestrated and carried out by people with a variety of disorders, for instance, psychopaths, sociopaths and narcissists. I am not aware of any study that has been conducted to establish what exact percentage is apportioned to which group. But if I were to hazard a guess I would say that narcissists will form the largest percentage and the largest group. If you happen to be really unlucky, your abuser could even be a narcissistic psychopath.

www.carolinestrawson.com states that, 'He doesn't have to hit you for it to be abuse. He can degrade, humiliate, blame, curse, manipulate, or try to control you. It's still domestic violence'.

So, for me I did indicate that mine was not completely void of any violence. I had the pushing, the slapping, the grabbing, objects thrown at me, and yes the tickling. Done allegedly in fun but not stopped when told it was too much, as it was becoming painful. His favourite though was the grabbing of me by the scruff of the neck and waving his fist in my face. It worked because I was always fearful that the waved fist would become a punch to my face. This action of his was enough to frighten me into believing that the fist flying and striking my face could and would happen at some point. I knew the triggers for his anger and aggression so I always backed down immediately or did not question him because I could never be sure that the fist would not fly. I think now with hindsight that this is the only reason why he was not violent towards me more often, because he had instilled this fear in me at the start and he had realised that this was an effective way to control me.

The first time I did experience anything physical was when I had emailed a work colleague and innocently signed it off with a customary kiss. This was normal for me on any email, text or letter to someone informal in my life. He knew that and it had never bothered him before. Another narcissistic trait where they can suddenly change their stance or their view on something. Such was his anger on this occasion at what I had just done in front of him that he grabbed me by the scruff of the neck and pinned me against the kitchen units. Of course, I was shocked! I had never experienced such behaviour against me in all my forty-four years at that precise moment. We had been living together for maybe just two years at that point. And of course, it was all my fault, I had deliberately wound him up, blah blah blah. I then got the usual 'End of the relationship routine' and the silent treatment that lasted for days and in the end I was the one who ended up having to apologise and grovel. The second time was not long after this first one and I had gone for a walk with my beloved Husky and the Nex was in a foul mood when I got back. I cannot remember what had caused his anger (many events were from a trivial start point), but on my return he went totally ballistic about where I had been. He tried to cover up his anger with an excuse of concern, but it did not stop him from preventing me from leaving the room we were in and then when he did finally let me pass he pushed me so hard that I stumbled. The third one I do remember well because it was the day before our wedding party in the spring of 2009. We had gotten married four months earlier and were throwing a reception the following spring. My parents were coming down and my beloved late father loved to play golf so the Nex kept telling him that he would take him golfing the day after our party (futureproofing). So, the day before, he informed me that he was going to ensure that he got pissed at the party and I simply reminded him that he was due to play golf with my dad the day after. Well, his response was shocking and unbelievable to say the least. He again grabbed me by the scruff and pinned me against the wall, waving his fist in my face and screaming at me. For the first time, I did feel real genuine fear, such was his venom. I seriously was expecting that punch to my face. Once he had released me, I put the dining table between me and him because I feared a further assault would be coming, but he simply justified his behaviour by telling me that it was my fault for winding him up and controlling him (that was a new one!) and that if he did not want to play golf with my dad then he would not. I should not have pushed it, should not have tried telling him what to do, should not have called him on it, should not have tried to control him and so on. Of course, none of this was true. You must realise at this point that this was only the third time he had shown violence towards me in four and a half years. So, to me, there was not a pattern there, the events were so random, and such is the narcissists conditioning of you through gaslighting, that yes you do believe that it must be your fault. That you made them do it. They make you feel sorry for them. Hence, you stay. You do not walk away. As I did on this occasion and all the others. This did not lessen how I felt though when the physical threat was made. It not only frightened me, but also shocked me, and made me wary and fearful as to whether he would ever do it and punch me in the face. I came to realise eventually after the second and third time he did it, that he was using the threat deliberately to control and manipulate me, and to make me shut up and back down. But because I never really knew for sure or not whether he would take it that far and the fist that was waved in my face would ever strike, I never put it to the test.

The next violent episode came again with a long period in between, five years to be precise. When I say long periods, I am only referring to the physically violent episodes. Trust me when I say that there were many more episodes and periods of abuse, devaluation, silent treatments and threatened discards in between. This next time, he had gone on holiday with his brother in the summer of 2014. You remember that I had mentioned the restaurant my friend and I had opened the previous year? Well, to cut a long story short we had been taken to court for reducing our rent because the building was in such a state of disrepair. On this particular day, we had lost our initial case which we did eventually go on to win later down the line in 2016 after we had had to close the business. So, I called the Nex to give him the outcome of the court case as he had insisted that I do this (pretend caring), and the response I got back when I gave him my news was downright absurd and completely, utterly irrational. He went ballistic at me, yet again. How dare I spoil his holiday, do not expect him to bail me out with money to pay the court costs, and so on it went. He finally slammed the phone down on me and proceeded to ghost and stonewall me for the rest of his holiday. He unfriended me and blocked me on Facebook (a favourite trick of his), blocked my calls and did not respond to texts. As this happened during the first week of his holiday I then had to endure approximately ten days of his beloved silent treatment towards me. I knuckled down and just got on with it. You must realise that by now after ten years of enduring them I was so used to them. I knew exactly what to expect. I actually enjoyed the peace and quiet on this occasion. Fast forward to his return home and he was civil with me but cold, responding in one syllable sentences. I pretended like nothing had happened, tried to give him a hug but he kept pushing me away pretending that he was busy doing something. At this point, I realised that he was still carrying a grudge and sure enough after I had made him some food and taken it through to him where he was sitting in the lounge, I then got the 'You spoilt my holiday, you're selfish, you're reckless, our relationship isn't working anymore (another of his favourite sayings) and finally his favourite one of all time, 'It's the end of the relationship'. For once I immediately just said fine, we will put the house on the market and then Wham! He threw the TV remote at me which hit, quickly followed by the bowl full of pasta in tomato sauce that I had just made for him. I did just manage to dodge that one. He proceeded to tell me that I had ruined his life, he switched on the crocodile tears and flounced off into the kitchen punching a hole in the door on his way. Wow I thought! Wow! You must realise that this was the very first time he did not get my usual response of trying to placate him, telling him that I was sorry and that I did not want the relationship to end. So that was his reaction. I had to subsequently calm him down and tell him that I had not meant it and of course I wanted our marriage to continue. Again, I was the one who did end up apologising to him! Little did I know that the reason he had reacted this way was because I had just caused him a massive narcissistic injury by agreeing to our break-up. The Nex had not received the cajoling and the apologies that would normally have come. But of course, once the victim role was played out by him, the crocodile tears flowing and the pity-play deployed, then he had succeeded in getting exactly what he had wanted all along! That is just how manipulative a narcissist is.

His reaction also provided him with his precious fuel and further acted as a way of regaining his power and control over me. Remember, a narcissist must 'always' have power and control. Again, nothing was resolved, no conversation was had, no resolution found, it was just buried under the carpet along with all the other many incidents.

I also now believe that his anger further stemmed as well from the fact that in that same year, 2014, I had taken my children to Italy for a holiday. This holiday was supposed to have been a 'family' holiday, and most likely the last one the 'kids' would have wanted to come on with us, but the Nex refused point blank to come. He stated that family holidays were now over for him because the children were young adults. He would not budge, so I ended up taking them on my own.

The final time he was this violent towards me was three years later, in 2017. Again, a very trivial event that had triggered it. The Nex had placed some CCTV under the bed in our bedroom, in the storage part and I had innocently asked him why he had moved it from downstairs and put it there. But I soon realised that it was also another weekend that I had just returned home from seeing my family and friends in my hometown. I do now believe that this was the actual trigger of his abusive behaviour and not the CCTV at all. He was jealous that I had spent my weekend with family and friends while he had chosen to stay home and do nothing. I therefore needed to be punished for this. So, while I was sitting in bed he stormed into the bedroom and grabbed me by the scruff of the neck and waved his fist in my face threatening to punch my lights out while the vile verbal insults just continued to flow out of his mouth. I really thought that this time the punch to my face was going to come, or he would strangle me or cause me some other physical harm, so for the first time ever I pushed him off me. He stormed out and went to sleep in the spare bedroom. And so, commenced yet another period of silent treatment for me. This one though lasted an entire week because for the first time ever I had really had enough. I chose not to try and cajole him in to talking to me this time. I chose for the very first time not to apologise for something that I had not done or caused. On the Thursday, four days into the silent treatment he disappeared and stayed away overnight. Nope, still no reaction from me as I knew that was exactly what he was wanting and that he would have simply gone to stay with a friend. On his return the next day, I did not ask him where he had been. On the day after that, the Saturday which was six days after the incident he finally came to speak to me. 'This was a first!' Never had he ever made the first move from a silent treatment before, not 'ever'. He said he was appalled that I had made no attempt to speak to him or care about where he had been that missing night. Looking back, I see just how laughable his behaviour really was. How ridiculously childish and pathetic. How typically narcissistic. I got the usual end of the relationship crap, with a new twist to it of him stating that these two friends he had stayed with had agreed with him that absolutely everything was my fault.

Now remember me mentioning the friends that I no longer spoke to?

Well, here now is the story surrounding this. I realised that I was right when I suspected it would have been these two friends that he had stayed with that missing night. Well, according to him they thought I was the Devil incarnate. He said that they no longer wanted to stay at our house because of 'my know it all' attitude; that they only tolerated seeing me for the Nex's sake. One of them was the same friend of his that I had helped win his own family court matters! In the Nex's opinion the solution was for me to continue to be their friend and see them but that I had to remain silent in their presence. Sit there like a little dormouse. Speak only when spoken to, problem solved in his eyes.

To this day I really do not know whether they had really said any of the things he claimed that they had said, because he was prone to drawing other people into his arguments and lying that they always agreed with him and that I was always the bad guy and that he was always the good guy. Because I did not know for sure of what was true here and what was lies, I could clearly see that it had rendered any further future friendship with them untenable for me. I told him as such. He was free to see them whenever he liked, but I would not. I never saw them again after that. Remember also that the Nex, being the narcissist that he was, had probably also Smeared me to them with a complete pack of lies and played the victim like only a Narcissist can. He did try over the rest of that year to make me see them by using direct threats towards me and by also using coercive tactics. I realise now that because I would not agree to any of his attempts he thus proceeded to punish me silently and 'silent treat' me for the next seventeen months, right up until we split up. I will explain more about this realisation later.

I did suggest that we seek couple's therapy on that Saturday and surprisingly he agreed only to turn around the night before we were due to go a week later and say, 'I don't think I need to go with you because there is nothing wrong with me and everything's always your fault. You should just learn to control your gob.' I went anyway and this was the very first time that I heard the term narcissist used but I did not pay it much attention right then.

Another occasion of violence after this was when the Nex punched me so hard in the back while I was asleep that I woke up in pain with my back smarting. He claimed that I was snoring, and he would not accept that a simple nudge to wake me would have sufficed. I was left with a bruise on my back from this. Looking back, this incident also occurred during the final devaluation phase and while he was punishing me silently for not speaking to his friends anymore. For whatever reason he had no doubt just been lying in bed absolutely seething and silently raging, so he struck out violently at me.

I think that because the violence was so sporadic and spread out over time I stupidly did not see it as true physical abuse. Because he always blamed me for absolutely everything and anything and because he gaslighted me into believing that it was all my fault I excused his behaviour. Justified it to myself. But most important of all, I did not leave.

Sexual Abuse: Rape, force, threats of harm, threats to cheat, ridicule, withholding sex.

My Nex certainly used ridicule towards me in the first few years before the sex ended. He used to bluntly state that I had a 'smelly cunt' (sorry, his words not mine) and often used this as an excuse to not have sex, of course it was never true, but he knew it greatly offended and hurt me. He would further comment on occasions that it was like dangling a 'Maggot in a Well'. This did used to deeply offend me and hurt me too, but it has recently made me silently laugh to myself because he did not realise at all that what he was in fact doing with this insult when fired at me was actually insulting himself by implying that he had a teeny tiny Todger! Oh, the Irony of it! You really cannot help but laugh at it now. For me, I could never get my head around how my partner, my husband could say such vile, insulting and abusive comments to me.

I have since learnt through attending the Freedom Programme with Women's Aid that this is not an uncommon comment for a narcissist to make to their partner. The label that the Freedom Programme gives the narcissist for this particular behaviour is the 'Headworker' and that it is common for them to use these types of offensive and insulting comments against their victim, depending on where you live in the country (UK). For instance, in Liverpool the narcissist will say that it is like the size of the Mersey Tunnel or another local one for my area is 'It's like driving a sausage up the M5!'. Learning this on the Freedom programme did further validate my belief that my Nex was and is indeed a narcissist and a headworker, and that his use of this vile abusive comment to me was par for the course when you are in a relationship with a narcissist, and that most importantly, it is deemed as domestic abuse.

For some narcissists, sex is a tool to use as a weapon against their victims. They will triangulate their partner and have multiple affairs during the relationship. If you ever challenged them on this and even had proof of their affairs they will just gaslight you and make you think that you are the crazy one. Fortunately, I do not think that my Nex did have affairs, but who truly knows? He did triangulate me other ways though. One of his previous girlfriends happened to work at the vets where I took my dog and once he knew this he befriended her on Facebook and told me he saw nothing wrong in meeting her for a coffee and a catch up. I told him that I was not entirely comfortable with him meeting an ex for 'coffee' and he informed me that it was not up to me, that he could and would see who the hell he wanted and 'How dare I question him about it!'. I do not know to this day whether he ever did meet up with her or not. I have since come to learn that he stated to someone while he was with me that he wished 'he'd never let her go'. Of course, we all know by now that this poor woman, who left him, had had an incredibly lucky escape!

In the beginning of our relationship, during the love-bombing and idealisation phases, the Nex informed me that he had never really been interested in sex or enjoyed it. He bullshitted me into believing that with me it was different. He stated that he now realised that he did love having sex, especially with me, and I would not be surprised at all now if he had churned this one out with all his victims.

Withholding Sex: Well at the time I did not think that this was the case but now I am not so sure? I am talking about after the Nex's bout of cancer. Because he had lost a certain body part he needed to take hormone replacement therapy. He refused point blank to have the yearly injection and instead opted to rubbing a gel into his thighs. He used to do this when he felt like it and I always knew when he was not applying it because he would become even more moody and aggressive. He was also given medication to help him 'Get it up'. He was diagnosed and treated at the beginning of 2010 and apart from once the following Christmas of 2011 we were never sexually intimate again! That is almost nine years of enforced celibacy for me. Do not get me wrong, I was a take it or leave it kind of girl by this stage anyway, but the one thing that stood out to me the most was the fact that it was 'never' discussed. We 'never' talked about the end of our physical intimate relationship and what we would and could do about it. In other words, as he 'could not perform' then neither could I! He made the decision unilaterally to end our physical relationship. Any opinion I may or may not have had was completely irrelevant, it was never asked for, never discussed and never sought. My physical capability had ended when his did. He never once thought to simply talk to me about this or explore how we could satisfy each other in different ways. It really was the end of our physical relationship in its entirety. Such was his selfishness that he did not give me a second thought. Oh, do not get me wrong I did suggest on several occasions that we take his pills away with us, but he always had one excuse or another as to why he did not take one. Usually that he did not like the side effects the tablets allegedly caused. Now I am not so sure that all these years were purely just excuses.

Why?

Because of what I have read about narcissism and that a lot of narcissists detest the intimacy that sex brings.

They are known to deliberately withhold sex from their partner as a form of control. This would fit right in with when not long before we finally broke up he passed a comment one morning that he had woken up with an erection or to put it bluntly, a hard on. Bear in mind that this was allegedly the first one that he had had in nine years! I did not react at all but simply said 'Oh really' without a single ounce of enthusiasm! I genuinely believe that he expected me to 'jump his bones' screaming 'It's a miracle' at the same time! When intimacy had been withheld for so long this was the last thing I was going to do, that is for sure! But most important of all is the fact that by this stage the devaluation was an almost continuous daily occurrence and getting physical with him was the very last thing on my mind for sure. As to whether he really did wake up with one or not, who knows?

I was either conned for the last nine years of our relationship where sex was concerned or the Nex will go on to con future victims.

Financial/Economic: Every single person who unfortunately becomes entangled in a relationship with a narcissist will lose out financially. A narcissist may have even targeted you in the first place because of what you could offer them from a financial point of view. They will steal from you, they will con you, they will take property from you, and they will even take your home away from you. You will ultimately always be the one paying for everything. Bills, nights out, weekends away, holidays and if you have children then financially they will be your sole responsibility. One of the reasons they do this is because of their overwhelming sense of entitlement.

Narcissist-abuse-is-real state, 'One of the nicest things about not being with the narcissist is that I finally get to keep my money. I never met anyone who was so content spending other people's money'.

For me, when I first met my Nex, I had a nice house in a nice area of the city where I lived. When I sold that house in 2005, I had made a profit of £105,000 once the mortgage was paid. The intention was that the Nex would sell his property too and we would buy a house together. This of course did not happen. I now realise that it was never his intention to sell. Oh, do not get me wrong there was a board at the house but no brochures and no viewings. He told me at the time that his house was valued at £210,000 and I had absolutely no reason to doubt him or question what he was saying. So, I handed over my

£105,000 to him to effectively buy fifty percent value of his property. I have to say that because I did not hand it over the minute it landed in my bank account I experienced what was probably my first real encounter of his venom. He was furious that I had not transferred it into his account immediately and I suffered his sulks until I transferred it the very next day. I never once thought 'Isn't it a coincidence that my profit is exactly half the value of his house!' The money was used to clear his mortgage and to put an extension on the property. My name never ended up on the deeds though as he said it was too expensive to put it on but that I could trust him. Oh boy if there was ever a time to 'not' trust him then this was it! As they say, hindsight is a wonderful thing.

Fast forward to after our split in June 2018 and I subsequently found out that his house had never been worth £210,000! At the time I bought into it in 2005, it was valued at £20,000 less, at £190,000! Can you begin to imagine what kind of devastation the discovery of this knowledge does to you? That the man you had loved and more importantly had trusted had deliberately lied to you at the onset just so he could deliberately con you out of £10,000 at the very start of your life together! Wow! Wow! Wow! What is even more appalling about this is that my late father had asked me if I could loan him a small amount of money to secure the purchase of a new vehicle. It was to only be for a short period until he could transfer the cash from his savings account and so I asked the Nex for £2000 of my money back so that I could give it to my father, and he point blank refused. He claimed that it was all accounted for despite it only being a few weeks since I had transferred it all over to him. I felt awful letting my father down and I never forgot it. So, to then find out post-split that the Nex had effectively conned me and stolen £10,000 extra from me at the onset just floored me and devastated me.

This was not an isolated incident though. Because he was a builder he built the extension himself while I paid all the bills, bought all the food, paid for all the nights out, and holidays. I even gave him £100 a week for 'pocket money' which he ended up using towards paying his labourer. This continued until towards the end of 2006, over a year later when the extension was finished. I never knew the true cost of the extension but now believe that it was far less then he had told me it was. You also get to learn later down the line how a Narcissist just loves to exaggerate. For the next three years, we then split the bills (it worked out at me paying seventy percent and him paying thirty percent as his pension was being paid out of the joint account too), but I still paid for the majority of everything else. I did not mind either of this as I was also supporting my children. During the extension build the Nex demanded that I took him out every Thursday evening for a meal and drinks at the local pub because he was cooped up at the house. Of course, I just did this and saw absolutely no reason not to, except for now when I look back on it and realise that the demand was made because of his Narcissistic sense of entitlement. Yet another red flag that I had missed.

Towards the end of 2009, shortly before his Cancer diagnosis, the Nex stopped his payment into the joint account for his share of the bills, using the excuse that his work had dried up. Now at face value there is nothing wrong with this because we were married, and we were a partnership. Except what was wrong, is that it was never discussed like a normal married couple would do. Instead, the Nex made the unilateral decision to cancel his Standing Order and he was then simply informing me of his action after. He did not think for one single second whether I could afford to pay for everything on my own, this simply did not matter. He was diagnosed two months later, and he did not resume work until the September of 2010. He did not resurrect his standing order though, and instead, I just carried on paying for everything. We subsequently moved to a new house at the beginning of December 2010 and because the house needed work on it we agreed that I would continue to fund 'all' of the bills, and as it turned out, the nights out, weekends away, holidays, etc., and I was to also pay for all the soft furnishings, the carpets and flooring plus all the new furniture while he would pay solely for the renovations. Another thing he did at the time of the renovations was to moan if I did not help him with any of it. It did not matter to him that I worked tiring ten-to-twelve-hour days, five days a week, did all the housework, cooked all the meals and so on, he still expected me to pick up a tool or a paintbrush and 'renovate' after 8 pm until I went to bed then go back to work at 7 am again the next day. Bear in mind that when he did most of the renovations he was doing it in the day instead of going out to work! I did help where I could by painting at weekends but as I had no building, electrical or plumbing experience I simply could not do any of these. Plus, my illness dictated a lot of what I could and could not do due to the physicality of the work. But none of this mattered to the Nex. If it gave him an excuse to have a go at me, then he used it.

Except the financial arrangement did not work out like that. Well of course, it did not. After all, this is a narcissist that I was married to!

I subsequently ended up paying substantially towards all the renovations as well.

Before I tell you what ripple effect this had on me when we separated I want to just tell you about two further significant incidents that stayed with me.

The first one is that I discovered shortly after my Nex's successful recovery from cancer in 2010 that he had savings of over £5,000 in a bank account! I was gutted. Blindsided and devastated because I had struggled so much financially during that year having to pay for everything myself, and when I questioned him as to why he had not told me that he had this lump sum his reply was simply 'It's mine and it's for a rainy day'.

A rainy day?! WTF?!

Did he not think being off work sick counted as a rainy day?! But his reply was no he did not. I silently sobbed my heart out from this reply as I was just so devastated. He went on to purchase a quad bike for himself with the £5,000 shortly after! His narcissistic sense of entitlement justified this as far as he was concerned.

The second incident was after we had moved house at the start of December 2010 and as I was still paying all the house bills by direct debit. I informed him one day between Christmas and the New Year that my salary would be late into my account because of the holiday period which meant a direct debit would bounce. I dared to ask him if he could put a small sum into the joint account to cover it. I can remember the event like it was yesterday. We were in his van driving back home from a DIY store and his reply to me which was spat at me in such a venomous way, such was his disgust with me for suggesting that he puts some money into the account was, 'You can fuck right off! Just because you cannot manage money I am not bailing you out. You're nothing more than a money grabber!' Oh Wow! Another WTF moment for me! I was totally and devastatingly lost for words. Again, the irony of what he was saying was completely lost on him. The fact that I had bailed him out that year, financially supported him throughout his illness and subsequent treatment and continued to financially support him 'after' this period and once he was back at work did not even feature in to how shocking, ridiculous and point blank cruel his response had been, especially by calling me a money grabber. I did not say anything, the conversation was over as far as he was concerned, but I never forgot that, nor will I ever, such was his nastiness towards me. And no, he did not put any money in the account, I borrowed from my parents instead. This was just how cruel and vile he could be at times.

After we had moved, we had to rent the previous house out because it would not sell and the Nex made a tidy profit from this income whereas I instead ended up out of pocket because I had to pay for landlord insurance and cooker insurance and when I raised this with him he immediately dismissed the topic, stated that he was entitled to the extra money and he even expressed annoyance that I had dared to raise the subject with him at all. This was yet another conversation that was just shut down dead.

So, I will touch briefly on post-split at this point and give you a little insight into the ripple effect that I mentioned earlier as it relates to the above about finances. After I had filed for divorce, the Nex agreed that we would share the sale of the house equity equally and retain all the contents that we had each purchased separately. This was a fair decision as far as I was concerned, even if I had paid more into the property then him in the long run. The contents were the easy part because apart from a couple of sofas and TV's that he had purchased, I had bought absolutely everything else. No surprise there then I hear you all shout!

I even had a legal document called a financial agreement drawn up at his request to reflect this. For the next six months, he led me to believe that he was still in agreement with this document until shortly after my beloved father's sudden tragic death. Then the Nex suddenly said no, he had changed his mind, he had finally sought 'legal advice' and he was now going to fight me instead. I do firmly believe that he purposely picked this moment when he knew just how broken, and grief stricken I was over my father's sudden death, and he thought I would just roll over and let him walk all over me for one last time. You must ask yourself what kind of despicable, nasty and evil person would do this kind of thing. I have to say the answer is a narcissist because a normal person certainly could not and would not. I also believe that it was done to punish me for telling him that I no longer loved him when he had asked me if I did, soon after my father had died. I had unwittingly inflicted a humongous narcissistic injury on him when I had said that I did not.

The Nex made it clear to me now that he wanted the majority share of the house. This was yet another property that he had kept my name off the deeds but had always maintained that it was not an issue as we owned the property jointly because we had both paid equally for it and we were married. You must remember that I never had any reason not to trust him, he was my husband and I never thought for one minute that he was capable of what he would go on to do and what would come next. He had also stated in several emails post spilt up to this point that of course the house should be split equally. Now, because he was so angry with me and he was out for revenge and wanting to destroy me, he decided that he was going to take out some inheritance money that he had put into the property a few years earlier and he became obsessed with wanting to take that out before we shared what was left. Forget my £105,000 input from previously, to him this just did not count! The Nex would not and could not accept that I had since contributed just as much as his small inheritance sum with this new house, if not more, albeit not in one lump sum, so the house should still be divided equally. Little did I know before I researched about narcissists the destruction and devastation they will cause after a discard or split from one. He became so bitter and twisted and fixated that he threatened to destroy me and said that he did not care if it cost him every single penny that he had, he would ensure that he took me down with him. This was sent in an email to me. I will not go into too much detail as we may revisit this later, but he subsequently went on to lie to the courts, he lied to all his friends and family, claiming the house was his in its entirety. Stating that he owned our house outright. He even committed perjury by lying on a signed court document and stating that I had not contributed a single penny whatsoever towards either property, and that he had paid for absolutely everything entirely. Luckily for me, I had overwhelming concrete evidence by way of extensive bank statements to prove otherwise. The worst part of all of this was the fact that his solicitor and counsel aided and abetted him in his lies in court! The SRA were not interested with this and nor was the court. So, it appears that they both openly advocated the Nex's perjury and fraud, or so it would certainly seem! Unfortunately, this does appear to be common in the family courts; orders that are breached go unpunished, perjury goes unpunished, and so on.

So, back to devaluation. Hopefully, you will have some idea of what this now entails and you maybe even be able to relate to some of my examples.

During the devaluation period as well as abuse in all its forms you will also experience from your narcissist some or all the following;

Gaslighting, blame-shifting, projection, word salad, mind games, provocation, smear campaigns, one-upmanships, dosing, triangulation, stonewalling, ghosting, silent treatment, invalidation, hoovers, trauma bonding, baiting, coercive control, control, manipulation, double standards, game playing.

They will literally throw 'the book' at you with some or all of these.

In the narcissist's eyes, you have fallen off your pedestal and you must now be punished. You must be brought to task. The narcissist must regain control and further exert their power and control over you. Neither does a narcissist see in all colours. To a narcissist, there is no existence of grey. Only black and only white. Only good and only bad.

No in-between. No middle ground. No halfway point.

I witnessed my Nex say to someone once, 'black is black and white is white and that is it'. I did not pay it much attention at the time but oh boy now I know for sure that I was hearing yet another 'Confession of a Narcissist' happening right there before me!

During devaluation, in their eyes you simply cannot do right for doing wrong. They will pick fault with you over absolutely everything you say or do. An argument will come out of nowhere. Knock you straight off your feet. A Narcissist will constantly pick on you over the smallest of things. But most of all, you will not be allowed to ever speak your mind to them.

A quote by Lundy Bancroft on hashtag, narcissisticabuse states,

'Your abusive partner doesn't have a problem with his anger, he has a problem with your anger. One of the basic human rights he takes away from you is the right to be angry with him. No matter how badly he treats you, he believes that your voice shouldn't rise, and your blood shouldn't boil. The privilege of rage is reserved for him alone'.

Again, in the early days after I had moved in with him and was regularly taking my children back to my hometown so they could see their father I would spend the weekend catching up with family and friends. I would call the Nex regularly and sometimes two or three times a day, or he would call me. We would be merrily talking away having a normal conversation then suddenly he would have a go at me over nothing. It would always culminate in him slamming the phone down on me and then proceeding to ghost and stonewall me for the rest of the weekend. I would then have to endure a worrying twenty-four or forty-eight hours wondering what the hell I had done wrong and what was I going to be walking in to on my return home. I now know that these occasions were deliberately orchestrated because the Nex was jealous that I was spending time with my family and friends and not with him. Especially if I was having a nice time.

During this devaluation phase, a narcissist will remain completely unaccountable of any perceived wrongdoing. They will abuse you in no end of ways be it emotionally, physically, sexually or financially. You may experience all or only some of these to varying degrees throughout your relationship with your narcissist. If you are a husband/wife or partner of the narcissist, your own devaluation will last the longest of them all. This is because you ultimately provide the narcissist with the most fuel, and especially the most potent fuel of all. Because of the nature of your relationship, it is quite literally 'On tap', readily and easily available and frequent. You might face a discard at some point following the devaluation, real or virtual. Think of the cycle I have talked about. Or maybe it will even be right back to a love-bombing phase if the narcissist feels that he could lose you because of his abusive behaviour. This of course will not stop the abuse from happening. The narcissist cannot ever stop this continuous cycle of harm towards you. It is impossible for them. Ultimately, they do go on to end up losing that current partner eventually. So, they do just simply 'switch off' and move on to the next victim, regardless of how many years the previous one had lasted.

Therefore, if the narcissist does realise that during this devaluation phase you are backing off from them, they will instantly flip to love-bombing/idealisation such is their fear of losing what is their best source of supply of fuel. You must always keep at the forefront of your mind, that all this chaos that a narcissist creates, is for one reason and one reason only, and that is to obtain this precious fuel (narcissistic supply) of theirs. Again, to a narcissist, his supply of the negative fuel that is provided during your devaluation phase is so much more potent and valuable than the positive fuel that the idealisation phase gives him. He or she thrives off your tears, your upset, your frustration, your anguish, your sorrow, your hurt and your pain. They really do quite literally feed off it and exist on it because without it they risk the fall of their mask so then all would be able to see what really lies beneath and for those insecurities to seep out of them, and that cannot ever be allowed to happen to a narcissist.

Whereas you, you will be totally blind-sided, confused and thrown off kilt by what you are experiencing because you cannot understand what is going on, but this is exactly what the narcissist wants. He wants to see you confused, insecure and downtrodden.

Why?

To put it quite simply yet again, it is because the narcissist will be able to retain power and control over you, and in the process, they will be guaranteed that their constant supply of their precious fuel will always flow! It is that constant supply of this fuel what keeps their false self in place. It is what keeps that false mask from slipping and revealing their true inner self.

You subsequently become conditioned to the continuous and endless cycle of idealisation, devaluation and discard, the abuse, the trauma bonding that is occurring, so much so that you just become numb to their behaviour. Once in the devaluation phase you will not be able to do anything right in the narcissist's eyes. They will pick fault with everything you say or do. They will constantly 'Pick on you' over the smallest of things. You just learn to walk on eggshells instead. You start to recognise triggers, you even still somehow believe that the 'nice' version is still in there somewhere and you just need to encourage it to come out more often, for longer, and worse still, you believe that it does not appear because it really is all your fault. Of course, it is not, but this is what your narcissist has led you to believe and ultimately conditioned you to believe through their consistent use of gaslighting.

Throughout the devaluation phase a narcissist will project, deflect, blame-shift and gaslight while remaining totally and completely unaccountable of any perceivable wrongdoing. Any hobbies or interests that you had when you first met them will be met with disdain. If you try and encourage them to join you in these hobbies the comment back will be 'That's not for me', despite them having shown an interest in the beginning. I remember booking a weekend in Brighton for our sixth wedding anniversary as a surprise for the Nex. I especially booked a slot to ice skate on the rink at Brighton Pavilion as a special treat for us. I had skated as a child all the way up to my teens and still occasionally went as an adult, taking my children when they were small. The Nex never wanted to come with us but instead always bragged that he would be good at ice skating because he had roller-bladed when he was in his thirties and that he had been so good at this and that ice skating was exactly the same, despite my comments that it actually was not. He would say, 'Nah, I don't need to do that, I can already do it because it's just like roller blading'. So, back to this Brighton weekend away and when he had learnt that I had booked this special event of ice skating at the Pavilion, he was not overly enthusiastic, claiming that he does not like surprises, but he duly donned his ice skates. Well, when we got on the ice I skated a few rounds while he was still holding on to the side, and I coaxed him off by offering him my hand and after quite literally only a couple of minutes of wobbling and trying to get his balance the Nex then used an excuse that his ankle had started hurting and he could not carry on because of the pain. I knew that this was just an excuse and in fact he had been rumbled and could not actually ice skate at all and I had inadvertently showed him up for one of his many lies and unwittingly called him out on it but being the narcissist that I now know he is, he would never have admitted to this.

Another example of devaluation that my Nex embarked on in the final year of our marriage was soon after we had put the house on the market. This was also during that silent punishment phase that I have talked about. I happened to mention to him about maybe looking at the possibility of moving to my hometown when we sold rather than remaining where we were, especially considering my parents' failing health. His reply was vile to say the least! His response and I quote was 'You can fuck right off if you think I'm moving to that shithole!' When I pointed out that it was one of the UK's most beautiful parts of the country, he again just said; 'I've told you, it ain't happening, end of!' And so, it was the end of that one-sided conversation and decision-making process with the Nex. Never to be mentioned again. Shot down, shut up and silenced as always.

On another occasion just two weeks before the split, it was Father's Day and the Nex was supposed to be coming with me to my hometown for it. He tried to make excuses not to come, even claiming his brother had asked him to go on a bike ride with him that day and he had really wanted to go with him but begrudgingly decided not to. Well, he eventually did come with me to my parents and that was the end of that or so I thought. His brother pitched up at the house a week later and I innocently asked him if he had had a nice bike ride the previous Sunday (Father's Day). He just looked at me blankly and said he had not been on one. So, in front of the brother I pointedly asked the Nex why he had told me there was a bike ride on that day and he was so flustered and just said that I had got the weekend wrong. Of course, I had in his opinion, after all a narcissist is never wrong. He could not possibly be at fault or be lying now could he, but of course he was!

With the mention of Father's Day, this reminds me of Mother's Day too. I never once got a card or present from my children that had been bought for them by the Nex. No meal cooked, nothing. It is not that he just did not think. Oh, he certainly thought about it okay. With his lack of empathy and his very narcissism, he derived pleasure at the thought that I would be hurt by my children not doing anything for me for Mother's Day. This started when the kids were young and could not get part time work because of their age and they only had pocket money. I remember on one occasion particularly when he gleefully asked me what they had bought me when he knew full well that they had not and could not buy me anything. I swear I literally saw him rub his hands together in anticipation at the thought of how this may upset me. Of course, it did not and would not. Especially when later my daughter presented me with the most beautiful hand-made card with a heartfelt message in it and then proceeded to make the evening meal for me. The funniest thing about his behaviour here was his yearly expectance of cards and presents on Father's Day from my kids, such was his narcissistic sense of entitlement.

Likewise, he never paid towards the children's birthday or Christmas presents whatsoever, despite that they were always given to them from the both of us. In fact, in all the fourteen years that we were together, he only once bought a token gift for them which he made sure they knew were from him alone. Again, this is a trivial example which at the time just seems like petty behaviour but once knowledgeable on narcissism I could see that they were in fact deliberate narcissistic traits and patterns being displayed by the Nex.

Once you start to realise that everything a narcissist does and everything that he says is purely designed with one intention and one intention only, and that is to gather this fuel from you and to keep their false mask in place, and once you acknowledge this, you will start to understand what really makes them tick. Why they do what they do. That everything is designed to maintain power and control over you and to ultimately keep that supply of fuel ever flowing because if God forbid it ever stopped, ever came to an end then their false mask would fall, and you would get a glimpse of the real monster that lurks beneath. Of course, you get to see glimpses of it during the devaluation periods but nothing like what really lies beneath. I am conscious that this is a theme that I repeat throughout this book, and it is because it is so important for you all to understand, digest and accept, to enable you to truly understand the actions and behaviour of a narcissist.

A quote by E S states, 'The toxic monster you saw in the end is who they really are, never doubt yourself again when they act nice'.

A few times the Nex would say to me, 'You'd better not talk to anyone about us'. In other words, I was to never mention his abusive behaviour towards me. I believe that this was because deep down subconsciously, he knew that his behaviour was unacceptable and unreasonable. I obviously told him that I did not but in fact I very much did. I regularly confided in friends at the start because I could not understand what was happening to me and I needed advice from them on what to do when I was threatened with the end of the relationship, because I really believed it at the time. Towards the end of my relationship with the Nex, my daughter became my confidant as she was living in Japan for the remaining three years of it.

Often on my return from my hometown the Nex would be seated on the sofa in the lounge. He would never get up to greet me but instead always expected me to be the one that had to go to him first. I had to hug him first, kiss him first and so on. If we were out anywhere, I had to hold his hand first or we simply did not hold hands. Again, I now know that this was due to his grandiosity and extreme sense of entitlement.

Another favourite saying of the Nex was that I was 'Like a bull at a gate'. He used it regularly to belittle me. It was never ever said in its true context but rather was used over and over because the Nex knew that it offended me and hurt and upset me.

I recently remembered another incident that occurred not long after we had moved in with him. We were invited to a pig roast, and we, as in the children and I, had never been to one before, we did not know what to expect. The Nex was rather evasive as to what it entailed, and my children and I dressed up as it was described as a party to us. He knew full well that it was not a party but rather an outside event, so we ended up being overdressed for the occasion and underdressed for the weather. He found this amusing and once we were there he just left us to our own devices even though we did not know a single soul there. I found it so hurtful at the time but that was an early taste of what my life was to become like living with a narcissist.

On another occasion, soon after we had moved down, we were invited to a friend's garden party, I was to meet these friends for the first time, and he categorically stated that my children were not allowed to come with us. I assumed that this was because it was an adult's only event. How wrong was I.

There turned out to be loads of children there. He could not understand why I was upset at the fact that he had not allowed my children to come with us.

In a later chapter, we look at why a narcissist does the things that they do, and the two above scenarios that I have already described will shed some light on this. But for now, it is because it made him feel powerful, in control, and he gained his narcissistic supply (fuel) from how upset I was.

Post-split, while we were forced to still live in the marital home until it was sold, the Nex was rarely seeing his latest victim because she lived some distance away, so he was clearly only receiving his positive fuel from her in drips. Therefore, he attempted on several occasions to generate negative fuel from me with Malign Hoovers via emails but the majority of the time I managed to ignore them and simply forward them to his solicitor, then to my solicitor when I needed him to let the Nex know that what he was doing was tantamount to harassment. Hence the most he was receiving was thought fuel which is a lot less potent than negative fuel. Another trick of his was to talk loudly enough so that I could hear him verbally slagging me off to just about anyone who would listen! The lies, confabulations and fanciful tales that I heard him telling were truly incredulous, but now knowing about narcissists, I saw them for what they exactly were. Of course, he did not dare devalue his latest victim during this period as she would have run a mile. Unfortunately, time will have to naturally unfold for her to learn the real him. I read many times over, comments on forums and support sites where the ex-victim would say she really wanted to warn the latest victim, but the general consensus from the readers was not to, as the latest victim would simply not believe them. Especially if they were still in the throes of the love-bombing phase. And especially if the narcissist had worked their magic with their smear campaign and painted their ex-victim as the crazy and abusive one. So, guys and gals, no matter how tempted you may be, do not do this. Walk away with your head held high, your dignity intact, and simply hope that the realisation for their latest victim comes soon for them.

The most important factor to remember about an abusive or toxic relationship is that the abuse will accelerate over time, it can take many years, but it 'will' get worse. In some, it can even lead to death for the victim!

I remember another incident that happened in the last couple of years of our relationship when we were due to meet friends for dinner. The Nex had been in a foul mood most of the day and was deliberately trying to goad me into a fight, but I would not play ball. We reached the restaurant first and he openly started picking on me by making derogatory comments which culminated with him informing me that I was worse than his ex-wife. His exact words were, 'Do you know what, my ex-wife was nowhere near as bad as you'. I got up and left the restaurant and texted the female friend of the couple and apologised for leaving at short notice and I did inform her as to why I had. After our split, I discovered that I had a mutual friend of his ex-wife, who had kept quiet about this connection and she went on to inform me of her concerns which had been passed onto her from his ex-wife during our relationship, as to what his controlling behaviour was like, but she never said anything to me because she did not witness the Nex's abuse and assumed that the ex-wife must have been treated differently to me.

A quote I recently read stated; 'A narcissist isn't horrible and abusive one hundred percent of the time. If they were, it would be easy to recognise the abuse, prove it to other people, and make a clean break with the support of your friends and community. They are horrible and abusive eighty percent of the time. What do they do with the other twenty percent? They try and convince you that the eighty percent isn't happening!'

Welcome to the world of gaslighting.

My Nex mentioned on a couple of occasions about some of his past brief relationships that were in between his four more significant ones, and from comments he made it was now more than apparent that these poor women were devalued and discarded very rapidly. One of the stories was of an ex-girlfriend who had kept showing up at his house, so he finally threw a bucket of water over her. Another one allegedly had a restraining order made against her. I never knew whether either of these tales were entirely true. Or, whether both incidents were just two great big fat lies that the Nex had made up to make himself look good and look like he was in demand and irresistible, full of grandiosity and superiority just like a narcissist does. A narcissist is after all a pathological liar!

It got to the point in my relationship that I felt I could not tell the Nex anything for fear of it causing a backlash, being used against me or me being needlessly blamed or ridiculed.

Hopefully now you are starting to understand this cycle of abuse that drives the narcissist. The devaluation that will always come in a narcissistic relationship. Why the narcissist must do it, what it hides, what it achieves and lastly, what is the most important thing that must never happen to a narcissist.

This is of course their unmasking to reveal the true vile, evil and nasty 'inhuman' creature that really lurks beneath.

I cannot deny that you do genuinely fall in love with your narcissist, and you do love them because they paint such a fantastic picture at the start of the relationship during the love-bombing, then the initial idealisation phase. This is because they are so good at what they do. They are so good at presenting this false image of theirs and what it promises that it sucks you right in. Such is their perfection at being a con artist. I defy anyone who has been involved with a narcissist to disagree with me. But therefore, it is so hard, because you do or did genuinely love them, and when you love someone you do not want to think anything bad about them. You do not want to believe that there could be anything wrong with them or is wrong with them. You do not want to believe that they are not good and that the monster before you during your devaluation is the same person that you love. So, instead you look for a million reasons as to why they behave the way that they do. The narcissist is so good at gaslighting you into believing that you are the problem and you do end up believing them because you do not want to think bad of them. This is how warped a narcissistic relationship is, and why you do not walk away. You are trauma bonded into believing them because you do not want to believe that they are not the person you thought they were. Effectively the narcissist has succeeded in conning you out of weeks, months and even years of your life.

HG Tudor sums this chapter up perfectly by stating that, 'The devaluation of the narcissist's victim is the most brutal of all. It continues for the longest, it can be years, even decades in some instances, and with this devaluation comes a whole host of manipulations and abuses which cover emotional, financial, sexual and physical'. HG Tudor believes that devaluation occurs, not only because the victim has slighted the narcissist, but also because the victim has failed to live up to the narcissist's expectations and ideals and therefore, their victim must be punished.

And of course, the negative fuel or narcissistic supply that flows for the narcissist during a devaluation is the most potent of them all.

Maria Consiglio states that, 'Throwing cups across a room, punching walls, screaming in your face, mimicking you, insulting you, telling you they could do better, telling you that you are useless and good for nothing, mocking you constantly in an effort to make you feel stupid, controlling your finances, isolating you and controlling who you socialize with... These are all various examples of psychological abuse and intimidation'.

A quote by Elinor Greenberg, PhD of 'IBelieveYourAbuse.com states',

'It is hard to maintain a stable and loving relationship with someone who says they love you and then when they become annoyed with you, suddenly turns cruel and vicious. A lack of object constancy is one of the major causes of emotional and physical abuse in intimate relationships'.

And to end this chapter with one final quote from Maria Consiglio,

'You could give your soul to a narcissist, and it won't matter. They will never reciprocate. If they need to put you down to make them feel better about themselves, they will do it. If they need to verbally abuse you to make them feel powerful, they will do it without hesitation. The only thing you will get from a narcissist is a broken heart and sadness that seems to go on to infinity'.

Chapter Four
What Is a Discard?

Just because your relationship with your narcissist is now over (hopefully!), finished and done with, this categorically does not mean that you are now narcissist free!

I think one of the most important things to realise with a narcissist is the fact that they 'will' destroy every single intimate relationship that they ever have, but nine times out of ten they will not just walk away for good. Be prepared for Hoover attempts, weeks, months and even years down the line. A narcissist sees you as his property.

Some of the narcissist's relationships will last a few weeks, a few months and even a few years. Some last even longer, especially where a covert narcissist is involved. I have read on some of the support sites of marriages lasting many years. I met a couple of women who attended the Freedom Programme along with me who for one of them her marriage had lasted twenty-four years and for the other the marriage had lasted a staggering forty years!

Wow you must think, 'These women deserve a bloody medal' because I sure as hell think that they do!

What they most certainly do deserve is the support that is not always out there for them.

Narcissism or more to the point narcissist, is becoming a somewhat popular and more easily recognised turn of phrase when describing someone and has even generated many articles, books and studies lately on the subject. There are even television programmes and dramas on the subject now. 'Dirty John' on Netflix for example. Yes, I have watched it, and yes it is particularly good! As I have mentioned before, every single one of us are on the spectrum of narcissism to some degree because a little bit of positive narcissism is indeed healthy. It is when we look at the ones who are at the far other side of this spectrum, even at the top of this spectrum that we can say with confidence that this person is a full-blown narcissist.

What is currently severely lacking in the judicial system in the UK is the support for the victims of narcissists. All too often a woman or even a man, will have to fight this evil alone. There are not many solicitors or lawyers out there that even know what a narcissist is and even if they do they do not educate themselves on what exactly they will be dealing with if their client is seeking a divorce from their narcissistic ex-partner or even custody of their children.

More importantly, neither do the Judges that preside over any court proceedings or hearings!

I have become appalled at the number of true accounts that I have read where children have been taken from their mother because of the lies the narcissistic husband has told the courts, especially if they are a successful powerful individual. Likewise, fathers that have not been allowed to see their children because the narcissistic mother has lied to the police and to the courts that the father has sexually abused the children, or harmed them in some other way, some of these poor men have even been imprisoned wrongly because of this.

On attending the Freedom Programme in the UK which while I found it extremely helpful, I was at first dismayed that the terminology of narcissist or even sociopath was not readily used and instead they referred to the 'perp' as a 'Dominator'. Then I understood that it was to keep the individual abuser neutral, but I do think that narcissism should still be taught because the one thing any victim of a narcissist, male or female, must realise is the fact that I stated earlier in the book which is that a narcissist will 'never' change. I think that it is vital during these sessions that everyone attending does learn about narcissism and narcissists so that they can recognise whether their abuser is a full-blown narcissist or just someone on the spectrum. I say this because another course runs alongside the Freedom Programme that is for the male abuser, called the Drive Project, this is there for him to challenge his issues, his anger and ultimately change his behaviour. It has been successful for some men. But of course, if it is a full-blown narcissist attending this course then he will not change, 'ever'. He may even have only attended the course as part of his bail conditions or court sentence. He will merely play along with the system. If a woman of one of these such partners is taught the difference and learns that no amount of intervention will change her partner, she can leave the relationship sooner and more importantly, permanently, which could ultimately save her life, and even that of her children.

Of course, the financial cost will always come into play here. In a perfect world, if narcissism was suspected in a partner/relationship breakdown then the courts could order an assessment to be carried out by a recognised professional in the field of narcissism on that individual, but this simply will never happen because of the cost involved. Instead, I really do believe that the way forward is for solicitors and judge's to be suitably educated on narcissism and narcissists, and other personality disorders that could be lurking.

I strongly believe that any man, or woman, who is abusive towards their partner does have narcissistic traits, and/or sociopathic traits, and/or even possibly psychopathic traits, or they have a mixture of all three. They could even fall under the category of 'Dark Triad'. According to Wikipedia, in psychology, the dark triad refers to the personality traits of narcissism, psychopathy and machiavellianism, meaning that the individual possesses all these traits. The term dark is because of the malevolent qualities involved. Wikipedia goes on to state that when you look at what machiavellianism is, it is characterised by manipulation, the exploitation of others, an absence of morality, unemotional callousness and a higher level of self-interest. I would argue that all these traits do sit squarely with a narcissist also.

So, back to a discard. When to expect one.

The simple answer is absolutely at any point during your relationship with the narcissist! Even if everything appears to be going extremely well. Also, be prepared for several and even many discards over the duration of the relationship, especially virtual ones, just as I was subjected to.

A discard – real or virtual – will generally follow a period of devaluation, even if you have not realised that this is what you were going through. It is important to realise that there is no exact timescale to the cycle that evolves with a narcissist. You really could be looking at weeks, days, minutes and even seconds. One minute all is well and you are being idealised and the very next minute you have inadvertently done or said something that the narcissist will perceive as a criticism of them, and you are immediately thrust into a devaluation phase that the very next minute after that could become a discard. You are now black and not white. You are now bad and not good. It really, truly can happen as quickly as that. If this is hard for you to get your head around, then think about how a narcissist only ever views the world in black or in white. You are either good or you are bad. Never grey, never in between, no middle ground. That is why he or she can flick that switch at the drop of a hat. You are white so you are idealised, then you go and challenge or pass an innocent comment that offends the narcissist, and you will suddenly become black, and so will begin your next period of devaluation. It could even be because the narcissist has grown bored of you and your positive fuel so they embark on a devaluation phase just to generate the more potent negative fuel that will flow during it.

According to HG Tudor, if you have inflicted a narcissistic injury on the narcissist, once you are painted black, you are now viewed through a black lens by the narcissist. Because they are controlled by paranoia, their overwhelming sense to control has been wounded. Their victim is not doing what the narcissist wants and so their sense of entitlement has been dented. This makes the narcissist feel like they are now losing control, so they now feel powerless and to regain this power they view you as black. Now whatever you say or do will be viewed as a challenge to their power. The narcissist will accuse you of trying to control them. It does not matter if the narcissist sees that their victim is upset, in their eyes it is the victims' fault. The narcissist now sees themselves as the victim. Your actions are what caused this so the narcissist is right, and you are wrong.

If you have been or are still in a long-term relationship or marriage with a narcissist, you will no doubt have been subject to several or even many of these periods of cycles and ultimately discards – virtual or real.

If you do remain in your relationship with your narcissist this, cycle will 'never' end. Even if you do every perceivable thing that you can think of to keep the narc happy with attention, admiration, adoration and so on, you will still trip up and do something that the narcissist perceives to be a slight against them. Or the narcissist will even orchestrate one deliberately just so he can draw negative fuel from you. So that devaluation that you now know about and understand 'will' still come. You cannot ever prevent it. Yes, you can limit their appearances, but you can never stop them. Is that how you really want to live the rest of your life? Walking on those limitless and endless eggshells and trying to stop the inevitable from happening? What kind of life is that? You deserve far more. After all, we only get one life and one shot at it.

A quote by narcissistic-abuse-is-real sums this up perfectly,

'I spent so many years walking on eggshells… never doing or saying the right thing. One day I decided I'd had enough and stomped all over them. Those broken eggshells cut me deeply as I walked away… but this… was the most beautiful pain I had ever felt'.

When a discard – virtual or real – does come, it will be used purely to exert power and control over you, to punish you and even in some cases purely for the narcissist's own amusement and entertainment.

As I mentioned only shortly before, a discard can come completely right out of the blue, a thunderclap from out of nowhere.

You could be in a relationship with a narcissist (but are obviously unaware of the fact that they are one) and everything is fine and dandy, then suddenly your partner demonstrates to perfection a Jekyll and Hyde personality flip and then they could even quite literally fall off the edge of the earth!

They have gone AWOL big time.

You cannot call them as it keeps going to voicemail, this is usually because you will have been blocked. That was one of the Nex's favourite tricks. An immediate block on the phone, defriending and blocking on Facebook and WhatsApp, and this was while we were still married and living together! You text and get no reply. Yep, that was me too. Nothing, absolutely zero, diddly squat. This is not a bout of the silent treatment that you are facing on this occasion, oh no, this is a bout of ghosting. For me, because we lived together and then married, the complete silent treatment would ultimately follow.

If you are not living with the narcissist at the time then they could disappear for days, weeks or even months. Sometimes permanently which will of course then become your final discard. But you will not know that for a while. Especially if they have done this disappearing act before. Closure with a narcissist just does not happen, 'ever'.

If you are living with your Narc, or worse, still married to them, then you are likely to suffer many virtual discards before the final and ultimate one.

A Narcissist will discard you for many reasons:

1. You caused them a narcissistic injury, real or perceived.
2. Another source of fuel is more potent, so you are temporarily 'shelved'.
3. The narcissist is seeking fuel from you, and they know that your worry and confusion will provide this for them.

4. It could well be your final discard.

As I said only a moment ago, one thing to know for sure is the fact that you will never get closure with a narcissist so it would be a complete and utter waste of your time to even attempt to seek one. The word closure is alien to a narcissist. This is too normal.

If you chase the narcissist for answers, explanations and beg him or her to come back to you this will just not happen. In fact, your very actions will be further providing the narcissist with fuel because they will envisage what you are doing, how you are feeling, and they will be 'Getting off' on it.

If your narcissist is a malignant narcissist, then they will mete out the cruellest of all discards that could even damage your health, your well-being, your reputation, your job and even cost you your life.

If your narcissist is a mid-range one like my Nex, their campaign of hate against you post discard will be intense, savage, and cruel because they will want to heal the perceived wound that you have caused them and to do this they will need fuel. This essential fuel will be gained from the smear campaign that they will unleash on you and by the narcissist playing the victim. The Nex certainly did both with a vengeance. I was painted as the Devil incarnate. At the start, he tried to make out that I had cheated on him, which was his firm favourite smear with every other previous relationship that he had been in, and it was clear that I was destined to follow suit. In fact, what was so laughable is that I knew exactly why his previous marriage had failed despite him always telling me that it was because his ex-wife had cheated on him. Not long after I had moved in with him I caught sight of his divorce papers and there in all its glory was the real reason that the marriage had ended, and it certainly was not adultery but rather his meting out of a silent treatment that lasted for two entire weeks that finally caused his first wife to walk away and end the short marriage. Remember me saying that he had spoken extraordinarily little about his previous marriage to me so knowing what I know now I suspect that it was not the first time that she had suffered one of these during their seven years together. I never told him what I had found out until after we had spilt. But after learning everything I did about narcissism and the use of the silent treatment I realised just how significant this 'discrepancy' was. Alas at the time, I was too ignorant to heed the great big red flag that I had just discovered.

The Nex's further previous two other long-term relationships had also ended in the women cheating on him according to him, but I have since learnt that again, this was not the case but rather that it was his cruel treatment of them that had ended those relationships too. Oh boy, do you not just wish that you could have learnt these kinds of important facts a hell of a lot earlier!

A mid-range Narcissist will also seek to replace you very quickly and the Nex certainly accomplished this after just a few weeks from our split, despite our fourteen years together, such was his addictive need for fuel, attention, admiration and adoration. What makes this even more ironic is that he played the victim so well but for a true victim of abuse (me!) the last thing you want to do is embark on another relationship so soon because you are still trying to recover from the toxic abusive one that you have just left.

The fundamental difference between an ordinary relationship breakup and a breakup with a narcissist is that theirs really will be sudden. The discard will come swift and hard. But most importantly, the narcissist will discard with every intention of hurting you in the process.

If this one really is the final one, then you will get the silent treatment, ghosting, stonewalling, smear campaign, insults and disrespect but all too tellingly they will move on to their next victim quickly, just as the Nex did.

If you have instigated the breakup then, oh boy, batten down the hatches because you are certainly going to be in for a very treacherous, stormy and rough ride! The above mentioned will be ten-fold, coupled with stalking, hacking your email accounts, your social media, and even your phone. Plus, you will be subjected to hoovers, most probably malign ones at that. I will give examples of these that I experienced later.

My Nex hacked my email account shortly after we had split up and I did not discover this until later that year when I had to change my password on not only one occasion but a further two more. He then went on to clone or hack my phone where he then had access to my calls, texts, emails, Facebook, WhatsApp and other social media accounts! God knows why because the Nex already had his next victim well and truly in his grip by this point! But then, God may not know why but I sure did know by now. It was because a narcissist will not just let go of you, even if they were the one that discarded you. Some experts even claim that you will only be free of your narcissist when they are dead, or you are dead! Oh boy, what a thought! I only discovered my phone hacking after my beloved father's sudden and tragic death at the end of January

2019. I must point out at this stage that we were still living under the same roof while the marital home was on the market. We had reached a truce (or rather he had decided to stop being abusive temporarily) at the end of November 2018. Following my father's death in the January 2019, in or around the end of February/ beginning of March 2019, the Nex started passing comments about certain things that could only have come from his knowledge of conversations that I'd had with friends and family. One particular comment really raised my suspicions as I knew full well that there was no way he could have had knowledge on what he was mentioning so I checked my logins for Facebook, and I was shocked to discover logins in different areas of the country where I had been allegedly logged in but most importantly when I had not been anywhere near those areas. But the one that stood out the most and confirmed and proved my suspicions was the one where I was logged in to Fuerteventura, in the Canary Islands over the Christmas period of 2018. I spent that Christmas at the marital home in the UK with my children, my mother and what was to be the last ever Christmas with my father, while the Nex was on holiday.

Yes, you have guessed it, he was in Fuerteventura!!

When I challenged him, he denied all knowledge of it and said he did not even know where that was and that he had never been there. Such was his ridiculous mentality at times, so I pointedly asked him where he had just been on holiday, and he had that 'Scared rabbit in the headlights' look on his face but quickly composed himself and replied 'Oh yes I was in Fuerteventura but not in that exact place where your phone thinks I was'. Seriously, you really could not make it up! It did not end there either because he disappeared up to his room then came back down five minutes later all animated saying 'Look, look, I've been logged in on Facebook in Cardiff, Wales and I never go there', quickly followed by 'You work in Wales sometimes don't you?' I could see exactly where this was going so I asked him when it had been, bear in mind that he did not show me this 'evidence', and he replied that it was recently, at the end of that January/ beginning of February. He really thought that he was being clever and covering his tracks until I pointed out to him that my father had died at the end of the January and to date, (the end of February/beginning of March) I had not travelled anywhere for work!

The look on his face was priceless!

But when you learn all about narcissists and narcissism as I did indeed go on to do, you learn that this is not only part of their pattern of blame-shifting and projecting, but also one of deflection. Such are their attempts to cover up because of course they can never be seen to be wrong or at fault. My Nex had been caught out with the cold hard evidence but rather than just suck it up and admit the truth like a normal person, instead he came up with this preposterous tale that he too had been a victim of phone hacking hence his ridiculous Cardiff story. A narcissist is not clever enough to cover their tracks, well the Nex certainly was not. From this point on, he denied it had ever happened and dismissed or ignored it completely whenever I raised what he had done. I on the other hand immediately went to my phone provider the next day who alarmingly informed me that it was easy for someone to clone your phone via Bluetooth. All they simply needed was your phone in their vicinity to be able to Bluetooth spyware on to your phone, and of course, because we still lived under the same roof, I was fair game for the Nex. I immediately changed my phone and put every Anti-Malware and Anti-Spyware app on my new phone that I could.

I guess what I am trying to point out to you here is the fact that even if they do allegedly discard you, you will still be a victim of their stalking of you, their smear campaign against you and every other kind of horror or bullshit that they can throw at you or against you. I do believe that my 'discard' by the Nex was never his intention to be the final one, but rather was his attempt to manipulate me into doing what he wanted but it backfired spectacularly on him because I then went on to make the decision myself that it really was indeed the final one. Hence why I then faced the nightmare vendetta against me that followed.

I also believe that it was a punishment for me allowing my daughter and her fiancé to stay in the same room while they were residing with us during a visit. My daughter, I hasten to add, was in her early twenties at this stage. Oh yes, we had that ridiculous scenario on a previous occasion where he refused to allow her to sleep in the same bedroom as her boyfriend, despite them already living together in Japan. I accepted his warped logic on that occasion because we had only just met the boyfriend for the first time, so I went along with his demand. But on the second occasion they were back in the UK the following year and engaged by this time, he again tried to demand that they slept in separate bedrooms. I stood my ground this time and said that I was happy for them to sleep in the same room. He tried to say that once they were married he would allow it as that was okay. So, I asked him if we should also stop his grown-up adult friends that cohabited together from sleeping in the same room when they stayed with us as well. But of course, this rationale was totally lost on him. Well of course it was! Remember, it is a narcissist we are talking about. With a narcissist, it is their way or the highway. Remember also, that they always live by their double standards.

I have another point to raise in relation to a disgusting and abhorrent act that my Nex did surrounding and directly relating to my father's death but again, this is easier to explain and divulge and relate to more appropriately in another chapter on post discard and the smear campaign.

After a discard that the narcissist has instigated or maybe you have instigated by finally walking away from your relationship with the narcissist, the worst thing, and I do mean the very worst thing that a narc can witness, is to see you, their victim, carry on with the rest of your life. To see you move on, heal and repair from the damage that they have inflicted enrages them. Such is their narcissism that they simply cannot understand how you can go on to live without them because in their eyes they are so good, so brilliant and oh so godly that it seems unfathomable and unthinkable to them that you can live and survive without them. The Nex certainly used to raise this in his Malign Hoover emails to me by claiming that I still loved him, that I could not move on and could not really let him go, such was his delusion. Even nineteen months after we had split and when the divorce was almost final he had emailed me about some garden hedges to which I did unfortunately break my 'No Contact' rule and after one or two emails back and forth, I eventually responded with a simple 'Oh dear, ever the drama queen' to him. His reply? That I still obviously loved him, could not move on from him, did not' want our relationship to be over, wanted him back, and on it went. How the hell he deduced all this simply from my 'Drama Queen' response I will never figure out! But of course, knowing that he is a Narcissist this was what he honestly believed, such is his sense of grandiosity and superiority. I mean after all, because he is so wonderful of course it was unimaginable that I could ever let him go, 'not'!

Even more bizarrely, this came after I had told him point blank to his face that I did not love him anymore. As I have mentioned earlier, shortly after my father's death, when I had challenged him on his stalking behaviour towards me, he asked me if I still loved him. I did not answer him immediately because

I knew that if I used platitudes of appeasement like, 'I still care about you', he would interpret this incorrectly and attempt to hoover me. So, I told him the truth and said out loud to his face that I did not love him anymore. This clearly fell on deaf ears, or more to the point, as the narcissist he is, the Nex chose not to believe this, because after all, he is the big high and almighty and how can anyone not love him? I do believe that this was the catalyst and another reason why he chose to then embark on a battle with me through the courts, because he wanted to punish me for telling him that I no longer loved him as I had caused him a massive narcissistic injury.

For you, the narcissist's victim, because that is what you are, a victim, this is the best thing that could ever have happened to you, or for you. You really must adjust your mind-set to honestly believe that, and you must start thinking that you have had a lucky escape, dodged the bullet that was the narcissist. For me, I devoured every available book and article about narcissists and narcissism that I could. Educating myself on what I had endured was not only enlightening, but it was also cathartic. The more that I read, the more I understood, and once the shock that my entire relationship of almost fourteen years was nothing more than a façade, fake, an illusion, a lie, and I could finally accept that the Nex had never 'loved' me, the rest came easily for me. I finally had the answer to the question that I had continuously asked myself, and occasionally had even asked him, over the years, and that was, 'Why could our relationship never be a normal relationship'. Now I finally had the answer. Now I finally understood why not. When I did ask the question to the Nex, his response was to automatically blame me and say that it was my fault, not his. That I was the problem, not him. Like many other men and women out there, I was sold a lie at the start of our relationship, and I naively bought into it.

It is natural to feel angry and hurt at first, because you did love and care for them, but you were conditioned to accept their appalling behaviour towards you through trauma bonding and conditioning. Throughout the relationship with your narcissist, it is extremely easy to paper over the cracks and let the world think everything is okay. You become accustomed to their behaviour through their use of gaslighting, projection, blame-shifting and cognitive dissonance.

This is a victim's natural response as a way of coping. You will try and convince yourself that it is not as bad as you think, that in-between the bad, everything is okay when really it is not. You are just experiencing the idealisation/devaluation phases. You will even think that it could be your fault and that maybe it 'is' your fault which just causes you to walk on even more eggshells throughout your relationship with your narcissist.

The main reason why victims remain with their narcissist is because of the trauma bonding that is felt as I have already mentioned at times throughout this book so far. To look at this in more detail I would say that this is due to the intense and often extreme emotional experiences that you have with your narcissist. Think of the cycle that I keep mentioning; the idealisation/love-bombing, followed by the devaluation of you, followed maybe by a virtual discard then right back to idealisation and so on and so forth. This continuous cycle, the seesaw that is in motion, the rollercoaster ride that keeps us tied to the narcissist because we are always seeking that 'nice' period. You end up changing who you are to accommodate them and their moods and feelings. You again walk on a continuous path that is littered with eggshells. But most important of all, you do not leave them.

I recently read a passage on Quora that someone had posted that said, 'Trauma Bond is like heroin addiction in that the relationship promises much, gives fleeting feelings of utopia, and then it sucks away your very soul'.

For me, I used to have to really think about what I said before I said it and when I say this I do not mean it lightly. I would run all kinds of scenarios through my head as to how he would respond to what I wanted to say. I would think of all the ways that I could say it so that it could not and would not be taken the wrong way and he could not and would not get offended by it. Ultimately though he would still do both. So, I learnt sometimes to just stay silent and not say anything at all. This of course was exactly what the Nex wanted. Without me realising it he was controlling and manipulating me. On these occasions that I said nothing at all, I would then get accused further down the line of not telling him anything.

I was damned if I did and damned if I did not.

Once the anger goes, and believe me that it will go, any possible thoughts of revenge that you may have had just disappear, evaporate, gone in a puff of smoke. You start to view your narcissist as nothing more than a stranger to you, someone you never really knew which is of course exactly what they were and are. The relationship you thought that you had was never real, it was fake, an illusion created by the narcissist purely for their own gain.

Trust me when I say that you even start to pity them because you know beyond all doubt that they will 'never' know the feeling of true happiness or even just contentment. They will go to their grave battling their inner demons and insecurities. No relationship will ever survive for them unless death takes them first.

If you believe in karma, then this is what I think it means to a narcissist's victim. The knowledge that despite whether he or she broke your heart in two or not, or robbed you blind financially, or cost you your job, your home and your reputation, or even years of your life, 'you', the real victim, 'will' get over this and you 'will' move on to a better, happier and essentially more peaceful and content life, but the narcissist simply will not.

Of course, a discard does not just apply to an intimate partner in a relationship with a narcissist. Oh no, everyone associated with the narcissist is fair game. Family member, friend and even work associate. The Nex routinely discarded family and friends along the way. Some were permanent discards and others were temporary, especially with his family. During my first few years with the Nex, he was building a house with his brother and they had a fallout, and to this day I do not know the real reason behind the fallout except to say that the Nex blamed his brother (of course he did!) but I can guess now that it was probably because the Nex would not be told what to do by his brother, or anybody else for that matter, (his brother was project manager for the build and the Nex was just helping him). Of course, the brother then got the silent treatment. You must also realise and recognise that many narcs, not all of them, but certainly plenty, will ultimately go on to work for themselves (or not even at all) simply because they cannot take orders from another person. Such is their narcissism. Others ultimately go on to be leaders (of course they do!) if they are in employment. Well, when the Nex fell out with his brother he did not speak to him for almost two years, that was how long his silent treatment against his brother lasted! At the time of the fallout, he insisted that I write a letter to his brother that basically explained everything the Nex had suffered because of his brother and how everything was of course his brother's fault. I felt uncomfortable doing this, but he rolled out the usual what kind of wife was I if I did not help him and that the letter was going to be signed by him, so it did not matter. Funnily enough this very brother and his wife are now two of the Nex's flying monkeys, such are the lies that he has fed to them about me and the black picture that he has painted of me, and of course his

109

smear campaign that he is the victim here and that I am the abuser. Such are the manipulation skills of the narcissist.

Still about flying monkeys, Maria Consiglio of '@understandingthenarc', sums up their description quite perfectly with a quote that says,

'Flying Monkeys are the enablers who support the NARCISSIST NO MATTER WHAT!'

I have to say that this is certainly true of the Nex's. She goes on further to state that the flying monkeys blindly side, encourage, support and even abuse the victim, to defend the narcissist. Even if they know the narcissist is wrong or doing very bad things. They are either blind to the narcissist's behaviours because of cognitive dissonance, or they just don't care! Either way they are just as guilty. Narcissists usually have a few flying monkeys that they count on for back up.

On another occasion long before I met the Nex, he fell out with his sister and did not speak to her for six months and it was only when she saw him on a night out and went to speak to him that they renewed contact. No doubt if she had not done this then his silent treatment against her would have lasted longer. Currently, as I write this book he has meted out the silent treatment to her yet again and he has had no contact with her for almost two years now just because she is still in contact with me. Except of course for a Malign Hoover attempt he made to her eighteen months in which I will save for later because it is more relevant then. She did attempt contact with him at one point, but he informed another brother that he 'Wasn't ready to speak to her yet'. Of course, he was not! This silent treatment meted out on his sister would only end when 'he' decided that it would. To this very day of writing this book, he still has not spoken to her, almost two years on. She is still very much painted as black. As I have mentioned earlier, the only real positive thing to salvage from my relationship with the Nex is the continued friendship that I do still now have with his sister. I am thankful for this, and that she is still in my life.

The Nex also had a friend that he had known for years but no longer socialised with, who did occasionally used to clean the Nex's vehicles because this friend was a professional Valeter. The Nex had also built a garage for this friend not long before this event that I am now going to tell you about. So, about eighteen months post build of this garage this friend rang the Nex to say that there was a problem with the garage, and could he come and look at it. The Nex immediately blamed the friend and said that if the friend had not insisted on cheap materials no fault would ever have happened, to which his friend replied that it did not matter what the cause was as the Nex must be insured. Well, I was not around when this took place but when I did get back the Nex let rip about what had happened and quite frankly eviscerated his poor friend as he was so enraged at his friend for blaming him. How dare he! The Nex proudly informed me that he had blocked the friends phone number, his email contact with him and defriended and blocked him on Facebook! Well of course he had! And yes, I know you are starting to see the familiar pattern here and realise that I was not the only one subjected to these outlandish knee jerk and most definitely childish over the top reactions from the Nex. I mean what grown man treats a friend of over twenty years that way? More importantly instead of reacting like a normal person and saying 'Yes of course I will come and have a look and see what I can do' instead the Nex reacted like the typical narcissist he is and took immediate offence because he thought he was being blamed and of course you must never ever blame a narcissist for anything whatsoever because it can never be their fault. How dare his friend do this to him! This friend went on to put a very public post on Facebook about his treatment by the Nex and what had just taken place with the telephone call but more interestingly, he commented that when he had on another occasion told the Nex that he could not clean his van exactly when the Nex had wanted it doing the Nex had become extremely angry and slammed the phone down on him. This is quite simply because of the narcissists extreme sense of entitlement and the Nex had expected his friend to jump and drop everything at the click of his fingers. For this particular friend, he got to see the mask slip and experienced a glimpse of what was really lying beneath the Nex's mask. I do not know whether to this day the friend is still experiencing the ghosting and silent treatment from the Nex? Or maybe whether the Nex has hoovered him back in. Who knows?

A narcissist's world really is one that is without boundaries of any kind.

I remember when the Nex and I used to go out for meals, and he would order whatever he had ordered but chips always featured on his plate. If I was healthy eating I would have salad with whatever meat I had ordered but still liked one or two chips, so on this one occasion I happened to help myself to one from his plate while asking him if it was okay at the same time. His reaction was to scowl at me and prevent me from getting one while stating that I should have ordered my own. I honestly thought he was joking at first, but no, he was deadly serious. He would not let me have one of his chips. I never asked again. What was so comical about this was that 'every' time we did eat out and I had finished eating he would 'always' proceed to then eat the rest of what was on my plate without asking me if I had finished! I told you it was like a comedy did I not?!

The narcissist will manage down their victim's expectations so that they ultimately end up not having to work too hard at anything in their relationship.

During both the devaluation and discard phases the narcissist will reveal their true self. You will get a glimpse of the abuser that lies beneath. The one that was there all the time.

I genuinely believe that the Nex realised that I was pulling away from him and withdrawing and this is when the mask could not stop slipping.

This was especially true for my children. Once he realised that I could see through him and once he knew that I was not going to keep quiet about it so all attempts at a cover-up was over, his 'gloves were off'. Not just for me, but also for my children. A variety of his actions confirmed this, especially when he had the audacity to call the police on my son who had only gone to the house to look after the cats when I had gone away for a few days and at that point my son was still speaking to the Nex and remaining neutral. But most of all because he had coldly discarded them too! After fourteen years of being a 'step-father' (in name only I hasten to add!), he did not care now if they saw that he did not care about them and never had. It had been blatantly obvious throughout our relationship that he 'favoured' my daughter over my son. I now know that this is because he was jealous of my son and saw him as a threat. He had made little effort once the kids had left home as well. He never contacted my daughter when she was living in Japan, nor wanting to visit her with me. Rather he just spared five minutes to say hello when I FaceTimed her. He never once picked up the phone to chat with my son because he felt my son should be the one to always contact him (remember a narcissists sense of entitlement). I have recently come to learn that he has pretty much wiped all memory of my kids from his life by classing himself now as having no children. That speaks volumes in itself. I also now know that he discarded his previous wife's children with the same brutal lack of emotion.

The very objective for a narcissist with a discard is to catch their victim off guard. To blindside them. To have the upper hand and most important of all, to have complete and utter control of the discard phase.

The way a narcissist tries to erase you once you have been discarded is one where they completely invalidate you as a human being.

Narcissistrecovery state that, 'A narcissist will hold hate, contempt and disdain for you, not because you've ever done anything to them, but because you have asserted your rights, have set boundaries and will no longer allow the disrespect and abuse, and because you recognised the abuse and exposed them, or have spoken up about the situation'.

I can bear witness to the above post 'discard' with the Nex. Except that because I was the one to ultimately 'discard' him he then proceeded to make my life hell because of the hate and contempt he now felt towards me because I had exposed him. His need for revenge was tantamount to him. A relationship with a narcissist will always end badly so you must be prepared for the inevitable that will follow. Your narcissist 'will' turn others against you, and they 'will' try to ruin your reputation. They 'will' also continue to deny everything, and of course, they 'will' blame you for everything.

When the only consistent thing about your relationship with your narcissist is that it is always on the brink of ending, then it really is time to get out.

On one of the forums, I belong to someone once asked, 'How do you really know if it is the final discard or not' and the response was – 'End it yourself!'

I really could not have put it any better.

I will end this Chapter with a quote by CiCi B that sums up the above,

'I think it all started when I stopped liking him. I still loved him, but I didn't like him anymore… and that's when I knew my mind was preparing my heart for that moment, the one where I would say 'I'm done' and really mean it'.

Chapter Five
What Makes a Narcissist?

As I have covered earlier in the book, we have described the biological and social reasons as to why and how a narcissist is 'born' and how they develop.

Here we will look at what exactly makes a narcissist. What distinguishes them from another human being. What exactly sets them apart? What are the warning signs for you to look out for?

Let us recap on what a narcissist must have,

Power, control, admiration, praise, adoration, desire, success, charisma, charm and of course the ever consistent ever flowing narcissistic supply or fuel.

In the narcissist's toolbox there is,

The need to be right, to have control over other people, no empathy or compassion, no remorse, no conscience, be over critical, have a lack of responsibility, anger issues, massive ego, jealousy, bear grudges, an extreme sense of entitlement, cruelty and manipulation.

A narcissist is basically nothing more than a spoilt and insecure child inside an adult's body. Albeit they can be an extremely dangerous 'child'. They are self-centred and hypersensitive to even the smallest of criticisms.

A narcissist will not work or help to solve problems or conflicts within a relationship. Rather, they will be the instigator. If you dared to challenge a narc, or criticise, or simply question, and worse still, God forbid, state that they are wrong/incorrect then they will unleash a torrent of abuse the like of which you have never experienced or seen before meeting them. As I have said before, this abuse will come in all manner of forms, be it verbal, emotional or physical. Depending on whether the narcissist is a lesser, mid-ranger or a greater, you will be gaslighted, blamed, mirrored, stone-walled, ghosted and blocked by every means open to the narc. And of course, if you live with them then welcome to the silent treatment, especially from the mid-ranger.

I cannot stress enough how 'nothing' is or can never ever be the narcissists' fault. A narc will 'always' blame their victim, however outlandish or absurd that blame is. A narcissist will 'always' see themselves as the real victim. Such is their distorted perception on life. Just to recap again, the birth of the internet has been the real victim's worst nightmare because it has led to the narcissist being able to cherry pick out their potential victims so much more easily. Just like picking candy from a candy jar.

As I have also mentioned earlier where the Nex was concerned, if a job he was working on developed a fault either during or after completion, he would immediately blame the materials, or his tools and sometimes even the customer but never, not 'ever' was it his fault. How could it be? He was Mr. Faultless. The narcissist really does believe what 'they' want to believe, truth or not.

With the Nex, any argument was my fault. Anything wrong in the house was my fault. Anything lost in the house was my fault. Anything broken in the house was my fault. Problems in our relationship were my fault. Relationship not working was my fault. silent treatment was my fault. He once hit a boulder whilst driving my car and immediately blamed me by saying that I had distracted him!

You really are onto a losing battle if you try to say that it really was not your fault, even if you can produce tangible evidence. Forget it, it will just not work. So, save yourself your time and energy and most important of all, your sanity, and just say to the narc if you are still unfortunately with them; 'That is not how I see it, or how I remember it'. Try to remain calm (easier said than done I know!) and change the subject if you can. Go 'Grey Rock' on them because if you deny, deny, deny, and worse still, challenge their lie, you simply will not win. The only thing that you will succeed in doing is stressing and upsetting yourself, but most important of all, you will be providing the narcissist with a supply of their precious fuel as they are feeding off your anguish and stress, and furthermore, you are creating an opportunity for them to devalue and abuse you.

My Nex's absolute favourite was to always blame my 'Gob'. He would say 'If it wasn't for your gob we wouldn't have had this row' or 'If it wasn't for your gob we'd be blah blah blah'. What he really meant was 'How dare you challenge me?' 'How dare you even speak to me and question something that I have said or done?' For a normal person, if I had indeed asked them an innocent question their response would be, 'I did this because', or 'Yeah I see where you're coming from with that question'. But as you are now probably coming to realise, or even already know, a narcissist does not and will not ever 'Do normal'. I would run out of fingers and toes if I were to count the number of times the Nex accused me of turning something around and making it all about me. Yet another favourite saying of his and of course another classic narcissistic trait.

My 'Gob' as the Nex put it was rarely challenging per se, or loud, or angry, or cross, or accusatory towards him. Remember, I had learnt from early on not to ask such questions, not to challenge him direct, not to unleash his wrath, but instead to walk on eggshells with absolutely everything that I said to him. But it never mattered because 'My Gob' was always his excuse. Rather what he really meant was that I had dared to stand up for myself, dared to deny his accusations or God forbid, worse still, had implied that it was possibly his fault. Another firm favourite of his was to say that I liked to 'Fight' everybody and everything. This was simply not true, but he knew that it would upset me and when told to other people, especially after we split, it served his purpose to paint me as the bad guy. I had email after email from him post-split spelling all of this out to me. I admit that like anybody, if something was wrong I would of course challenge it, for example, faulty goods, and service, an injustice and the like of, but the only real true fight I ever fought for myself was the court one my friend and I went through except that we did not start that 'fight' but instead merely defended ourselves when we were the ones who were taken to court. I did fight plenty of battles for the Nex though as this of course was expected of me what with me being his wife. Parking tickets, faulty goods, planning consent, even one of his friends' fight in the family court. They were always my fight according to him, except of course they were not. What I mean is he made me fight them for him. The best one of all was the planning application fight after it had been turned down in the September/October of 2016. It transpired that an objection from our neighbour had been made to the planning department (this was not the reason for a no answer but rather because the design was too big) and he was absolutely enraged that it had been refused. I had my parent's and daughter staying with us at the time as my father was recuperating from a heart attack in the August, and I was right in the middle of our business court battle and on my return from a day in court he thrust the letter from the council at me before I had even got through the door. No mention of my day at all or how it had gone, but this was normal behaviour for him. That is another thing you soon come to realise about a narcissist that anything and everything is 'always' about them, never about you. So, he went on and on ranting and raving to the point where he insisted I went round and spoke to the neighbours about it (apparently they did not like our hedge and had not liked it for five years but failed to ever say so!) I explained that I could not go right then and there as I was busy and needed to get the evening meal cooked for everyone. Well, you have never heard anything like it. In front of my parent's and daughter he screamed at me, and I quote, 'What kind of fucking wife are you?!' 'Get around there right now and say something!' He would not let up. My elderly parents of course were shocked at the tone and venom of his voice. You must remember what I have said previously about the Narcissist's mask, his or her false persona that they put on to the rest of the world and how crucial it was that no one else ever saw what was really underneath this mask. The fact that his mask had now slipped, and others had gotten a glimpse of what he was really like only served to feed his rage and fuel his anger further. It was so bad that I immediately stopped what I was doing and obediently obeyed his command and went around to the neighbours because I really did not trust what would happen next if I did not go. My parents never spoke to me about what they had witnessed. I think they were so shocked by it all. Whenever I questioned him on why I was always the one who had to do things he would say that it was because I was good at 'that kind of thing'. Ironically, the 'one thing' he thought I was good at was then always used as a weapon against me later, especially after we had split up by him constantly claiming that I liked to fight everyone! Yet another classic narcissistic trait, and yet again, damned if you did and damned if you did not!

The simple fact of the matter was that his original design for his garage was far too big and grand and ostentatious, so much so, that it was never going to be passed. He reduced it slightly two more times, but it was still too big and so was refused again and again. It featured an upper mezzanine level with windows and the roof pitch was almost the height of the house. It was only supposed to be a bloody garage but looked instead like a second house. His narcissistic sense of grandiosity and entitlement left him feeling that this is what he should, could and would have. The Nex of course, insisted that I lodge an appeal for him and when I said that I would rather not as it really was not

117

my 'fight', I then got the verbal abuse and comments like, 'What kind of wife are you if you don't support me?!' The appeal was subsequently rejected, and he was informed that he could have a smaller garage at the side of the house, but this of course was not enough for him. This rejection from the planning department caused a massive narcissistic injury to the Nex and I ultimately paid the price for that.

In the narcissist's perceived defence, they will use a combination of favoured methods to confuse you and to deflect the blame away from themselves. They will use; word-salad, confabulation, gaslighting, blame-shifting, deflection and projection. I remember one incident clearly though not what started it because as I have said before, they usually came from out of nowhere and for some very stupid and trivial reason. So, on this occasion I had left him downstairs and gone to bed following one of his usual onslaughts. Of course, the light was off in the bedroom and for all he knew by this time I was asleep, but it simply did not matter to him. I did not matter to him. He flounced into the bedroom and switched the main light on (I wear a sleep mask so I was not blinded by this action) and I could just about make out from under the bottom of the mask that he was rummaging in his wardrobe. He then threw a suitcase on to the bed straight on top of me and proceeded to put clothes into it. I laid there stock still and silent until he finally zipped the case up and put it on the floor. I then got out of bed, pointed up to the top of my wardrobe and calmly said, 'There's a bigger suitcase up there if you like which I'm sure will fit more of your clothes in'. I then left the room and went to sleep in my son's bedroom for the rest of the night. Except of course I did not sleep. I had managed to stay calm up to that point but once in my son's bedroom I was shaking so much, and my heart was pounding and beating irregularly (symptom of my illness). So much so, that I seriously contemplated calling myself an ambulance! He of course did not come after me. Surprisingly, he did in fact tell my daughter about it the next day when I was at work, making a joke out of it, and telling her that I had left him gobsmacked when I had told him where he could get a bigger suitcase from. Of course, he was quick to follow this with a further comment to her that him and her mum may have these 'fights' but that we would never ever split up. I must stress to you that this conversation never took place between the Nex and I. I only knew about this because my daughter told me. In fact, my daughter and I did have a little giggle about it a few days later because, come on, let's face it, it was such outlandish and childish behaviour from him that it was in the end funny! The look on his face when I had told him where to find a bigger suitcase really was priceless! At the time though, it was far from funny. Nothing more was ever said about the incident to me, and I think that because I had calmly told him how he could pack a bigger case, this was enough for him not to unleash a silent treatment on me that time or an 'End of the relationship' scenario because he could not be sure that I would not agree with him on this occasion! After this event, I have to say that a little something inside of me that I felt towards him did die and did continue to die with every single episode after that. I think this is because at some point during the relationship with a narcissist you do ultimately reach your breaking point. After all, we are only human and can only take so much abuse before we finally react.

Again, I will reiterate that it is a complete and utter waste of time trying to get a narcissist to ever see things from your point of view. You really will just be wasting your breath and your time and your energy. You will stress yourself out and probably even escalate the situation. The narcissist will not and cannot see or feel your pain, your anguish or your torment. All that they will see is the Fuel that your reaction will provide for them. I do not mean that this is done on a conscious level but instead all they will know and perceive is that your pained and upset reaction makes them feel better. They may even go as so far as to feel that what you have done has instead caused them an injury. Again, this will not be done on a conscious level, but you will have triggered a narcissistic injury which will have hurt them. Do not be surprised if on these occasions you are the one who ends up apologising to the narcissist, such as I did, many times over.

You will discover or have already discovered that it will be you, the victim, that will spend most of the time apologising, even if it is not your fault, such is life with a narcissist.

Because a narcissist is 'never' wrong, 'always' must be in control and you cannot 'ever' tell a narcissist what to do, how to think or what to say.

He or she will do exactly as they please when they please and how they please. Your thoughts, opinions or feelings will not feature anywhere in the equation.

A narcissist will spoil every event or occasion if the focus is not solely on them. I have told you already about my graduation. Well, when my son graduated, even though the Nex did attend my son's ceremony, he certainly did not congratulate my son on his achievement at any point. Well of course he would not because it was not about him! These examples were not the first nor were they the last time an event, birthday or Christmas was spoilt. The Christmas of 2016 my son had bought his very first brand new car using money for a deposit from his earlier 21st birthday present from me. He bought the car just ten days before Christmas and because he was so proud and excited he wanted to tell the Nex himself and surprise him by arriving in the car when he came to us for Christmas. I was excited for him too. My parents and my son arrived together but in separate cars and the Nex had seen them arrive and opened the door to let them in. Obviously, he saw my son's car immediately. I was in the kitchen at the sink, and he subsequently came in and sidled up to me and said, 'You didn't tell me about ****'s car'. I said, 'No he wanted to surprise you, but isn't it great news and he's so proud of what he's done and I'm so proud of him too'. The Nex immediately replied angrily and stated that he did not like surprises and that I should have told him about it because he was my husband, and I was his wife, and I should not keep secrets from him. He would not accept that it was my son's surprise and was not mine to tell but his reply to this was that it did not matter. I had betrayed him. He then had a go at me about the money, said he bet that I had bought the car for my son, and I was paying for it, on and on he went. I told him no that was not the case and that my son had decided to use his birthday money instead of using it for the holiday he had planned to go on and he then set up the finance for the car all by himself with absolutely no help from me at all. It really did not matter what I said, he was fuming. He was going to believe his 'version' of events and no one else's, so much so, that I got the silent treatment from that moment on, the evening of the 23rd of December, right up until Christmas Day morning. He only relented then and spoke to me because he wanted his Christmas presents and he knew that the attention would once again focus on him. I know that as you are reading this you must be thinking that surely I am exaggerating because it sounds so stupid but trust me I am not. Every scenario I tell you about really did happen exactly as I am telling it. This was not the first or last Christmas that an 'event' happened neither.

In relation to Christmas, the Nex found it amusing to buy me cheap toiletries as presents several years in a row. This was done as a not-so-subtle dig at me because he would state that I smelt. The reason for this is because I did not shower at home every day but instead chose to often shower after work

120

because it was easier, especially if it had been a long day for me. Well, in his narcissistic wisdom he decided that this was not true, and I could not possibly be showering at work so instead he tried to insist that I had to shower at home every day. I refused. So, he would insult me, call me names, make out like he was not going to hug me because I smelt and so on. I became so paranoid that I asked family and friends if they thought I did but they could not understand why I ever needed to ask this of them and of course I did not smell. So, the purchase of the toiletries at Christmas was to cause me offence and ultimately hurt and upset me and put a dampener on my Christmas. Of course, his relentless onslaught about me showering at home yet again highlights and demonstrates his need for control over me.

In relation to the Christmas period, it was only in the last few years that he allowed anyone to arrive to stay before Christmas Day. So, my poor parents' who lived over two hours away could only ever make the journey on Christmas Day morning up to this point. He used to use the excuse that Christmas Eve was family time, though it never really was, because he would simply do his own thing and I would be getting things ready for the next day. I now know that this was simply yet another form of control by him, and the first time he did finally allow my parents to come the day before, he made sure that he spoilt it for me.

Another previous occasion that I can recall, was the Nex's birthday in the October of 2010 following his illness and loss of his mother. We had already lost most of our animals, and my beloved dog had died only five days prior to his birthday, and I had already purchased an expensive Bengal cat for him as a surprise for his birthday. I really thought it was a nice thing to do for him, especially following his illness, but nope, not at all, not in his eyes. I took him to see the kitten on the day of his birthday and before we were meeting up with the rest of his family, as I had arranged a surprise meal with them for him too. He acted weird when he saw the cat and did not really say a lot about it until we were back in the car and then the anger came. How dare I do that to him! How dare I buy a cat without his knowledge or input! (We had previously had three cats between us and still had mine at this point). The upshot was that he refused point blank to have anything to do with the cat and he refused point blank to have it in the house even when I said that I would keep it for myself instead. He said that if I kept the cat then he would leave.

Boy, I wished I had put that to the test now that is for sure! I would have certainly saved myself a few more years of grief, abuse and a shed load of money! What I had effectively done was inadvertently taken control away from him by purchasing this cat without his knowledge or permission. That was the crux of the matter and nothing else.

I had spent over £500 on this cat and accessories for it, and I ended up just giving the cat away to our next-door neighbour instead. There was nothing else I could do. I was devastated. He even told his family what I had done at the meal and tried to justify his behaviour. It is something his sister never forgot nor ever understood, and nor could she ever believe to this day just exactly how he had overreacted to it. From his point of view, me purchasing this cat had taken control away from him and as you now know, a narcissist must always have total control. Again, at this point I had not even heard of the term narcissist, I just knew that his reaction was not normal behaviour at all.

After my cat died a couple of years later in 2012, he went on to not allow me to have any more pets for the next three years. He refused to even discuss the prospect if I ever brought it up. It was his decision, and his alone, and I now see that it was yet another way he could control me by not allowing me to have anymore. When we finally did get two rescue cats, his immediate reaction had been to say no, then he relented, for whatever reason I will never know, and said he would think about it, then he finally said yes. The point I am trying to make is that we never discussed it like we would have in a normal relationship, every aspect of it was down to him, he always had to have complete and total utter control. I guess that on this occasion that I had asked I was being treated to an idealisation phase without realising it.

Another example is when we changed broadband provider and they accidently changed our telephone number by mistake at the same time. The Nex went mad and demanded that I had to sort it out immediately and that every day that went by was costing him money because he was losing business because the landline was so vital to him. We must not allow our number to be changed. So, I obeyed and went to another provider who allowed us to retain our original telephone number. He went on to never use the landline. What was most laughable about it all was that when the phone did ring he never answered it because he stated it was never for him, so he did not see the point in answering it! His customers had always preferred to reach him on his mobile.

122

Yet another act of control was to do with something as simple as shower gel. The Nex liked a particular expensive brand and if I ever bought a different one to try, even a more expensive one that was on offer, he would point blank refuse to use it and proceed to moan and force me to go out and buy the one that he liked. To him it was as simple as that.

What this demonstrates is the fact that a narcissist often picks a fight just to create drama and so that they can be the centre of attention. This is a prime example of being goaded into fighting his battle for him. A narcissist will also bend the facts and twist logic to make it seem like they are right. You can be left many times of fighting a battle on the wrong side.

Can you remember the title of this book at this point? Go on, look at it again. Digest the meaning behind the title. Why do you think this title phrase stuck in my head after it had been said and why it was one that I never forgot? Because it was 'never' going to really happen. Ever.

Why?

Because a narcissist 'always' must hurt you to enable them to draw fuel from you. They must punish you if you have dared to challenge them. They must ensure that they are 'always' in control. 'Always' have the power over you and you are 'always' feeding them their supply of fuel.

A narcissist will never feel what we feel purely because they cannot.

They simply learn how to mimic those emotions.

The only true feelings a narcissist can feel are hate, loathing, despise, malice, jealously, anger and ultimately power when they receive their precious fuel that has been provided to them via praise and adoration or on the flip side, from their destruction of their victim during the devaluation phase. This Fuel makes them feel better about themselves. Your destruction brings them pleasure.

A narcissist also seems to have a vocabulary that comes straight out of a dictionary that has especially been written for them.

For example, 'I am broken', or, 'You always manage to turn this around', or, 'You always make it all about you', or, 'You started this', or, 'It's all your fault because you shouldn't have said or done this'. The latter ones were always used not only throughout my relationship with the Nex but also on a regular basis after we had split up. The first one, 'I am broken', the Nex saved until after we had split up then meted it out on a regular basis, especially by email. I think he just liked the way it looked written down and of course liked the way it made him appear as the victim. Or how it made him feel more like the victim. Another favourite of his was. 'You made me do it'. I bet all of these are sounding familiar to you by now are they not? This is because all narcissists really do sing from the same hymn sheet. Bizarrely they really do use the same modus operandi (MO).

And finally, those three little words that a narcissist can say so easily but ultimately do not know how to truly feel for another being, 'I Love You'.

To a narcissist this really means that he or she loves your fuel provision, and they love the control and power that they have over you. They love how they can manipulate you. They love how good they feel about themselves when they have hurt you.

HG Tudor mentions in his literature that the analysis of his therapist is that he purely remains in a relationship with someone simply to punish his partner for letting him down and not doing enough for him. Of course, this is his perception of his victims rather than that they really do let him down.

For a lesser or a mid-range narcissist, their responses to what they perceive as wrong doings or criticisms of the victim are purely instinctive and correct because in their opinion their victim is the one who is in the wrong.

As noted in Joseph Burgo's book, 'The Narcissist You Know', a narcissist is so committed to his 'truth' that his lies may not be conscious. In other words, as I have already mentioned in other chapters, the narcissist really does believe that what he is saying really is the truth. Such is the level of disorder of this kind of personality. Joseph Burgo has further noted in his book that the narcissists drive to always be the 'winner' renders the truth completely irrelevant.

A narcissist really believes that they are the best and they want everybody else to believe the same about them too. Remember that they are never wrong, never at fault, nothing is ever their responsibility because to them, to accept blame or responsibility will chip at their false façade and they simply cannot and must not ever let that mask slip to anyone else. They cannot ever let the world see their true vile, evil inner self.

As an expert on narcissism and a narcissist himself, Shmuel 'Sam' Vaknin states that a narcissist has lost their true self and that it has been replaced by a false self, which is a delusion of grandeur. Therefore, he believes that a narcissist cannot be 'healed' because they do not exist as a real person but only as a reflection. The false self-replaces the narcissists true self which is intended to shield them from any hurt or narcissistic injury. Therefore, the narcissist pretends that his false self is real meanwhile keeping his or her real-life imperfect true self hidden away.

Another personality trait of a narcissist is their innate sense of entitlement. They truly do think that they are entitled to anything and everything whether it is your love, your attention, your adoration, your home, your car, your money, your friends or even your family. They genuinely believe that they are owed all of this. You must constantly provide a drip feed of attention and admiration (fuel) for them to simply just exist in the world as we know it. They are 'never' sated. If there is a drop in this attention/admiration, then you will feel the narcissists wrath. But of course, if this did happen, you will still be providing them with their fuel during this phase too, albeit you are now in the devaluation phase and simply providing them with a different kind of fuel, but nevertheless, that supply of fuel is still ever flowing.

With me, the Nex would say 'You never give me any attention anymore' or, 'You never praise me anymore'. Both were false, and it did not matter how much I protested he would still say it. It got to the point where I started to praise him more publicly so I would then have proof that in fact I did praise and admire him. So, I would put posts on Facebook praising work that he had just done on the house, or I would post some other endearing comment about him, but he would still say the same thing over and over. I even had to put posts on if we had been out somewhere or done something nice because he expected me to announce to the world what a wonderful time I had had with my husband. I never understood the relevance of this at the time and that it made him look good to other people, and so he was getting a hit of his narcissistic supply (fuel) from all the likes and comments. Again, the main point to remember here is that these were moments before my knowledge of narcissism. So, the cycle would continue to play out, I praise, he denies it, I get upset, he receives fuel. Over and over and round and round we would go.

Quite simply you become trapped on this hamster wheel where the more you give, the more they want, and the more they will take, so that wheel just keeps on turning.

After we had spilt up, he would then say 'If you had given me more attention' or on another occasion he even said. 'If only you had fought for me'. Both comments truly just say it all.

You will also have noticed or found or will find that you cannot have a normal conversation with a narcissist. Especially if there is nothing in it for them and more importantly they are not gaining fuel from it. You will feel drained and even exhausted at the exchange you have just had with your narc simply because it will have become all about them, and they will have ultimately taken the lion's share of the conversation.

On the flip side, if you are dealing with a victim narcissist, like the Nex is, then they will portray an act of vulnerability and neediness, they will try to play on your sympathies. A good example of this which I witnessed from the Nex was when I was paying any attention to my beloved husky dog. If I was found to be saying 'hello' to the dog and giving him a cuddle then the Nex would immediately say 'If I got down on all fours and starting barking and panting would you give me some affection too' while at the same time of saying it he would literally bark and pant and hold his arms out like the forelegs of a dog. I am not kidding you at all, he did this on several occasions! But if you ever told him he was acting jealous then oh no not him, he was never jealous, not ever! It was not as if he did not get affection neither when he used to say this. Bear in mind my dog died towards at the end of 2010 and up until near the end of our relationship in 2018, I was always the more attentive one towards him, constantly praising him and doing things for him. But he hated it if I gave the same love and affection towards anyone or anything else, especially my children or my pets. He also insisted that my dog and cat were to live outside when I first moved in with him, just as he had made his cats do, something that was alien to me and that I had never wanted to happen.

I have a thing about hairy chests on a man and absolutely love them! Therefore, I loved to touch the Nex's chest and at first he did not have a problem with it. Fast forward further into the relationship and suddenly he did not like me touching it anymore. He suddenly claimed that he had never liked it being touched by anyone and knowing what I do now I believe that that this was not true at all. Rather, because he knew it was something I liked doing he denied me the action on purpose as a form of control and because this is what a narcissist does when playing with your mind.

They behave this way because the narcissist requires their ego to be continuously stroked. They need constant praise and attention, including the covert narcissist. This behaviour is just as harmful for their victim. The narc will try and manipulate you with guilt, just as in my example above with my dog, they will say things like 'You never praise me'. Just as I have explained previously that the Nex did over and over so I would deliberately then publicize the praise for my own proof. Such are the levels you go to because you become sick and tired of always being painted as the bad 'guy' and always being accused of not doing something that you know full well that you do. This is a prime example of cognitive dissonance, which is the uncomfortable state of mind caused by the presence of two opposing beliefs about a subject. This is also a classic example of gaslighting.

As described by Maria Consiglio @ understandingthenarc, she describes Gaslighting as,

'A technique that is used to manipulate people by instilling doubt in them. It conditions victims to doubt their own memories. It also conditions them to doubt their own eyes. This manipulation leaves victims feeling unstable and racked with confusion. It teaches victims to lose trust in the most important person of all, 'Themselves'. It really is a form of crazy making that is meted out deliberately (not consciously) by the narcissist.'

At the start of a new relationship, a narcissist loves the way that the person (victim) makes them feel. They are genuinely not interested in that person as such, rather what that person can provide to them by way of fuel, praise, admiration, security and financially. I remember the early telephone calls with the Nex, before we met, and he asked me about my home, my job, if I could cook, etc. I stupidly assumed that he was just interested in me as a person but now I realise that I was being 'interviewed' for the prime position of his next victim.

Again, you must always keep in the forefront of your mind while reading this book that a narcissist needs to always have his constant supply of fuel. If it were to ever dry up or is not being provided by their intimate partner (their primary fuel source) or if you dared to challenge the narc, you 'will' cause them a narcissistic injury. As I have said before, this could be through a conscious act that you have done or an unconscious innocent act that the narc has perceived to be a slight against them.

The most ludicrous and ultimately abusive one that I can recall that I endured, was a weekend when I had been to my hometown to visit my family and friends. It was probably around 2016. I returned home on the Sunday all bubbly and in a good mood because I had had a lovely time with my family and friends. The Nex had his brother there visiting him when I got back. I think that because I was in such a good mood this immediately angered the Nex. Remember what I have said before that everything must be about them, and woe betide you if you are happy and they are not. Well, his anger was not apparent and 'on show' but I could tell by the way he was with me and the way he spoke to me that he was not happy. Clipped responses, tone of voice, etc., they were all giveaways that he was not in a good mood. He of course tried to cover it up in front of his brother, but I think that on this occasion even his brother could see something was wrong with him. The Nex passed some dig about being cooped up at home, so I suggested we go out for lunch and to the cinema. Once his brother had left we set off out towards town and I could tell by now that the Nex was really spoiling for a fight. It did not matter what I said to him he just tried to make me react to a slur or a dig that he passed my way. I deliberately ignored his attempts and kept being nice and pleasant to him. We parked up in town and got out of the car to start walking towards the cinema. I turned around and saw him just stood there looking at the ground. I said, 'Come on let's get going, what are you waiting for?' and he just looked at me then back at the ground. I then asked him if he still wanted to go to the cinema or not and he then launched his tirade at me. 'How dare I have a nice time that weekend while he was stuck at home! How dare I'! I pointed out to him that it was his choice to stay home rather than go and visit friends or family, but it fell on deaf ears. His shit weekend was my fault, end of. It was as simple as that to him. Couple that ridiculous and absurd belief of his with his jealousy that I had had a nice time and he had not, and you start to see the forming of a narcissistic injury. It really does only take something as stupid as that. So, I said okay we will go home, and he then refused to get in the car with me and he promptly marched off. I got in the car and drove round the one-way system and then saw him walking down the road. I pulled alongside him and asked him to get in the car and he said, and I quote, 'I'm not getting in the car with a fucking ugly selfish bitch like you!' and he stormed off again. So, I could not do anything else other than drive home, which was about a fifteen-minute drive away.

Once home, I got a call from him and an absolute maelstrom of abuse down the phone with him screaming, 'How dare you fucking leave me stranded, how dare you just drive off and leave me, what kind of fucking wife are you?, Get your fucking ugly arse back here and pick me up now!!'. He then promptly slammed the phone down on me. More importantly he had not told me exactly where he was. I called him back, but he did not pick up, I texted to ask where he was, and he ignored me. What the F??!!

How was I supposed to pick him up if I did not know where he was?!

Of course, it was completely lost on him that it was him that had refused to get in the car with me and told me to fuck off. But of course, it was now all my fault. His narcissistic default mode was to automatically ghost and stonewall me hence his refusal to answer my calls to find out where he was so that I could pick him up. Such was his stupid mentality!

I drove back to town then home three more times in total, picking a different route each time but I could not find him en route. It was like looking for a needle in a haystack. Each time I had called and texted but still did not receive a response from him. On the third time I arrived home, he finally called, and I had to literally hold the phone away from my ear because he was screaming obscenities so loudly down the line at me. He finally told me where he was and demanded that I go and pick him up immediately. So, stupidly and obediently I did.

He was sat on a bench when I got there and without a word he got in the car, slamming the door after him. I was then treated to the most vile and abusive onslaught from him. It really is too vulgar to repeat here but I am sure your imagination will do the work for you. I sat in silence, gripping the steering wheel because my hands were shaking. I had gone past anger by this stage and a cold calm shock had descended over me. When we pulled up on the drive, he said that the least I could do now was go and take him for lunch, so I was ordered inside and told to fetch my purse (yes of course I was!). I got out of the car and left him in it. I went into the house and immediately called my friend and asked her if I could come and stay with her and that I would explain everything when I got there. This friend was my restaurant partner and knew full well what the Nex could be like as not only had I confided in her in the past, but she herself had witnessed snippets of his personality. I threw a few things into a bag and was in the cloakroom getting some shoes and coats when I heard him come in. I hid in the cloakroom then when I heard him go to the toilet I quickly ran out to the car to leave. As soon as he heard the engine he was out of the door in a flash and physically blocked me from driving off. He asked me where I was going and why was I going (yes he really did ask!) but would not let me leave. Every time that I revved the engine he put his hands on the boot of the car to stop me from moving. He really could not understand why I wanted to leave! I told him that I was not going to tolerate that level of abuse anymore from him and he quickly gave me a false apology which was then quickly followed with a 'Well it was your fault for having a nice time when I didn't' excuse. I learnt later that this is the classic narcissistic trait of blame-shifting and projecting. He then turned on the pity play to try and justify his behaviour. Ultimately I did eventually get out of the car and remain but a little bit more of what I felt for him inside of me had just died just a little bit more once again. Of course, the incident was never mentioned again and in fact for the rest of that day he acted as if nothing had happened. In the terms of his fuel provision that weekend, the positive fuel I was providing him with the attention he got on my return was just not enough for him, such was his perceived narcissistic injury. Because he was so incensed that I had had a good weekend when he had not, he needed more than positive fuel to satisfy him, so he commenced his onslaught that I have described above, and he received the more potent negative fuel from me because of his appalling behaviour. This is a good example for me to demonstrate to you a little bit about the fuel a narcissist needs and to show you how it is obtained and why. I did go and see my friend later that week and filled her in on what had happened. She asked me pointedly how many more times I was going to let him treat me like that, but more tellingly she asked me if I still loved him. For the first time ever, I hesitated when I answered her, and she noted this.

The Nex and I never spoke about that event again. Not even straight after it had happened. It was as if the switch had been flipped and everything in his world was alright again. I now know that this is typical narcissistic behaviour and I had inadvertently provided him with a hefty dose of his precious fuel, so he was temporarily sated. I was no longer black but instead I was now once again painted white. Discussing things was something that the Nex and I never ever did because the Nex would always immediately take offence and shut the conversation down dead if I ever tried broaching anything with him. No argument was ever resolved in the entire fourteen years that we were together. Rather, the Nex always won, I always was the one who backed down and had to apologise and thus control and power was always then restored to the Nex.

When you first really see the narcissist and their true colours it can be a shocking thing to witness because you finally see what really lies beneath their carefully constructed mask. I did not ever see what the Nex could be truly capable of until after we had split up. Oh boy, if I had felt his behaviour during the marriage was abusive and bad then I was certainly in for a nasty shock of what was to come post-split. He threw so much at me that I will explain more about later, but the one most shocking incident that I will tell you about now came around the time of my beloved father's death and just after it.

I will explain to you shortly about the Nex's behaviour when he used the death of my father and the period of profound grief for me to renege on a financial agreement that was agreed and in place between us.

For now, I will tell you about what happened just before my father died and while he lay dying in an intensive care hospital bed we found out that the Nex had unfriended both of my parents on Facebook. When I asked him why he had done this he lied and said that Facebook had deleted all his friends by mistake. Unbeknown to me and my family he then tried to cover his tracks by sending a friend request to my dying father who was at that point in a critical condition and in a coma in intensive care. I only discovered this a week later, after my beloved father's death, when my brother and I went to collect my father's car and mobile phone from where he had collapsed. Large as life on my father's phone screen was a notification from Facebook that the Nex had sent a friend request to my father. Both my brother and I were shocked and appalled to say the least. When I asked the Nex why he had done this, he saw nothing wrong in his action whatsoever and he claimed that he thought one of us would simply see the request and accept it! Such was his monstrous mentality! Forty-eight hours after my beloved father's death he demanded that I come home from my mother's house to give him parcels that had been delivered which I had left locked in my office for safe keeping. He really could see no wrong in asking for them, and in fact went one further and lied that the eBay sellers now needed paying and he could not pay them until he knew for sure that the goods had arrived. Everyone who has used or does use eBay knows for a fact that you 'always' must pay for goods first before they are delivered to you. Such was his mentality in telling such whopping great big lies! But more importantly and for sure most telling of all was the fact that the Nex was displaying absolutely 'no' Empathy for me whatsoever, for the loss of my beloved father. Plus, this is also a prime example of his sense of entitlement. He wanted the parcels there and then, he was entitled to have them there and then, that was all that mattered to him. How dare my father's sudden death deny him of this!

I have mentioned before about the sense of entitlement that a narcissist has and right now seems a natural point for me to give you another prime example of this displayed by the Nex which relates directly to the death of my beloved father again.

Of course, following what I had discovered the Nex had done with sending my dying father a friend request simply to cover his own back, I could not even bear to look at him let alone anything else. So, on my return home from my mother's to collect a few more clothes for myself as I had literally only the clothes on my back that I was wearing when I had got the call to tell me that my father had collapsed, the Nex did attempt to 'comfort' me. I averted this move and made the excuse up that I did not want any form of comfort as I was trying to remain strong, pretend that it had not happened and so the Nex proceeded to have the audacity to immediately take offence with me, he pulled a face and then stormed off and subjected me to yet another silent treatment for the next two weeks. He felt entitled to comfort me, I should be grateful for his comfort, how dare I refuse it! For the very first time I was so relieved for the silent treatment. He then only spoke to me when I later challenged him in the February, after discovering that he had hacked my phone and social media accounts and logged me in, in Fuerteventura where he was over the holiday period.

So, by the time of my father's funeral in the February three weeks after his death there was absolutely no communication between the Nex and I whatsoever and the 'truce' was well and truly over. I of course did not invite him to the funeral as he was clearly not welcome. Not just by me but also by the rest of my family who knew exactly how he had recently behaved. He was livid at this and of course he felt entitled that he should have been able to go which I explain in more detail about in another paragraph. Can you imagine the complete and utter devastation that I felt when I finally discovered that he had hacked my emails and social media, so unbeknown to me, he could see all the private arrangements, funeral directors' correspondence, private messages from family and friends, and posts/comments that were all directly related to my father's death. All the things that were private and sacred and details which he was the last person on earth that had a right to know anything about. Because he had breached my privacy, he was able to see everything, and know every single detail. When I realised this, I felt like I had been emotionally and mentally raped!

It is important at this stage to also point out that despite the Nex still having contact and a 'relationship' with my children he never once offered them his condolences for my father's death. For their grandfather's death. In fact, he never once mentioned it to either of them. Such was his lack of empathy the thought of offering them any sympathy was alien to him. Just like when one of his friend's wife was killed in a tragic accident. He was uncomfortable when this friend came around, to the point where he actively asked me to 'deal with his friend' because the Nex 'wasn't good with that kind of thing'. Now I understand why. Lacking empathy makes it extremely difficult for someone, especially a narcissist, to feel, show, experience, demonstrate or give empathy to another person.

The next incident to follow this was soon after, in the March, when he decided that he would kick me when I was at my lowest following my father's death and put a stop to the financial agreement we had drawn up and thus proceed to fight me through the courts. He of course told me everything was my fault, just as a narcissist would do, but then proceeded to tell me that he would never ever forgive me for not letting him go to my father's funeral! He stated that he was entitled to go. Such was his complete and utter sense of entitlement! It did not matter what I said about it being my father's 'day' and all about my father and not all about the Nex and that if he had gone it would have been too uncomfortable for my family and friends who were attending. He simply did not care about this. In his warped entitled narcissistic eyes, he had every right to go. So much so that he said at one point that he was just going to have just turned up with his brother. Thank God he did not! He truly felt such a sense of entitlement that he said it was his right to attend and that this superseded everything else. I will give you more examples of his sense of entitlement later in this book but for me this was by far the worst of them all. I strongly suspect that this is what also triggered his need for revenge and why he chose to then fight me through the courts.

You must be wondering by now why the hell did I not get out of this abusive relationship a hell of a lot sooner?!

But hopefully I have begun to address and help you to understand why not.

What primarily keeps a victim with their narcissist for so long will ultimately depend on what kind of Narcissist they are and what you are dealing with. For example, are they an overt or covert narcissist? Are they a lesser, mid-range or greater?

Because all narcissists use the three-phase cycle of idealise/devalue/discard it will not all be bad one hundred percent of the time with them. In fact, with a covert narcissist such as what the Nex is, you can have lengthy periods of normality. As I have said earlier in reference to the climb of percentage from ten percent to twenty percent to thirty percent and continuing upwards over the course of the relationship it sometimes is not until the very end that you finally 'jump ship'. Remember also that you are in the throes of the 'Frog in the Boiling Pan' scenario too. For me, what climbed from three to four incidents a year in the beginning to steadily three to four a month to finally in the final devaluation period was daily, will give you an insight into this.

Once the devaluation phases start, you may well be already living with them, married to them or even have a child with them.

You are not their first victim, nor will you be their last victim (unless the narc dies!) and over the course of all their relationships the narcissist has learnt how to hide their true self better. How to have improved their mask. What pitfalls to avoid with their next victim.

And of course, by the time you do start to realise that there is something seriously wrong with your partner you are already in too deep and already on that hamster wheel of cycles that ultimately keeps you tied to your narcissist.

Even though I was with the Nex for almost fourteen years, I never really felt like it was a proper partnership, especially once married. I did not have the support, respect or understanding from my partner. The Nex was not someone I could turn to for support, he was never really there for me. Pretty much the entirety of the relationship was all about him and his wants and needs. The attention always had to be on him and if I dared to mention anything that related to me he would respond by saying, 'Oh yeah, that's it, make it all about you!' So, of course, it would always remain all about him.

I think that my definition of a narcissist is a soulless, evil demon that lurks beneath a mask of feigned normality. Their sole intention is to destroy their victim by feeding off of their emotions and sucking the life out of them in the process so as just to make themselves feel better. So that the narcissist can feel something, anything, because they are empty and devoid of any feelings like we have. Feelings of love, joy, happiness and contentment. Instead, they are constantly seeking it and constantly draining it from their victims.

I will end this chapter with a quote I once read by Ramani Durvasula that goes,

'The narcissist is like a bucket with a hole in the bottom… No matter how much you put in, you can never fill it up… You are not enough… No one is… Nothing is…'

Chapter Six
How to Recognise How a Narcissist Operates?

So, how do they operate?

What is their Modus Operandi? (MO)

@narcissist.sociopath.awareness2 states,

'Idealisation, devaluation, discard. These three little words will turn your whole world upside down. Narcissists swoop in with adoration and attention until you are hooked. They will begin passive-aggressive insults and then ramp up the bad behaviour. They will leave you at the most inconsiderate time without an explanation while smearing your name. This is the blueprint for their life and is the only way they know how to live'.

This is every narcissists MO.

As I have mentioned before, online dating is 'the' best tool that was ever invented for a narcissist. When a narcissist selects a victim through one of these sites, they will not be alone in the selection. They will not have been singled out. Rather, they will be one of many that the narcissist is in contact with. The narcissist will syphon through all of them, including you, to establish which one exactly will most meet with their fuel requirement. Again, I cannot reiterate enough that this will not be done consciously, as to who will provide the most fuel, but rather who ticks most of the boxes as to who can be manipulated the easiest, who can be controlled the most, who appears to be the most empathic and the most pliable of all of the narcissist's targets, who has the most to offer the narcissist. Simply who is the best candidate to be their next victim.

As I have also mentioned previously, a particular game that a narcissist will play is to engage in online conversation with you, even texting you and calling you via mobile phone, and as it was in my day, using the webcam through the online dating site. It will appear that you are getting on enormously, then the narcissist will then just suddenly disappear. This leaves you confused, you cannot for the life of you think of what you have done wrong or said wrong. You rack your brains trying to figure it all out then you finally put it behind you, and you move on.

Poof! As if out of nowhere they are back again. The narcissist contacts you. As I have already said earlier in the book this is a deliberate ploy to mess with your head and put you through a test. If you do not question them on their absence, you have passed the test. The narcissist now knows that you will be easy to manipulate. For the duration of your 'shelving', the narcissist was already putting another potential 'candidate' through their paces and advancing their attempts to what will have appeared to the narcissist to be a better candidate than you.

As previously indicated, you must watch out for what a narcissist looks for in a potential candidate (victim). To pass the ultimate test not only must you meet the above requirement for manipulation, but you must also be someone who is financially secure, successful, have your own home (rented or owned) and it is also important that you must be vulnerable and pliable. For some narcissists, their main aim is to con you out of money, property and any other valuables that they can.

As was the case with the Nex at the start when he took £10,000 more than what fifty percent share value of his house was. Likewise, for the duration of the relationship where I paid for almost everything. I ultimately learnt post-split that his intention was to stop working, then live off me entirely for the rest of his days. He drew on a private pension not long before our split, made out that it was only worth £6,000 but I discovered post-split that it was closer to £20,000. I, and the marriage, never saw a penny of that, even though I had paid the premiums solely myself at one point for over a year. It was not reinvested for his future retirement or anything like that, nope, he splurged out on a brand-new motorbike and a sports car with the money.

When things turned acrimonious and he forced the court proceedings, he subsequently went after everything from me that he could. I mentioned earlier that he had lied to the courts, committed perjury on his Form-E by stating that I had not paid a single penny towards either property, and that he had paid for everything entirely. He went one step further and lied that I would be inheriting a large sum of money as my mother would be dying shortly. Yep, you certainly did read that correctly! Yet again, this statement was documented on his official court Form-E, written by his solicitor. Just four months after losing my beloved father so suddenly and so tragically, and the Nex was now trying to manipulate the court proceedings for nothing more than profit, by telling vile, diabolical barefaced lies about my mother purely so that he could get more financially. My mother had been diagnosed with vascular dementia shortly after my father's death, but this most certainly did not mean that she would be dying shortly! Nor would I be receiving any large sum of money from her in the future in the unlikely event that any money she did have was not used for future care home fees.

Are you starting to understand now just how incredibly vile and evil a narcissist really can be, and is?

The levels that they will stoop to just to serve their own purpose and their own overall extreme sense of entitlement and to exact revenge and destruction on you. The Nex did not stop and think for one nano-second of just how hurtful this lie would be so soon after my father's death. Of course, he did not! I repeat, narcissists lack empathy. I have email correspondence from him that stated that he was now going to destroy me. He stated that he did not care how much it would cost him as long as he took me down with him. He also stated that he now had to work longer than he had intended (yes he did actually put that in an email too!), would have to work until retirement now when his intention had been to finish work in his mid-fifties, and so he was now going to go after any meagre pension that I may have had and also spousal support from me. This is when I realised that his ultimate goal all along had been to retire soon and then become totally dependent on me financially and that despite my degenerative auto immune disease, I was the one that would have to work well into my sixties while he just sat back, did nothing whatsoever except live of my hard earnt wages. This I believe is what had ultimately pissed him off when I had called his bluff at his discard which he had never intended to be a final one but one which I ultimately made final. This was his punishment for me now. How dare I foil his plan! How dare I make him start again and find another victim? Because by now he was well in his late fifties. That is why he was now out to hurt me. Such was his need and his bitterness for revenge on me and ultimately for him to destroy me, totally and completely.

I did of course have enough knowledge by this point to recognise what was happening and why it was happening. Unfortunately for me though I still did not recognise Malign Hoovers, so I unwittingly used to get embroiled in an email argument with him and I mean they used to sometimes span fifty emails at a time! It is extremely hard to not defend yourself when you have wild accusations flying at you, when you are being told that you, the victim, has serious mental health issues, that you are the crazy one. That you still love and want the narcissist back. None of it is ever true but they are now engaging full pelt in all their narcissistic arsenal because you have finally sussed them out and called them on it. When you do start to realise that this is what they are doing, and you understand more about narcissists you will slowly become empowered. Therefore, I put a stop to all this at the end of May 2019 when I finally went 'No Contact' with him, not easy when still residing in the same house but fortunately for me, in his attempt to play the role of the victim this had meant that he stayed in his bedroom when at home as he had set it up as a bedsit style scenario. He still used the kitchen and bathroom, but it was easy to avoid bumping into him. Everything now went through his solicitor only. He did send a few more abusive malign emails after that, but I just forwarded them to his solicitor and logged them with the police.

@awakeningwomensupport state, 'Invisible abuse is the most harmful kind of abuse because covert narcissists are so good at making you look like the 'crazy' and 'unstable' one for reacting to their abuse and no one else sees it'.

So back to the title of this chapter and looking at how exactly a narcissist operates.

A narc will throw a temper tantrum, they cannot help themselves. It is like watching them morph into a spoilt child, it really is. They will dole out the silent treatment after they have called you abusive names, vilified you, and they may even have resorted to violence against you. These will be reactions to something that you have inadvertently said or done, even in all innocence, but which will have ignited their fury. Because you have caused them a narcissistic injury you must now be severely punished for it.

I am tempted to say that if you are still in your narcissistic relationship then when this happens just picture your narcissist stood there in a great big dirty nappy, having just tossed their dummy out of their pram and now proceeding to throw a temper tantrum, just like a baby or small child would. Hopefully for you, you will just laugh and then walk away. This is the worst thing you could do to a narcissist because you will have stopped them in their tracks. But it will be the best thing you can do for you, because their onslaught cannot continue. You will have diffused it. Be careful though if you think that your narcissist is a lesser as they may be violent if they see you laugh. Instead, just walk away laughing to yourself.

On one occasion that I can remember that demonstrates both temper tantrum and sense of entitlement was another weekend that I had come home from visiting my family. Shortly before bed on the Sunday evening, (I had an early start for work the next day) the Nex stated that the bed sheets needed changing and I simply replied that I would do it the next day. Well, you would think that I had just taken his favourite dummy away from him and dumped it in a great big pile of shit! I obviously had not (lol) but he certainly did spit his dummy out of his mouth and way across the room in his anger at my response. He demanded that I go and change it right there and then and followed it up with the threat of sleeping in the spare bedroom until it was changed. The best part about it was the fact that he had had all weekend to change it himself but oh no, this was beneath him. He did not 'do' housework; that was my job! I had to wait on him hand and foot. Such was his sense of entitlement. I was nothing more than the housekeeper in his eyes. So, obediently, I just quietly went and changed the bed. I was just too tired for an onslaught from him, too tired to face the silent treatment that I knew would ultimately come if I did not change it. Are you starting to see the pattern here? That the narcissist knows exactly how to control and have power over their victim. How to get their own way using continuous abuse and manipulation.

As I am writing this book I am also starting to see a pattern that a lot of his tantrums always followed a weekend of mine away visiting family and friends. Oh wow! This realisation is quite literally only just starting to dawn on me. But as it does, I am not in the least bit surprised. The Nex clearly hated it every time I had a nice weekend, and he probably did not. Hated it when I was happy, and he was not. Hated it when I had attention and he did not. Hated it that I had not been at home pampering to him, adoring him, praising him and so on.

The narcissists overall sense of entitlement is of course what resulted in the above 'changing of the bed' example because they see any menial task as below them. Housework, oh no, as my Nex stated, it is not his job because it is 'my' job. 'you' must pamper to the narcissist, serve them, clean the house, cook their meals, wash their clothes, buy their food and on it goes. In their opinion, they are entitled to all this. I have not used the phrase of housekeeper

140

earlier lightly at all. In the last few years of our relationship, I did genuinely feel like I was nothing more than the Nex's housekeeper. When I once pointed this out to him, he ironically went on to say that he felt like he was nothing more than the builder. Well of course he did! Classic example of narcissistic mirroring and projecting and deflecting.

It is difficult at the time to recognise that any of these responses mentioned above are the actions of a narcissist. You will not think, 'Oh, I am dealing with a narcissist here'. It may take months and even years before all these behaviour patterns and behavioural red flags begin to make any sense or logic to you. Look at me, I always knew that our relationship was not 'normal', but I did not know exactly why for almost fourteen years! I just knew that I was dealing with a very immature and at times irrational controlling adult.

So, if your partner reacts in an irrational, over the top, and illogical way whatsoever, then please mark and identify this as a great big fat red-flag. Your own common sense will tell you what a normal response is. Your gut instinct may even be screaming right at you. Other relationships that you have had in the past or do have with family and friends will be a good indicator for you. If you even find that family and friends are warning you about your partner, then please take heed. They will not be doing this just for the hell of it but rather because they have witnessed the narcissists behaviour towards you and even maybe recognised the red flags that you have not recognised. I have had several people after the end of my relationship turn around and tell me that they had not liked my husband and found him to be arrogant and manipulative. One friend whose own husband had met my Nex only once, then went on to refuse to ever have the Nex in their house. Can you begin to imagine how I felt learning these kinds of things out after we had split up?

Once you realise that it is narcissistic abuse that you have suffered from it is like a puzzle or a jigsaw, and all the pieces start coming together so you can finally see the bigger picture and you start to realise that you were right all along. That your relationship was not normal, and most important of all, you start to understand why it was not normal and this is one of the first steps on your road to recovery.

Some favourite methods of narcissistic traits that the narcissist uses are the silent treatment, ghosting, stonewalling, gaslighting, projecting, blame-shifting, victim playing, pity plays, word-salad, mirroring, discards, love-bombing, devaluation, victimhood and smearing. I know that I have mentioned all of these in previous chapters, but I cannot stress enough of how important it is to recognise and identify these so I will keep using them as examples for the duration of this book in the hope that by the end of it you will know exactly what I am talking about and understand what I am describing.

We are currently looking at how a narcissist operates and their use of 'all' the above which at some point in your relationship with a narcissist, 'will' be used against you.

It is also important to keep at the forefront of your mind why a narcissist operates the way that they do, and as I have stressed before, this is to, control, manipulate and extract fuel from you. I know I keep mentioning the narcissists need for fuel and hopefully by now you are understanding the meaning of this. I will also explain more about it in another chapter as well.

When we look at control and the use of it, we must acknowledge that a narcissist must always have total and absolute control. This very fact will give you early indicators what to look out for. Remember, a relationship is supposed to be a partnership of equal value and equal respect for both involved. If your new partner starts to try and control you, tell you how to look, what to wear, where to go, what time to be home by, and so on, then they are trying to control you, and this is 'not' acceptable at all. This is disrespectful and controlling behaviour towards you. If you tried to challenge them then you will be verbally, emotionally and even physically abused and none of these are acceptable either. If a narcissist does not have control, then he will also have no fuel. Fuel is what has kept him in control. Of course, you must not forget that there are also other covert insidious forms of control that the narcissist will use against you that are harder to recognise. The silent treatment 'is' emotional and psychological abuse, but more importantly, it is deployed purely to control you and have power over you.

Jackson MacKenzie at Hashtag/narcissisticabuse states that a narcissist will punish you with silence, so you learn to blame yourself.

If you dared to challenge a narcissist even with good cause, if they perceive this challenge to be a threat, or an insult, they will react with anger and fury, and possibly even violence. They will first attempt to deflect, project and blame-shift by using gaslighting and possibly word-salad against you then if this does not stop you challenging them and in fact you are seen to be getting upset, angry and frustrated then they will unleash their full fury against you. Just think about the amount of precious fuel that is now flowing out of you to them. You have challenged them which has fired them up and provided them with challenge fuel, but this is still not enough for them to regain control and bring you into line. It is still not enough to satisfy their thirst for this narcissistic supply, so they unleash their anger, you react, and hey presto they are now getting negative fuel flowing out of you which is by far the most potent fuel of all. Then they must regain power and control over you, so you will be possibly discarded, ghosted, stonewalled, abused, delivered the silent treatment and even endure a bout of the smear campaign. And so, the abusive, toxic cycle continues, over and over, and round and round.

The comment which may have ignited their fury may have started with some totally innocent comment or question that you made to them. A good example I can tell you about to demonstrate this was on one night in 2015 that the Nex, myself and my adult son went for a curry. Innocent enough occurrence you are thinking no doubt. Well, it certainly was right up until the Nex had kept moaning on that his garlic and chilli naan was not strong enough despite him asking them to add extra chillies. So, on the next mouthful he coughed, started reddening up in the face and sweating. He had bitten on a whole chilli! Well, my son and I burst out laughing because it was funny, like something straight out of a comedy sketch. The fact that the Nex had spent the best part of ten minutes moaning that it was not strong or hot enough for him then Bam, the next mouthful certainly put paid to that! Well, the Nex laughed too but only until we got home later, then he let me have it both barrels! How dare my son and I laugh at him! How dare we! I tried to explain that we really were not laughing at him, but rather instead it was with him and at the comical situation, and I pointed out that he had found it funny too but oh no, that was not how he saw it. So, I had the 'We aren't working', and 'I think our relationship is over' routine followed by the silent treatment for the next few days until I apologised and grovelled. I still have Messenger messages I sent to him apologising to him and saying that I was sorry we had laughed, sorry that he was offended, and sorry that he saw it to mean that we were over. This event took place long before I learnt anything about narcissism. Again, I knew that his irrational response was not a normal one, but I just did not know why at the time. I now know that a narcissist always takes laughing or criticism as a personal attack. This is just an example to show you how quickly this narcissistic fury and subsequent injury that a narcissist feels can come right out of absolutely nowhere and more importantly come when you least expect it to and also when everything is okay just before the event happens. Post-split, he would spit out at me 'What kind of crazy person keeps messages?!' and, 'What a total weirdo you are!' when I called out his behaviour in the relationship. Of course, this was classic blame-shifting and projection at play.

As stated earlier, if a narcissist is wounded through actions or lack of action, or words and insults then his or her anger and fury will be ignited, and you must be severely punished. Total control and power must be restored and regained by the narcissist and your punishment will be delivered (abuse, ghosting, silent treatment, stonewalling, even discard, etc.). This is to stop the pain the narcissist is feeling and to also absorb the fuel you are giving out in response to his abuse against you which in turn will make him then feel better. So, the perceived insult leads to a narcissistic injury which leads to a loss of control which then leads to anger which unleashes abuse which results in your punishment which ends with the provision of fuel for the narcissist. The above story I have just told you about with the curry night is a prime example of this.

I hope you are now truly starting to understand how this all works. When I have explained this to friends, you can see that some of them just do not get it. They cannot get their heads around the fact that there are some human beings out there that behave this way, and why they behave this way. And I get that, I totally get it. If I had not experienced it myself, had not educated myself on narcissism or reached the point where I knew the Nex was a narcissist, I would probably still be right there, in the thick of this toxic abusive relationship, not understanding what was happening but just knowing that it most definitely was not normal.

A narcissist wants to cause you fear, confusion, pain, hurt and ultimately have you walking on eggshells around them. Again, I must stress that this is not a conscious action on the narcs' part. Merely that their actions do lead to you walking on eggshells because you do not want to anger them or upset them. You are forever wanting the idealisation phase to return. Thus, the narcissist then feels important, empowered, sated (fuel), but most of all, in control.

J Brock states that a narcissist wants to see you falling apart, so they will do shit on purpose to destroy you even more. Just like the most recent examples I have just given you, for instance, the cinema episode and the bed changing one and the curry one. He goes on further to say that people like that find strength in other people's weakness, it distracts them from the horrible way they feel about themselves on the inside.

A narcissist is also selfish, moody, weak, has trust issues, turns their backs on those who love them and starts arguments out of nowhere all for their own gain, agenda or game. They are arrogant, childish, petty, play the victim, play mind games, manipulate, control, lack empathy and will not apologise, 'ever'. I know it is not a pretty picture that I paint of them, but this is it. This 'is' a narcissist in all their glory. No nice image, no true love, no caring thoughts, no positives whatsoever. The initial love-bombing is the mask and the false façade that they portray to you at the start of the relationship simply to ensnare you. When you are entrapped you, then get to see the real them, their mask slips, they are now in control. The love-bombing stage is extremely important for the narcissist because it determines to them just how many boundaries you will willingly allow them to violate, so that when the abuse starts, you will stay.

I recently read on Quora a comment someone had put that said to be aware of a mask less narc. They go on to state that they are the most hideous of all demons. Once you see a narcissist for who they really are, you will never see the person you thought you knew them to be ever again. You will only see the demon, and it will send chills down your spine.

Once you have grasped the whys and the hows you do start to understand what is happening or did happen to you. This leads to a recognition of what you are going through or went through which in turn helps you either get out while you can or achieve closure on what you did suffer. I am not going to pretend that you will instantly recover from the abuse you suffered at the hands of a narcissist. Some women never fully recover. Developing PTSD is common. Such is the destruction and devastation that a narcissistic abusive toxic relationship can do to you. The key is to get out as soon as you can or better still, learn the red-flags and avoid a relationship with a narcissist in the first place.

I am sure that most of you who are reading this book will be able to relate to some if not all the examples I have told you about. Maybe not the exact same story obviously, but certainly the behaviour pattern and the abuse will be easily recognisable and identifiable and will even ring true with most of you.

What else you will witness from a narcissist is their deployment of all the 'Tools of the trade' associated with narcissism, used against you, their victim, for the sole purpose of masking their real selves. To be able to apportion blame on another individual because as you must have learnt by now narcissists are completely blameless and faultless. It is never their fault, not ever. How could it be when they deem themselves to be perfect, superior to all others, even godly. To maintain this false persona they will intimidate, manipulate and ultimately control their victim, gaslighting them along the way so the truth becomes distorted, and the victim is painted as crazy. With of course slithers of kindness littered throughout just to keep you confused, and ultimately bonded to them. And so, the cycle just continues, and the phases just play on.

I really cannot stress enough of how the narcissist will 'always' appear to be the victim in other people's eyes because of the smear campaign that they have unleashed against you. It is not a question of if but rather 'when' they turn others against you with their lies, they will attempt to ruin your reputation. They will deny everything you say and blame you entirely by playing the victim themselves. What you must remember the most about a narcissist is that they 'always' believe their own lies to be the truth, even as they are making the lie up, by the time it leaves their lips, to them, it 'is' the truth!

HG Tudor states that all his kind see themselves as victims, but one kind takes it to the extreme and that is the victim narcissist. He goes on to say that they will use pity plays more often and more intense. I can certainly testify to that being true.

Another 'Tool of their trade' which I have mentioned briefly before is the narcissist's use of hoovers. These can come in many forms and will be deployed both during the relationship and after it has ended.

A hoover, as I have said before, derives its name from the good old vacuum cleaner because it does the job of 'Hoovering' up the dirt or sucking it up/in.

In a narcissistic hoover, the aim is to suck you right back into the relationship or contact with the narcissist and there are several methods that can be deployed against you for them to try and achieve this.

The positive hoover: used during a relationship, will come after a devaluation period and after a 'virtual' discard and possibly even after a final discard if the narcissist has grown tired of his latest victim and they are not shiny and new anymore. HG Tudor describes this as an 'Initial Grand Hoover'. With a positive hoover, the narcissist will contact you and bombard you with a period of 'love-bombing'. They will give false apologies, promises of changing their behaviour, promises of a better future with them, undying love claims, you are their soulmate and so on and so forth. It is clearly designed to 'suck' you right back into the relationship again. By hoovering their victim, the narcissist can utilize his or her exceptional skills of manipulation in order to regain control of their victim once again.

The malign (negative) hoover: This will come post discard phase and if it is the final discard then fasten up your seatbelt because you are in for one hell of a ride!

HG Tudor describes malign hoover as being any of the below or many of the below examples:

- Repeated texts, calls, emails all containing abuse, insults blame, etc.
- Following you
- Stalking you on social media
- Getting their flying monkeys to abuse you
- Threats of police, social services, courts; all against you
- Hacking or cloning your mobile phone
- Leaving note/messages with threats
- Slashing your car tyres
- Throwing your possessions away or destroying them
- Harming your pets or threats to harm them
- Hanging around your place of work or home

These listed above are just a few examples.

For me, as I have already explained in greater detail earlier, the experience I had of my email account being hacked, my mobile phone being cloned so he then had access to all my social media accounts, WhatsApp messages, text messages and phone calls. What had happened when I had first challenged the Nex about my Email account to which he claimed that I had left it 'open' on his iPad. I duly changed my password. He hacked it two more times. I discovered everything else when he kept making comments about things I had posted on Facebook or snippets of conversations I had had with other people. Such was my suspicion that when I checked my logins on my Facebook account. OMG! I had been 'Logged in' on an unknown device in different parts of the UK where I had not been. But the biggest give away was the login in Fuerteventura, Canary Islands over the Christmas period of 2018. I was not there! I was spending Christmas and the New Year at home with my parents and children! You have already heard that story by now.

I have other examples of both positive and malign hoovers to share with you, but I am saving them for the post discard chapter.

The best course of action when dealing with malign hoovers is to not respond or react because that is exactly what the narcissist is wanting from you. Remember, they must get their daily dose of their precious fuel! If you do feel that you need to do something, especially if you feel threatened or in danger, then go to the police, or apply to the courts for a non-molestation order and even if necessary, a restraining order. I cannot stress enough that the only lesson a narcissist will learn from their failed relationship after failed relationship is how to hide and conceal what they are better. How to avoid being unmasked. And of course, how to extract Fuel more efficiently. None of these are done at a conscious level, by that I mean that they do not recognise that they are a narcissist, or acknowledge this fact, but rather that the narcissist knows that some of his or her previous behaviour and actions resulted in the loss of that relationship. Thus, the narcissist will mask it better next time round.

I have previously mentioned that there is a continuous debate going on as to whether a narcissist is aware of what they are doing or not. Are they aware that what they are doing is wrong?

The conundrum here is that some experts state that the very fact that the person is a narcissist stops them from processing this fact, because as we all hopefully know by now, a narcissist is 'never' wrong.

So, the big question is 'Is that a conscious thought process of theirs, or a reactionary thought caused by their narcissism?'

Some would argue that yes, to a degree, they 'do' know that they have done something wrong, but they simply will not admit to it because to do so would require an apology and to a narcissist this would be admitting a weakness. To apologise is to lose control and most importantly, to lose power, and this is something that a narcissist would never want to give up.

Other expert views and opinions suggest that because a narcissist 'always' believes their own version of the truth (even when it is a lie) this then naturally and unconsciously implies that together, they really are not in the wrong.

Personally, I leave my own mind open on this debate. I see logic in both points of view. And if you believe HG Tudor's analogy that there are different cadres, i.e., a lesser, a mid-range and a greater, then this very conundrum would certainly apply.

Why?

Because a lesser would not know or accept that they are in the wrong, such is their placing in the narcissism hierarchy. Whereas a greater – well yes he would definitely know that he was in the wrong, but he would still vehemently and emphatically deny it because to allow such a thought to be right or true – would cause him a narcissistic injury and it would also dent his or hers perfectly structured façade. This simply just would not do.

To a greater also, he will be deriving pleasure from the pain his wrongdoing had caused his victim, and this would likely be a conscious feeling, whereas to a lesser, it would not.

Another important fact to recognise and remember in how a narcissist will operate is, they will always use a weakness against you. For example, if you are concerned about your weight they will 'tease' you and make inappropriate comments while making it appear like it is just, a joke. By calling you a 'chubster' what they are doing is deep down they are deliberately targeting your weakness.

For me, the Nex would often use my mother because he knew that it would upset and offend me. He would make nasty comments about her weight, about her smelling, about any trivial argument she may have had with my beloved late father. Such was his glee that he had found a weakness of mine that he could deliberately target, that even when she was under investigation for dementia, he still ridiculed and belittled her.

Another example was using my son. He would often call him my 'Golden Child' or 'Golden Boy' and continuously state that I mollycoddled him, when all I was simply doing was being a mother. He was jealous of my son, jealous of his youth, his looks and of any attention my son received from me. When my son went to university, he was cock a hoop, not with pride for my son, but because he saw his 'rival' leaving the home. Due to a cock up at the university my son returned home after a week and when I informed my Nex I was bringing my son home he went ballistic. Again, I had the 'End of the relationship routine' followed by a week's silent treatment. I knew that this was 'not' a normal reaction but at that time did not know why. To the Nex, my son coming home meant my attention would not now be solely on him, my attention would at times now be elsewhere again. This was enough to cause the Nex a narcissistic injury, hence his irrational reaction. My son went on to go to university the following intake.

The Nex would even make me feel guilty if I simply fussed the pets. I have given you an example of this earlier with my dog.

Another sign is the narcissists' use of passive-aggressive behaviour. This is a favourite of the mid-ranger like the Nex is. They will sulk at the slightest little thing, causing an almighty row or just dole out the silent treatment on you.

Whenever the Nex instigated the silent treatment and because we were obviously living together he could not really do a disappearing act. So, instead he would barricade himself in the spare bedroom, or my caravan that was parked on the drive. This was to prevent me being able to talk to him and instead mean I would have to speak to him through a closed door. He never responded to me obviously. It was always a futile one-sided conversation. Of course, he would then appear when called for meals and such like, but would not utter a single word to me, even if I spoke to him, he would just completely blank me, not even look at me but just take the food away and return later with the empty plate and once again make his way back to his bolthole. He would just absolutely ignore me completely and totally. I would be unfriended and blocked on Facebook and other social media platforms, all calls diverted, and text messages ignored. This was all the while that I was bloody well still living in the same house with him! Can you see now just how absurd a narcissists' behaviour towards you really is? How childish, immature and destructive it is. I am sure that there will be a few readers out there that can relate to what I am saying and even have accounts of similar treatment towards them. It is by no means normal behaviour, but rather abusive, controlling and manipulative behaviour.

The use of gaslighting towards you, another firm favourite of the narcissist, is used to deny or minimize their abusive behaviour towards you. It is also used to make it appear that you are the crazy one, that you are imagining things that it did not happen the way that it really did, that you need help. It is again a form of manipulation.

You must get it out of your head if you believe that the narcissist will ever miss you post discard or split, They will not miss you, the person, but what they will miss is what you provided them with, most importantly the constant steady supply of fuel that you were providing to them. Next they will miss the material side of the relationship, be it the nice home, car, holidays, gifts and money, followed closely by of course the adoration and admiration that you once provided to them.

Another indication is the fact that a narcissist is a chameleon. They will mirror their latest supply. For instance, whatever music or films you like, so will they. This will be most noticeable during the love-bomb/idealisation phase. If you are left thinking that your new relationship is a match made in heaven and that you have truly found your soulmate, then be incredibly careful that this is not a narcissist lurking underneath.

You must also look out for signs that where once your narcissist liked your strength and confidence, they will later, always go on to use it against you.

A perfect example here with the Nex was the fact that he always wanted me to fight his battles for him with parking tickets etc., but then would use this against me by stating that I always like to fight people. This was most prevalent post-split.

Likewise, my gob. He liked it when I spoke up or out if it benefitted him but if I used it to defend myself against his false accusations and blame-shifting he would then state that everything with us would be okay if it was not for my gob. What he really meant was if I never answered him back, never questioned him, or God forbid disagreed with him and defended myself, then all would be 'normal' in our relationship. Of course, it would not be! Normal is having mutual trust and respect. Normal is being able to speak up without fear of repercussions. Normal is not having to go through life walking on eggshells like I did!

As I have already enlightened you to, another firm favourite of his was always saying that I was a 'Sayer and not a Doer'. It would always be said in a very condescending and belittling way. He realised very early on that this would upset me especially when I would try in vain to point out to him that this was not true and that the biggest ever 'Do' of mine was packing up my entire life as I knew it to be, to be with him, but it just fell on deaf ears. The irony of it was that over the course of the relationship I proved many times over that it was I who was the doer in the relationship and that it was the Nex that was really the sayer with his constant use of futureproofing.

Something else that you will quickly come to realise is that you are in a 'competition' with your narcissist. I do not mean this in a physical way and especially not in a way that you know you are. Absolutely everything about your relationship is a game to a narcissist. It is a competition that the narcissist must 'always' win.

Therefore, you will find that the Narc will never recognise or acknowledge any accomplishments or successes of yours. They hate to see you succeed in anything because they perversely perceive this as a diminishment of them. They are the ones who must always be satisfied, pleased, winning, approved, 'the best' and so on.

Life to a narcissist is one big fat competition. A continuous game of one-upmanship.

My Nex would often say that he had won me over something, or one nil to him and he would give the one up finger sign to me while saying it. This was especially true post-split when he openly and gleefully stated that he had won. Seriously, once you realise that you are witnessing narcissistic behaviour, it really is the funniest thing to witness. You laugh at the absurdity of it all.

Another trick a narcissist will use, especially a covert narcissist, is to make snide comments to you. If you dare to pull them about it, they will then protest that they are only joking with you. This is still emotional abuse. They will have a favourite scapegoat for this behaviour and if they are in a relationship unfortunately it is usually their intimate partner.

I remember at our wedding party, people were calling on the Nex to make a speech, but he kept refusing stating that 'he did not do things like that and that it was not his kind of thing to do'. So instead, I was made to speak. Bear in mind that this was just one day after the violent onslaught that I had received in relation to the golfing incident, so I simply obeyed. Now I see it. It was not that he was shy or not confident that he did not want to speak but rather because he genuinely could not feel those emotions or think those thoughts that people expected him to stand up and say. He could not profess a love for me that he did not feel. These words of emotion were just not there. He was incapable of making them as they were not inside of him, because of his lack of empathy, and because of his narcissism. I did find it strange at the time because normally he was outgoing and talkative, but to shy away from giving a speech to his family, my family and our friends, I now see why he did not do it as clear as daylight.

I feel it is really important that you have an understanding on what a covert narcissist is and looks like because these are the type that can and will 'get under your skin' before you know it and you will then find it much harder to get away from one. Think of the 'Boiling frog scenario'. Therefore, looking more specifically at a covert narcissist, just like my Nex is, I read a passage on Quora which still resonates with me now that I must share with you.

This passage is in response to a question someone had asked about whether all narcissists do indeed go back to a previous victim. The answer was,

'I know this question is old and there are several good answers, but I wanted to add an additional answer to this question. It is a myth that every narcissist comes back and Hoovers. Narcissism and its associated disorders occur on a spectrum, and everyone does not always hoover 'or' come back. Covert narcissists, specifically, are a different type of narcissist. A covert narcissist does not mean that they are discrete. A covert narcissist is a narcissistic type where the person is more reserved than a typical narcissist. They are not overly extroverts and are 'much' more difficult to spot than typical narcissists. Typically, people who encounter covert narcissists will not know them as such 'unless' they develop an awfully close relationship with them. These types are significantly more introverted than 'normal' narcissistic types. Their motivations are also different. Their 'flights' unlike a lot of narcissists who are trying to juggle multiple people, are typically 'not' caused by their desire to see other people and covert narcissists can and 'do' stay in relationships for long periods of time without ever being unfaithful'. I am pretty much certain that my Nex never physically cheated on me, but I do believe that he may virtually have. By this I mean, he still dabbled on date sites. He often used to disappear back to the hotel room in an afternoon when we were on holiday, making excuses that he needed to lie down, but he was actively online during these periods. I think he was seeking fuel from these date sites by other women admiring him and so on.

While certain types of narcissists do 'not' discard people permanently, covert narcissists 'do' have the capacity to do permanent discards and will. In fact, they can go to extraordinary lengths to ensure that they 'can' discard a person permanently. Unlike typical narcissists, covert narcissists experience extreme 'fight or flight' responses and, when they take 'flight' and run, they run hard and fast. They exist in this space with one foot in and one foot out of the relationship. In fact, people who have been in a relationship with a covert narcissist have likely noticed that the covert narcissist has tried to 'leave' several times before. Covert narcissists do this when things get overwhelming for them. Running is a coping mechanism for them. You can see this illustrated even when you are talking to them about something they find uncomfortable. When they are getting panicky and want to get out of the conversation they will do things like:

1. Move towards the door while you are speaking
2. Walk out of the room while you are talking
3. Refuse to answer when you ask them something
4. Turn their backs to you while you are talking
5. Intentionally move far away from you while you are talking
6. Refuse to look at you while you are talking and just continually shake their heads while you are speaking

All these things are designed to signal their discomfort and to force you to end the conversation.

Once discard is in place with a covert narcissist, they will work hard to erase you from their lives, as if you never existed. Typical narcissists want to maintain a source of supply, but a covert narcissist sees themselves as the true victim and you as the abuser. A covert narcissist will file things away and hold a grudge, while a normal person will just tell you what is wrong, let you respond, resolve the issue and just move on. A covert narcissist will not do this, 'ever!' They have been stewing and brewing on it and when it does eventually come out their actions will be crazy and over the top. This is because the covert narcissist has been reliving the nightmare things they perceived that you 'did' to offend them repeatedly in their heads. 'You' are doomed, you just did not know it. It will not matter whether you really did do anything wrong or not, if the covert narcissist perceives that you did do something wrong to them, it is their perception that only matters. They are unwilling to entertain or try to understand the root cause for why something has happened especially when it is usually their behaviour which most likely will have started the problem.

A covert narcissist starts being mean to you so that they can feel justified in treating you as though you do not exist post discard. It is what is known as a Scorched Earth Policy. They want to burn that bridge, scorch the earth and make sure that you do not want them or chase them after it is over. They will go to extraordinary lengths to make sure they stay away and to prepare themselves to disconnect and push you away, so you stay away and do not try to reconnect.

The covert narcissist will then treat you so badly that when you do reach 'boiling' point and you do react to their behaviour towards you they then point to your reaction and say this is 'the' reason for their behaviour or as proof that you are crazy and unstable and that you have anger issues and so on.

They will pretend that your relationship never existed. They will perceive you as the abuser and consider that 'you' were abusing them. This is because they are extremely sensitive so they will perceive exceedingly small slights in an exaggerated way internally.

A covert narcissist is the king or queen of the blame game. A typical narcissist will blame others in a general sense, but a covert narcissist is vastly different. The extent of their blame runs deep and they, unlike some others, genuinely believe that 'you' are the issue. They deflect and convince themselves of this throughout their own false narratives. They are extraordinary drama queens and kings and are also extremely negative individuals. They have extremely fragile egos and get mad at the slightest thing, or the slightest real or perceived threat. They internalise and personalise almost everything, even when things are not personal. They hold grudges for an extraordinary length of time. To them, if you did something at one point, you would 'never' escape from the negativity associated with that in their mind. This means that they are continually holding on to a lot of baggage and a lot of anger and hurt. This is one of the core reasons why they can be so miserable with their partners.

Covert narcissists will also say something and then deny that they said it. This creates an off-balance feeling in their victim and often makes the victim question his or her own sanity.

When the covert narcissist does finally leave, it is typically over something ridiculously small. This is because the covert narcissist has worked themselves up over time because of all the grudges that they hold. They do not ever truly forgive. Instead, they file things away and move past it temporarily. In essence they stop talking about it, but they do not forget it. They hold on to all those negative emotions and will unleash them time and time again, at the next argument, the next devaluation phase. Something that upset them in year three is resurrected in year five and so on. Because of the covert narcissists inability to truly forgive and let things go, they simply file it away until the next time. There will come a point, years down the line when they will 'trot' out all the things they think you did wrong, one after the other, over and over, like a broken record. Someone somewhere likened a narcissist to a volcano. In that, they are always just one explosion away from the next saga. The grudges build one after the other and so does their anger. This explains perfectly why you see the percentage rise from ten percent to twenty percent to forty percent and so on until like me, you reach the point where you are at ninety percent because they have held on to so many grudges against you. Your relationship was always doomed, it was always a question of when not if, with a covert narcissist.

All of this perfectly explains the behaviour of my covert narcissist, the Nex.

I have mentioned other factors that point towards narcissistic behaviour, for example, their lack of boundaries, always right, no responsibility, manipulation, no interest in you, your work etc., deliberately winds you up, play mind games with you, judgemental, no empathy and of course last but certainly not least, their innate sense of entitlement. We will look more at this last one in more detail in the next chapter because it is this very sense of entitlement of theirs that leads to a lot of their behavioural patterns.

When you hear someone telling you about their crazy ex who is acting psycho, just stop and think that it just may well be really the victim who is telling the truth about their abuser.

Narcissists often pick fights to create drama and to be the centre of attention. They may goad their partner into fighting their battles for them, just as my Nex did. A narcissist also bends the facts and twists logic to make them seem like they are right.

For a victim it is extremely frustrating when you are the only person who can see just how destructive, evil and abusive someone is and especially when everyone else is blind to it.

A passage I recently read states, 'Narcissists, sociopaths and psychopaths will tell you they are romantic, heartbroken souls, who were hurt by their previous partner's, but 'it is a lie!' These relationships failed because 'they were abusive'.

Narcissists Schmarcissists also quoted, 'There is no one more deranged than a narcissist posing as a victim'.

Bookofallquotes.com also quote, 'It's so frustrating knowing how terrible a person actually is, yet everyone loves them because they put on a good show'.

Another one by @Breaking-Free-From-Abuse stated, 'Trying to explain the secret living hell you were put through as a narcissistic abuse victim is like trying to explain colours to a blind person'.

Convincing others of what you have gone through is probably the next hardest thing you will have to do after finally plucking up the courage to leave your narcissist.

It is so especially important to educate yourself about narcissism and narcissists. Learn to recognise red-flags, warning signs and other indications that something is not quite right.

If your gut is screaming this at you then go with it. Whenever has your gut instinct been wrong?!

Chapter Seven
Why Does a Narcissist Do the
Things That They Do?

So why does a narcissist behave the way that they do, and more importantly what drives their behaviour?

A 'normal' person wants to live their lives peacefully and with minimal drama. They want contentment and even happiness. This is normal human instinct and for the most part, is achievable. You find a job that you hopefully enjoy, a partner you love, children if you desire them, maybe get a pet, a hobby or interest, or even take up a sport, and surround yourself with friends. You fill your life with all the things that you know, and hope will make you happy, and help you achieve the contentment you desire. This is normal life.

Whereas a narcissist, well what exactly does a narcissist want?

Certainly, none of the above and not for the reasons a normal person does.

Maria Consiglio states, 'People have to understand that neglect is a huge form of abuse. Constantly ignoring a person's needs, making them feel insignificant, or unimportant on a consistent basis, has huge consequences to a person's spirit. Narcissists want to kill your spirit, so there is nothing left of you, and it's all about them'.

Primarily, everything that a narcissist does or says is to gain their narcissistic supply or fuel.

This is their very life source. It is what keeps their world turning. What keeps their inner demons at bay, keeps their false image in place, keeps their true insecure and loathsome self, hidden away from the world. It makes them feel good about themselves. They truly are parasitic, and need the drama that they create, the upset that they cause and the emotional fallout they receive just to simply function.

We have already looked at what 'creates' a narcissist. The causes underlying their narcissism, the outcome this creates, their false façade, and finally that with the use of power, control and manipulation and of course their fuel, then their mask, their false façade, or 'construct', (HG Tudor) will remain securely in place.

Quite simply, the fuel that they receive from their behaviour does succeed in keeping all of this in place for them. This fuel is their life force. By using control, power and manipulation, it ensures that fuel is continuously being generated, thus the false mask remains firmly intact.

A quote by Drglotfi goes,

'With a narcissistic spouse, every argument about the smallest of issues like a simple disagreement turns into a relationship ending level row. All the important and irrelevant issues for them is a disaster and a deal breaker'.

This completely explains the well-used 'End of the relationship' routine that the Nex always pulled on me.

I have often mentioned fuel throughout this book, otherwise known as narcissistic supply, and now we will take a closer look at what exactly this is and why it is so crucial to a narcissist and the role it does play.

Basically, there are three types of fuel that a narcissist relies on. At this point, I must stress what I have said before to you, that this is not a conscious action by the narcissist. All they know is that by being praised and adored, or seeing you upset or creating an argument with you does make them feel a hell of a lot better. It is like an 'unconscious' drug to them. Just like when I heard the Nex say that 'it made him feel better' when I described it in the chapter about 'What makes a Narcissist'. Right out of the mouth of a narcissist. Now we can take a proper look at the three types of fuel in turn, starting with what is known as positive fuel.

Positive Fuel: This is of course generated when the narcissist receives positive feedback from someone. Praise, attention and adoration. Obviously the most potent source is from their intimate partner, but it will also come via friends, work colleagues, even the man in the petrol station. Any words of adoration or encouragement instantly feeds the narcissist with positive fuel that instantly makes them feel better about themselves. Indicators here are their constant use of self-profile images on their Facebook or Instagram account. They are purely seeking positive comments to the photo and lots of likes for the photo. This does not of course mean that everyone who uses a self-profile photo is a narcissist! But the consistent use of such a photo, over and over and changed on a regular basis, especially if it is a male topless one, or one showing off their muscles or a female pout pose, etc., but most importantly is just a 'selfie' with no one else in the shot, then this is a good indicator that the profile may indeed belong to a narcissist.

Negative Fuel: Of course, this is provided to them when you have reacted in such a way to one of their put downs, or their use of gaslighting, blame-shifting, projecting, deflecting, silent treatment and ultimately their abuse towards you. When a narcissist sees you upset, angry, frustrated, crying and full of anguish they are receiving a flow of negative fuel from you, and this can often be a far more potent fuel to them then the positive fuel that they have previously received. If this is the case, which unfortunately with a lot of narcissists it is, then you will suffer a higher degree of the devaluation phases of the cycle just so that they can obtain this type of potent fuel from you again. In other words, they will deliberately generate chaos and drama for this very purpose.

Challenge Fuel: This comes in the way of threats towards them or more importantly what they perceive to be threats against them. For instance, if you question them, criticise them or simply disagree with them. Ultimately the narcissist will have frustrated you at some point, and they then perceive your body language, how you look, your expression and the tone of your voice to be a challenge to their superiority. Again, the potency of this type of fuel and how it makes them feel can be addictive to a narcissist so they will 'wind you up' even more in the hope that your reaction will then allow them to release their rage which will then generate the negative fuel supply.

Fuel is ultimately obtained by the narcissist by however and whenever you interact with them, how they react to us and interact with us, and even from their environment. As you have no doubt learnt by now with my use of the phrase, narcissistic supply, this is the formal terminology for fuel of which you will probably read this terminology more than the phrase fuel. Thought fuel is another type they obtain by thinking about how you may react to something that they have done or said. This is more prevalent post discard when you are not with your narcissist. personally, I prefer the term fuel as it describes perfectly what you are 'feeding' the narcissist with.

An article I read recently stated that the 'ego fuel' or narcissistic supply (NS) that a narcissist requires from their relationships is to maintain their fragile psychological innards. Because a narcissist exists without a solid core identity due to factors that have stemmed from childhood, in order to fill this psychic void, they will spend the vast majority of their daytime energy 'mining' for emotional reactions from the people in their lives. As I have stated above, this comes in all forms, and is used to 'top up their gas tank of ego fuel'. The article likens the negative fuel supply as a 'high form of emotional propane'.

According to HG Tudor, a narcissist must always have control of their environment and of all the people within that environment. They must own every passing second and every passing moment. This is because once upon a time they did not have control. Without control a narcissist feels weak, exposed, powerless and vulnerable. He goes on to say that the combination of a genetic predisposition and the imposition of this lack of control created narcissism as a coping mechanism. He states, 'These two ingredients combined and gave 'birth' to narcissism as a means of coping with the world'.

My Nex absolutely loved to wind me up as another way to gain his supply of fuel. He would deliberately goad me with words or actions then sit back in glee when he had succeeded.

On one occasion in 2014, I bought him an expensive pair of Ray-Ban sunglasses on a trip to Spain for his birthday. He proceeded to tell me that they were fake and despite me showing him the certificate and even the receipt he just would not accept it. He had realised that by saying that the sunglasses were fake, it had upset and offended me so he continued to bring it up time and time again by saying things like, 'Remember when you bought me those fake sunglasses and pretended that they were real' or, 'I can't believe you bought me fake sunglasses for my birthday'. He refused to wear them, and I ended up just keeping them for myself. He had found yet another way to wind me up, to upset me and to ultimately keep that fuel supply flowing. Looking back now I do believe that his 'devaluation' treatment in relation to my present to him was nothing more than punishment because I had just been on a long girlie weekend for one of my friends 40th birthdays. Interestingly it was the same girl as the one in the 'blackout blinds' incident and this was before he allowed her back into our home!

On another occasion which was his 50th birthday, I bought him a real brand-new replica scooter. He initially showed delight in it until a couple of weeks later when he then passed a sarcastic comment stating that he would rather have had a genuine one but the fake one would have to do. I was so upset at this as I has saved so hard to buy him this for his birthday, and I also threw him a party, which was not cheap either. But once he saw that this comment had upset me, he deliberately saw it as an opportunity to wind me up, so he used it more and more to the point where he even started pointedly saying things like 'What on that pile of shit?' if I asked him if he was going to go out on a ride on it. He subsequently went on to go out and buy himself a real Vespa instead not long after this. This incident perfectly displays the narcissists lack of empathy. He did not care if his comments upset me. He did not care how I felt when he went out and bought himself a 'proper' one. He did not care how I would feel whatsoever because he had achieved his goal of generating yet more fuel from me. The below quote sums up this scenario perfectly.

A quote by Elinor Greenberg, PhD states that a narcissist punishes you for feeling hurt. She goes on to say. 'It's actually a very simple and predictable cycle of events. They hurt you, but because they lack emotional empathy, they do not care. You care. You complain, then they feel attacked by you. That they care about. To protect their self-esteem, they attack your self-esteem. The goal is to hurt you badly enough that you do not dare rebuke them again'.

Another example was with his birthday party that I have just mentioned, the Nex insisted that everyone was to dress smart for it. No casuals and absolutely no denim whatsoever. My family were travelling from my hometown to attend the party and one of my brothers did not do smart. He had denim of course and smart Chino style trousers which he planned to wear but my Nex said no. If smart trousers were not worn, then my brother could not attend. So, my brother and my adult niece and nephew (his children) did not come. I felt so awful but could not say anything as the Nex was adamant that these were his rules. On the night of the party, one of the Nex's friends then did turn up in a pair of jeans and was welcomed with open arms! The photo of this friend was obviously then seen on Facebook by those family members of mine who were naturally so upset that they had been banned from the party if they did not wear smart clothes only to then see a photo of someone there in jeans. My brother and I did not speak for the next few months after this because he was so upset, and I had stupidly defended the Nex to him! As for the Nex, he had done nothing wrong in his eyes. So, what if he had banned members of my family from attending but then allowed one of his friends to pitch up in the wrong dress code? This was his prerogative!

After we had split up, I realised just how much I had lost sight of how important my family was to me, but most important of all, I recognised that the Nex had achieved success in deliberately distancing me from some of my family.

This is also another classic narcissistic trait where they try to alienate you from family and friends. On this occasion, my Nex had succeeded during this episode for sure.

I always wanted to have a tattoo in memory of my beloved dog, Nanook, but the Nex said he 'was putting his foot down' and he forbade me from ever having one done. I had two tattoos before I met him and even when I said I would cover the one up on my shoulder with this new tattoo he was adamant that I was not to do it and if I did then I was not the woman he thought I was and so he would leave me. I of course never got one done because he had simply controlled and manipulated me by using his usual 'End of the relationship' routine. I have to say though that post-split I did indeed go out and get one done on my other shoulder and this one small act felt so liberating to me!

I could fill the rest of this chapter with continuous examples of how the Nex would deliberately wind me up and try to control and manipulate me, but I will try and limit these to those that really count and use the ones that will provide you with an understanding on why a narcissist displays this kind of behaviour towards you and why and how it can affect you. Hopefully, some may resonate with you, some may not, but they are all examples of abusive behaviour.

Nine times out of ten a narcissist will state that their victim is trying to control them, knowing full well that this will upset their victim who in turn will try to defend themselves. What the narcissist is really doing is projecting their own behaviour towards you on to you. What the victim does not realise is that the more they protest their innocence, the more upset that they get, the more fuel they are providing to the narcissist. The Nex regularly rolled this one out. 'Stop trying to control me'. 'Stop controlling me'. 'You're nothing more than a control freak'. These were his favourite expressions to say to me.

Always remember that a narcissist thrives on chaos, hurt, pain, anguish and despair.

Also, what drives them and what they thrive on is drama, conflict, control and power.

A narcissist is the exact polar opposite of a normal person.

Once you begin to learn more about narcissists and narcissism, the more you begin to understand. You will even get to a point where you will be able to 'diagnose' if they are a covert or overt narcissist. Which cadre they are, lesser, mid-range or greater. Whether they also play a victim narcissist, or worse, a malignant one. 'Your' narcissist will display classic traits but some of these will be more obvious than others. Some of the different cadres will use some traits more than others. For instance, a lesser's trait is to react with a knee jerk reaction to what they have perceived to be a criticism, with a punch to your face! This is purely an instinctive act by the lesser narcissist. He or she has not punched you because they know that they are a narcissist. No, they punched you because your totally innocent comment wounded them, and the fist flying was purely an instinctive result of this. Your subsequent reaction to the punch, your pain, your upset, and even possibly your anger provides him or her with a sudden hit of fuel for them. The narcissist does not consciously know that this is what is being provided. Purely what they know is that the punch and your reaction to it makes them feel a whole lot better.

To anyone who is not a narcissist they will know that this is not normal behaviour but to a narcissist, they will simply just not see this.

According to HG Tudor he states that a lesser narcissist does not know that his hurtful comments or actions have wounded you because of his complete and total inability to feel empathy. What this means is that to a narcissist, 'It is what it is'. They do not feel guilt at what they have done or the harm that it has caused you, the broken jaw or black eye, the cruel and vindictive words, they will not accept accountability for any of it. Instead, they will say that it was your fault, you made them do it, etc. It really will be as simple as that to them. I also think this can apply to the mid-range narcissist as well. Certainly not all the time, because unlike the lesser, the mid-range does know that his harmful words do hurt you. But on some occasions they may say something that they have not perceived to be hurtful, but it subsequently is. One of the Nex's relatives did not speak to him for eighteen months because he said something offensive to her and he did not realise this. More importantly, he did not even realise that she was not speaking to him, let alone for that length of time. Such is the narcissists self-centeredness in their world. The Nex was often two-faced and bad mouthed or slagged friends and members of his family off to me and to others too, but he was completely different to their faces. This is yet another classic narcissistic trait.

Also, according to HG Tudor, the lesser narcissist lives by the motto 'His way or the highway', But I would conclude that this does in fact apply to all cadres of narcissists. The Nex, who is most definitely a mid-ranger, certainly lived by that philosophy. It was always his way or the highway. I lived my entire fourteen years with him this way and by his double standards.

A narcissist will lie, exploit, scare, isolate and ultimately try to destroy you. They will change the rules, move the goalposts, mock you, insult you, wound you and force you to walk on eggshells around them. They will do all of this to try and control you, to exert power over you and to manipulate you into doing what they want. Of course, with all of this and while all of this is going on they will also be extracting their precious fuel from you.

What a narcissist will do is; they will never support you, care for you if you are ill, acknowledge an illness or help you. With the Nex, if I had a cold or a headache or some other minor ailment you could bet your life that he suddenly had one too! This was purely to ensure that he could exonerate himself from tending to me. It became so bad that I would pass comment to a friend that I could never be ill on my own and that the Nex always had to 'Highjack' my illness. Of course, back then I did not know about narcissism, I just knew that it was totally weird behaviour.

Another thing he never did was pay me compliments on anything. If I had cooked a special meal for us, I would have to ask if he had liked it and he would reply, 'It was okay'. If I asked him how my hair looked after I had had it cut he would say, 'I can't tell you've had it done'. If I asked him how a new outfit looked he would say, 'It looks okay', or 'It'll do', but never that it looked nice. Yet on the flip side he was always expecting me to tell him how wonderful he was or how wonderful he looked. In our early days a few people told him that he was 'punching above his weight', a saying that I had never heard before, and neither had he, but when he discovered what it meant he was really pissed off!

Another thing the Nex used to do in the first few years of the relationship which I found extremely uncomfortable and now can see exactly why he did it, was to remove his glasses slowly when he looked at me. He did it in such a way that it made me feel insecure and that he was removing them because he could not bear to look at me through his glasses, so he was taking them off because he could not stand to see how I really looked and so that I did not look so bad when his glasses were off. I know that this sounds absurd and even like paranoia but trust me when I say it is not. This was genuinely how it made me feel. Anyone reading this who has been in a narcissistic relationship will know exactly what I am saying and will fully understand what I am describing. A narcissist will use all kinds of methods against you to knock you off your feet, to destabilise you and to make you question or doubt yourself.

We looked briefly at entitlement earlier, but I did not go into too much detail then. Now while looking at 'Why Does a Narcissist do the Things that they Do', the relevance and importance of this comes to the front.

Due to a narcissist's grandiosity and sense of self-importance they have this enormous all-consuming sense of entitlement in every single aspect of their life.

If they could, they would expect you to bow to them such is their delusion.

Because they feel entitled they will expect you to do all the housework, cook all the meals, pay for all the bills, pay for all the holidays, days out, evenings out and weekends away. I told you about the Nex and how I did indeed pay for almost everything almost all the time we were together. I recounted the day to you when he called me a money grabber. Well on another occasion, in June of 2017, I had recently changed my job and would be receiving less money. All works on the property had ceased nearly two years earlier yet the Nex did not offer any kind of contribution to the household bills nor offer to resume paying half towards them (he ceased paying at the end of 2009). So, I asked him if he could start contributing towards the bills again. A simple, perfectly acceptable request for a wife to ask her husband you would think, yes? Oh no! Anyone would think I had just asked him to slit his own throat! He went ballistic with me. Told me that I could not manage money, and why should he contribute and so on. I held my ground and he finally flounced off upstairs and came back down with a bundle of cash which he proceeded to throw at me. Yes, it went everywhere. I simply picked it up and said thank you. I asked him if he could set up a direct debit or standing order as I did not want to be made to feel guilty every month when every time I would be forced to go to him and ask him for it. Of course, his answer was no. (Think of the power he would feel every time I had to go 'cap in hand'). At the same time, I also asked if he could pay it on the first of every month and I would set up the current direct debits to reflect this and he again went ballistic with me and stated that if he did that he would then be two weeks out of pocket as it was the eleventh on this particular day. I was gobsmacked! The fact that he had not contributed towards the household whatsoever in any shape or form for nearly two years, except for the planning fees, and certainly nothing towards bills or food in total, for eight years by then, was completely and absolutely lost on him! In his warped illogical mind, he was not going to be left out of pocket if he backdated it by just two weeks. All he could see was that he would be paying two weeks more than me. I am seriously not making any of this up or exaggerating. This is truly and sincerely what happened! Yes, you are right. His wishes of course prevailed. He did not pay from the first, but instead from the eleventh and of course in cash which was never forthcoming but only given when I asked for it. Think of the fuel that this produced for him every month when I had to ask for it. The power and control that he both felt and had over me.

His overall narcissistic sense of entitlement was that he felt that I should simply carry on paying for everything. He should pay for nothing. It was like this for the entire fourteen years that we were together. I have more examples of how this behaviour was ramped up big time post-split. Yes of course it was! But more on that in the chapter on post narcissist phase and the smear campaign. As I have said before, I do strongly believe that the Nex's intention had we not split up was to stop working altogether and finally live off me full time and I honestly believe that this is what pissed him off the most when we split up.

Such is a narcissists sense of entitlement that they will constantly and openly freeload off you for as long as you let them. But woe betide if you ever challenged this.

Again, because of the narcissists sense of entitlement, they will explode if you do not bow to their wishes. They will throw a temper tantrum, sulk, stamp their feet and generally display the behaviour of a two-year old child. Such is their immaturity. When you recognise that this is what is playing out in front of you, it really is comical and laughable to witness. To them, what they want is what they can and will have. They feel entitled to say what they like, do what they like and act how they like.

For the Nex, he also always felt entitled to my undivided attention and woe betide if anyone or anything else received it. Hence the barking dog episodes.

But worst still he hated it if I gave either of my two children attention, especially my son. He felt especially threatened by him and jealous of him and I was acutely aware of this even though at the time I did not know why he felt like this towards him, but of course I do now. And woe betide if I gave the kids money, he really hated that with a passion and made his feelings known, often. In relation to my children, the Nex felt that he was entitled to just walk into their bedrooms without knocking first, and this is when they were adults! He would just barge straight in, and it would not occur to him whatsoever that they should have been given any privacy. When I once asked him why he did this and why he did not knock first, his response was that he could do whatever he liked. He had zero respect for anyone.

One totally ludicrous example of the Nex's sense of entitlement was our first 'family' holiday together in 2005. The Nex's alleged mild fear of flying suddenly took a dramatic turn for the worse. He insisted that he could not possibly fly being sat in a seat on his own, next to strangers. My children were twelve and ten at the time. I offered to sit in the seat across the aisle from the three of them but no, this was no good. The only solution he could see that would save him from his fear was if I sat next to him (of course it was!) and my son, the eldest child sat across in the aisle seat on his own. You must envisage that we were already on the plane trying to get seated when this all played out. Over the following years to ensure that this seating arrangement continued, he would take a mild sedative for his 'fear of flying'. And so, it did continue for the next few years until the children had grown up but more importantly, until he went on a long weekend break with a friend to Spain.

Miraculously, on this occasion, suddenly he no longer needed his sedatives and could now fly anywhere in the world medication free! What a recovery hey!

Such was always his sense of entitlement that he had to have me seated next to him and this was how he found a way to achieve that. A perfect example of narcissistic manipulation at play.

Another example is in 2010, one week after I had lost my beloved dog, and I was still reeling from this plus his appalling behaviour only three days prior with the Bengal cat purchase for his birthday present. It had been my son's eighteenth birthday and I had bought my son a small, inexpensive car (yes of course only paid for by me!). We had all travelled up to my hometown as it was also my daughter's sixteenth birthday the day before my son's eighteenth and was also my birthday the day after my son's! The plan was that the Nex would drive my son's car back home later that day and I would follow the next day in my car. I was taking three other passengers back with me and the Nex was travelling solo. Well to cut a long story short when he had set off in my son's car he had only gone a few miles when part of the exhaust dropped. He came back and insisted on taking my large 4x4 car for himself and leaving my son's small car to get repaired and subsequently for me to use to drive the four of us back once it was repaired. This of course could have been any length of a delay for us. Bear in mind that the Nex is self-employed and can work whenever he decides to work. Oh no, not on this occasion. This time he could not possibly stay another day and when I suggested that maybe he could he went ballistic at me (of course he did!) I dared to call him selfish and off he drove in a strop and so ensued another bout of the silent treatment against me. I managed to get the car fixed the next day by an apologetic garage that I had bought the car from and the four of us squeezed into this tiny car and drove the two hours home. It was a comical sight all of us squeezed into that tiny car at the end of the day, and I can laugh about it now but at the time it was far from funny. We returned on the day of my birthday and the Nex had already stonewalled and ghosted me and subjected me to the silent treatment since the day that he had left. Screw that it was my birthday! In fact, he no doubt derived more fuel for that very reason. It took a further two days after my birthday before he finally spoke to me again. He did not care that I was grieving for my dog, that I was exhausted, both mentally and physically from having cared for him only a few months prior and dealing with what turned out to be my own undiagnosed illness. Such was his sense of entitlement that he did not think about the rest of us and how we would get back home. All that mattered to him was that his needs were met, and of course, they were. But also, all he cared about was exacting punishment on me too. Punishment for being nice enough to buy him a Bengal cat for his birthday. Punishing me for daring to call him selfish. Now you know a little bit about narcissistic supply, aka fuel, imagine the amount that was flowing towards him during this episode of events, the pleasure he was deriving from his punishment of me. Bizarrely, when he did resume speaking to me he gave me for a birthday present a small plushie husky dog with angel wings. Can you imagine how that left me feeling! I had had my birthday totally ignored, suffered from the silent treatment until two days after it, only for him to then do something as 'thoughtful' as that. Welcome to the gaslighting world of a narcissist!

In relation to my birthday, apart from my 50th, it became a habit of his to always plead poverty just before it. This ensured that if any present was purchased for me, it was always small and cheap. Likewise, it also always ensured that I was never taken out for dinner for my birthday or even taken out anywhere. Neither was the evening meal ever cooked for me. To the Nex it was just any other ordinary day.

Something else that may sound familiar to you is the fact that he always expected me to be the first one to show affection. He felt that it was his entitlement to receive it first always. A prime example of this came in the last few years of our relationship. I consciously decided to put it to the test. From the start of our relationship, it was always me that would snuggle up to him in bed, always me that would say goodnight first and always me that said 'I Love You' first. This one night I decided that I would not but rather that I would wait to see if he for once, made the first move. Of course, this was pre-narcissistic knowledge. I just knew that it was always me that always had to make the first move and I was starting to wonder why, and even felt hurt by it. Well as you have no doubt guessed, no he did not snuggle up, say goodnight or tell me he loved me. He simply went to sleep. From that night on up until when we then split up, we did not snuggle up together ever again in bed. I continued to say goodnight first, but the routine was over. I had proved a fact to myself, but I just did not know then what that fact was. Likewise, when we used to sit on the sofa together. It was always me that snuggled up to him, leaving my position on the sofa to do so. Again, around the same time, I decided to consciously not do this one night to see if he would make the first move and yes you have guessed it again, no he did not. We never snuggled up together on the sofa again. We sat like bookends from that day on. As I have pointed out previously, that for the last seventeen months of our relationship I was subjected to the punishment of what was the silent 'silent treatment' and he even went so far as to not sit in the lounge with me at all in the evenings, instead choosing to sit in another part of the house where there was another TV.

When we were out and about it was always me that took his hand to hold, never him taking mine first. Tiny little memories like this come flooding back and you realise that even a simple gesture like this held a hidden meaning.

I have given you several examples of the Nex's entitlement perception but more importantly it is about looking at why he felt like this.

Why do all narcissist's feel this way?

Quite simply it is because a narcissist sees themselves as the most important person on the planet. Because of this warped perception of theirs they honestly believe their superiority warrants special treatment. They should receive more than anyone else, regardless of what that is. Be it money, respect, adoration, praise, admiration, credit and even Love. They would take your car to use without asking you, screw if you needed it to pick up the kids from school or attend a hospital appointment. You do not count. Your needs do not ever count. The narcissist comes first, end of.

Such was the Nex's sense of entitlement and feelings of superiority that at times his behaviour was so trivial in his actions. For instance, on one occasion he ate my chocolate Easter Egg that my parents had given me one Easter. He did not just have one piece. He ate the entire lot! This was a person who always proclaimed that he did not even like chocolate. When I returned home from work and found it gone, I challenged him on why he had felt that it was okay to eat all of it. He just could see nothing wrong with it whatsoever. His response was 'What's yours is mine'.

If I had shopped and bought a pack of two desserts and I pointed out that there was one each for us mine would soon quickly disappear too, devoured by him, before I even had a chance to eat it myself. I know I can hear you laughing at the absurdity of it. I am laughing myself as I write this. It is funny. The narcissists childish behaviour is so laughable at times because it is so ridiculous. The plausibility of their behaviour and the logic behind it is also ludicrous but laughable.

Just like the treatment the Nex meted out to his friend, because he did not drop what he was doing and wash the Nex's van when he had wanted it washed.

All the behaviour patterns displayed that I have referred to over and over all point to a narcissist's superiority complex and ultimate sense of entitlement.

If you are in a relationship with a narcissist you, will be giving far more then what you are taking out of the relationship. This will also apply to a friendship with one.

Often, a narcissist will simply feel sorry for themselves if they are not receiving what they think they are entitled to.

So, lets now turn our attention to some of the other things that a narcissist does and why.

A classic and essential one is to blame-shift. A narcissist will do this because of course according to them they are always right. It is you that is wrong. They blame-shift to avoid responsibility. To obtain fuel, and of course, because they feel entitled to. In their narcissistic opinion, they are superior and in their warped mind it simply was not and could not have been their fault. This then means that it must have all been your fault. Such is their black and white outlook on life. You are idealised or you are devalued. It is always one way or the other, never in between. A narcissist can never view a person as having both good and bad qualities, it is one or the other that flips back and forth depending on how they are currently feeling towards you.

When a narcissist blame-shifts, they are also then using another trait called projection. A narcissist projects to shift the blame away from himself. They also do this to gaslight you, to blindside you and to confuse you. But ultimately it is to acquire fuel and to control you, beating you down in the process. They lack accountability because in their eyes they are superior to you. Ultimately they are controlling and manipulating you.

They are also known to use deflection. By deflecting the guilt or blame on to you, they are no longer accountable. They did not do it. It is not their fault. They are good and you are bad. You are black and they are white. It is almost laughable when you do present the narcissist with something and their automatic and instant reaction is to say, 'No, it wasn't me', or, 'I didn't do that', and they could be stood there with the very evidence dangling from their hands! They will still categorically deny it.

About six months before the Nex and I finally split up I met an old friend of his who just happened to be the boyfriend of a work colleague of mine. I was away with work and went out for dinner with them both. This old friend of the Nex had been in business with him when they were in their twenties, a part of his past he had never told me about but that is also normal with a narc, and apparently the Nex had pissed someone off so badly that he had had a bullet shot into the bonnet of his car! I was seriously like WTF?! Can you imagine discovering this bombshell information about someone after being with them for almost fourteen years?! To learn about a part of their life like this from someone else. It truly was incredulous! When I asked the Nex about it he went really quiet and finally stated that it was actually five bullets that

172

were shot into the bonnet of his car, but he then immediately switched off and said he could not remember anything else and did not want to talk about it anymore. Well of course, he did not!

Another important trait that we have already looked at is empathy. A narcissist lacks empathy in totality. They do not feel it. They do not even understand what empathy is. I have given you examples in relation to the death of my beloved father, the death of my beloved dog and my mother's dementia diagnosis. Another example of this on a much lesser scale is when my son (a teenager at the time) had stayed over at a friend's house and there were no buses running on the Sunday, the next day. My son phoned me and asked if I could pick him up. I of course said yes but the Nex went ballistic and insisted that he was to walk home. That he had to learn that I was not available 'at the drop of a hat'. This would be a four-mile walk for my son along country lanes to the nearest train station for him to complete his journey home by train. I protested and said that it simply was not fair making him walk this distance and especially that it really was not safe. The Nex was having none of it. He forbade me from picking my son up and I was so fearful of his temper as this was soon after his first physical episode against me that I did not dare disobey him. I could not stand the thought of the treatment that would follow, especially the silent treatment that I knew without a doubt would ensue. My son walked. I have never forgiven myself for not being stronger at that time. As a mother I should have stood up to him and bugger the consequences. A lot of you will not understand this but those of you that have experienced the abusive treatment and behaviour you suffer with a narcissist will.

In a narcissist's eyes if you do not comply, do not provide them with their fuel and dare to stand up to them you will be viewed as a disappointment to them, you have just been painted black. If you have not provided them with the amount of attention and adoration they feel entitled to and subsequently got the good old fuel juices flowing, then you are a disappointment and painted black. Of course, the abuse will then follow.

A normal person will think 'Ah bless she or he must be tired, they are working so hard, that's why they don't want to cook tonight'. They will then probably order a takeaway or even cook themselves. A narcissist instead will punish you by creating a drama, an argument, dole out the silent treatment, even discard you, real or virtual. They may 'silently' punish you by withholding sex or affection. Play mind games with you like hide your stuff around the house.

This will be for not one, but for two reasons; 1. You have not cooked for them, and they are entitled to this. 2. They feel no empathy for your plight.

A favourite of the Nex's was to move furniture around, particularly on one occasion, it was a coffee table which I innocently put back in its place only for the Nex to move it again. And of course, the many mind games that ensued post-split which will be detailed in that chapter. Another thing he did was to download an app on his phone that controlled the TV volume. He derived such pleasure from turning the volume up and down when I was watching the TV so I would then think that the TV or the remote was broken. I eventually caught him doing it and he passed it off as a joke.

Maria Consiglio states that, 'Narcissists have a sense of entitlement. They believe they have favour over other people. They do not play on equal grounds. They can say, do and have what they want. and you cannot. On a surface level, they believe they are special. They are shocked when you oppose them. They expect you to abide by their wishes no matter what. Even if it is hurtful, damaging, and unfair to you. They will get angry if anyone oversteps their Boundaries. 'How dare they?' They are appalled at anyone's unfairness, but they could do the same things or worse and it is perfectly fine because it's them'.

Keeping these two traits in the forefront of your mind, lack of empathy and extreme sense of entitlement, a narcissist will play out their three-phase cycle against you relentlessly, over and over. This is designed to keep you on your toes, to increase the trauma bond with you, to make them feel good and empowered and most important of all, to draw their life force of fuel.

Do not get me wrong, you will have experienced waves of intermittent kindness, fun and even gentleness from the narcissist, as part of that cycle, but you can guarantee that it will always be followed by the abuse, the anger, the hurt, the blame, the silent treatment, the gaslighting and so on. What is so laughable about the Nex is the fact that he honestly believes that he is a kind, honest, genuine and likeable bloke. I have heard him say it over and over to a variety of people and I often wonder whether this is done to convince himself that he really is all these things, or I suspect more likely that he was saying them because he genuinely believes that he is all these things. His very narcissism makes him believe this.

174

From a scientific point of view, the brain of the victim responds to this incessant irrational roller coaster with neurochemistry that increases the bond you have with your narcissist. This pretty much sums up what trauma bonding is and why you do not leave them sooner. It has been described by psychologists and the FBI as 'Intermittent Reinforcement Manipulation Tactic'. In a narcissistic relationship, the fluctuation of feelings tends to be love and fear (you) or hot and cold (the narc). As I have explained when I described the percentage ratio to you before, the positive recedes and the negative increases in frequency. If you look at 'Stockholm Syndrome' where the victim develops an empathy towards their abuser to the point where they will defend them, this is also what can make it so difficult for you to leave the narcissist.

This causes the trauma bond.

Hashtag, narcissisticabuse state that trauma bonding is when you are so heavily attracted to a toxic person, that you are willing to maintain a relationship even at the expense of yourself, for the few and far between highs. The loss of the love makes you crave more. You are dependant in the same way a heroin addict is.

HG Tudor states that the victim does not leave because they are bound by the hope that the golden period (idealisation) will return. He claims that the ties we have to the narcissist keep us in place, despite the abuse that will come. He also states that the bond that a narcissist creates with their victim is so powerful, so deep and so long lasting that it is often the aftermath of the ties that bound us that hurt more than the abuse itself. He asserts that this is how dangerous a narcissist is.

Effectively you are an addict to your own brain and the narcissist is your dealer. You crave the positive times because your brain releases chemicals, the love-bombing and the idealisation phase, so you are addicted to your narcissist, and this then makes it extremely hard for you to walk away.

If you do manage to walk away, going 'No Contact' can be extremely hard because the victim feels emptiness without the narcissist. I have witnessed this on different support sites. So many go 'No Contact' only to fall weeks or months later and respond to the narcissists current hoover attempt.

Therefore, if you do suspect that your current partner or ex-partner is a narcissist it is extremely important to learn all that you can about narcissism and narcissists, the three-phase fork that they use and trauma bonding, and how vital 'No Contact' is for you.

It really is true when they say that knowledge is power.

Especially if you have young children with them because you need to navigate how you can go 'No Contact' when still having to make contact re childcare arrangements. This is when the 'Grey Rock Method' will really help you. Because the narcissist craves chaos, by using this technique you are removing the drama that any interaction you have with them can cause and this is diluted or even non-existing. They will hopefully become bored and seek the chaos elsewhere and your exchange with them will become less harmful or hurtful to you. What you are essentially doing is setting a boundary, something that is alien to a narcissist, which in turn will allow you to remain grounded. Shannon Thomas, author of *Healing from Hidden Abuse* has referred to this as 'Detached Contact'. With the Grey Rock Method, you will not react to any attempts made by the narcissist to bait you. When having to react with the narcissist your responses to them will be dull and boring. You are essentially taking a step back and observing rather than defending yourself from unwanted attention or even verbal attacks from the narcissist. You will be non-responsive and boring to your narc, pretty much just like a rock. This is what is termed as emotional detachment and serves to undermine the narcissists attempts to lure you in and manipulate you, so hopefully they will become uninterested in you and bored.

It is not uncommon to find that victims of narcissists suffer from PTSD, anxiety attacks and depression.

I am currently under treatment for trauma PTSD, but this not only relates to my narcissistic relationship but also the trauma surrounding my father's sudden death. I do not doubt for one single second that if I had not endured the post-split nightmare of abuse that ensued from the Nex my PTSD may not have been so severe. I was taken to some very dark places where I struggled to find a reason to carry on.

I personally believe that the only way to move forward and recover is to go 'No Contact' and to learn absolutely everything you can about narcissism and narcissists. I will keep stressing to you over and over just how important this is for you to do. If I had not learnt all that I did I would most certainly not be writing this book but moreover I would not have understood exactly what I went through which for me was so important for my recovery process. The only way to deal with a narcissist is by going 'No Contact' for then you are effectively starving them of their fuel. No emotions from you, short responses and minimal interaction if you must, but most important of all, 'No Contact'.

Back to the chapter title again and looking at 'Why Does a Narcissist Do the Things They do'.

As you have learnt already, they must win at all costs. To achieve this, they will lie and manipulate. The narcissist must succeed in everything. From the most trivial and mundane to the most substantial. To lose or suffer defeat of any kind is unthinkable to a narcissist and it must never happen at whatever cost!

To achieve this, they will project and call you the abuser and claim that they are the victim. They will state that you are controlling and manipulating them. That you are belittling them.

When I called the Nex a narcissist, not long after we had split up, he immediately mirrored and projected this on to me and stated that it was I that was the narcissist instead. Bear in mind that at this point I had read so much on the topic that I knew I could state it confidently to him. He on the other hand, did not even know what a narcissist was let alone could describe the traits of one. To this day he is still telling all and sundry with his smear campaign against me that he is innocent and that he was abused for years by me and that it is I that is the real narcissist. The big difference between both accounts is that mine are true and his are not. I can back up all my accounts with evidence. Funnily enough when I pointed this out to him he then retorted with the comment 'What kind of weirdo keeps their messages and emails?' Typical example of a narcissist projecting and blame-shifting, but this was totally lost on the Nex. Likewise, at other times when he performed classic narcissistic traits and I pointed them out to him he had no clue what I was talking about! He had and still has absolutely no concept of what a narcissist is.

The narcissist will blame you for everything. I know I have said this before, but I will keep repeating it because it is an important trait of theirs to accept and acknowledge. Their sense of grandiosity prevents them from owning their own part in any problem. They lack the skills to reach a solution in a disagreement. They will not accept that you, their victim, has rights too, and that you are entitled to an opinion. Because of their lack of empathy, they cannot even begin to envisage how their behaviour, actions or comments can affect another person. The focus is always on them. It really is 'All about them'.

Also, when you catch a narcissist in a lie, they will continue to cover up that lie. When they see that this does not work, they will fly into a rage and somehow it is now your fault that they lied!

In the case of a covert narcissist, like the Nex is, they have a serious sense of victim mentality. When he attempted to assault my daughter, that was my fault. When he bumped my car, that was my fault. Or it was 'my gob' that caused the problem, the argument, his abuse, his behaviour, and so on, always my fault. All my fault.

Another favourite was the use of what I call 'Parrot fashion' speech. This was where the Nex would use the exact same words that I had just said to him and he would then spit them right back at me, or if it was a text message he would literally just send the exact same message back to me. He could not come up with a genuine thought of his own. It got to the point where it wound me up so much that I would do the same back to him to try and get him to see how ridiculous he was being, but it never worked. I now understand that this behaviour of his was projection and mirroring.

I have also now learnt that my response, noted above, was a classic form of reactive abuse that a narcissist's victim does. Reactive abuse is when you have suffered so much abuse, covertly or overtly, from your narcissistic partner that you react angrily right back at them. You respond to them with anger, emotion, verbal insults or even violence because of how they have behaved towards you. They will then gleefully state that you are the crazy one. They will not recognise that it is their constant abusive behaviour towards you that brought about your angry response. This is often known as 'Crazy making.' The most prevalent thing to recognise here is that when this does occur, the abusive partner will often be very calm when you are angry and upset. This is because they now have the power and control over you in response to your anger, upset and hurt. This was especially observed by me after we had spilt up in our email correspondence between each other.

By playing the victim, the narcissist can secure a new supply and gain support from others. I have no doubt whatsoever that all the Nex's friends and family have been informed that he suffered such terrible abuse by me and that he is very much the victim. What they have probably failed to do is to ask him for examples of my alleged abusive behaviour because of course, he will not be able to give them any because they do not exist, and also because the Nex is ultimately lying and projecting his behaviour on to me. If he did manage to conjure any 'examples' up, they will of course be lies and fabrications.

Just like when he told me that 'all' his previous exes had cheated on him. All lies.

What a narcissist fails to realise is that they 'always' get found out by their latest victim because once the love-bombing is over and the devaluation begins, which it will without a doubt, the narcissists mask can and does slip. The latest victim will start to notice discrepancies in what the narc is saying compared to how they are acting. If the latest victim challenges them on their behaviour, which they will, the narcissist will respond as only a narc can, by attacking them verbally, emotionally or physically, or worst still all three. The latest victim will realise that the narcissist is 'not' the victim and never was. But this will not stop the narcissist from using gaslighting against their victim. In fact, they will probably ramp this toxic behaviour up because they are aware that their victim is starting to see the real them. So, the victim is gaslighted, subjected to crazy making, have the inevitable blame shifted on to them through projection and so on. As I have stated before, this can take the victim many years to finally reach this point in their abusive toxic relationship, especially if dealing with a covert narcissist.

So, this did not happen with me at the onset of my relationship with the Nex because of course the Nex had 'got away' with it by using the cheating theme against his previous exes. Therefore, I was blind to his previous behaviour, I just knew that what I was enduring was not normal. It was not until after we had split up that I started to learn about his abuse in his previous relationships. Whereas with me, because I had forced his narcissism out into the open, he had discovered that by enacting a typical narcissistic trait of projection, (I know you really could not make it up!), he could reverse this by claiming to be the victim himself. He will no doubt dine out on this for the next few relationships that he embarks on, probably while claiming that his next victim is a narcissist too, and so on rather than a cheater! He has probably realised that he gets more fuel by playing the role of a 'victim' of abuse rather than a victim of adultery.

Every relationship that a narcissist has is built on lies. By them playing the victim, they can exert control through manipulation. Just like the Nex did play the victim of alleged adultery in all his previous relationships. At the time, I just thought that he had been extremely unlucky. That is how gullible I am!

Also, like the Nex who is a mid-range victim covert narcissist, he genuinely believes that he is a good person. He has said as such to me in numerous emails and text messages. He genuinely believes that he is nice, charming, kind, honest (that is the biggest laugh!) and a wholesome kind of guy. This warped belief of his further ensures his belief that he is the victim and not the abuser. I would like to say do not get me wrong he is not always like this. He could be nice and funny and charming, at times, which is true, but of course it was not real and never was real. It is and was merely his false behaviour at play to hide his true inner self.

HG Tudor states that when a mid-range narcissist lies they do not know that they are lying because their narcissism prevents this. Their narcissism causes them to believe that their lie is the truth. They will deflect and blame-shift onto their victim. HG states, 'When a mid-ranger gaslights he does not know he is doing so, he may be contradicting what he said five minutes ago but his narcissism blinds him to this, it has to so that his defence mechanism remains intact and affective. Therefore, he genuinely believes that what he is saying is correct and moreover you are wrong and therefore you are the problem'. He goes on to say that therefore they honestly believe that they are a good person and that you, the victim is the one at fault. This is also why the narcissist goes on to label you as the abuser and them as the victim. Why they go as so far as to accuse you of being the narcissist instead, they really do believe that this is the case. HG believes that the narcissist does this so that their responses and actions have total conviction and the best possible chance of a successful outcome. Which of course is the supply of fuel and the control. Therefore, the manipulation just continues with absolutely no prospect of the narcissist changing whatsoever. We look at this concept that they cannot and will not ever change in more detail in the next chapter.

I now know that the Nex did not put my name on our property's title deeds so he could exert power and control over me. But more importantly so that if we ever did split up, he could 'steal' and con even more money out of me then he already had throughout our relationship.

On another occasion after we had split up, he had the audacity to say that he would never forgive me for not lighting a candle on what would have been his late mother's birthday, something I had done every previous year. The important fact to note here is that he himself had never lit this candle for his own mother, and despite our break-up, he still felt entitled to it being my responsibility to light it for him. On this occasion, I was not even at home as I was flying back from a holiday! Such was his warped logic, his sense of entitlement and his blame-shifting and projection because the candle never got lit. He just did not think to simply light it himself.

I have recently been sorting out some photos on a couple of my old phones and found old messages between the Nex and I. On reading them through again, I could now blatantly see the narcissism pouring out of him with every word that he had wrote. The blame-shifting, the gaslighting, the projection, the deflection. Back then of course I had not even heard of the term narcissist, but my responses were as expected without this knowledge, upset, confused, hurt and so on. Again, reading these now just further validated all that I had gone through with my narcissistic abusive ex.

An article by @narcissist.sociopath.awareness2 states, 'They love your kind, nurturing nature, your sensitivity. They think you are brilliant and feel lucky to have you. But in time, the things they once loved about you become the things they resent and loathe. They are angry because you put others before them, you're too sensitive, or you think you're smarter than them. They hate you for being everything they are not'.

It is such a shame that a narcissist cannot better themselves once they have been told what they are, but I guess it is because they already see themselves as 'the' best!

When I started my new job in 2017, although the Nex feigned pleasure for me in achieving the role in the beginning, he hated it especially when he could see that I was doing so well in it. He tried to say that I had changed when I had not done. He was merely jealous that I had succeeded in getting such a good job, and that I was really enjoying it, and that I was being praised and rewarded for my hard work. He could not stand to see me happy, to see me enjoying my work, to see me receiving praise, so instead he blamed my job for any issues that we had, stating that I had changed. If I had changed in any way, it was that I was a lot happier with my job, I was less tired, less stressed, less exhausted and was enjoying my life more. This is what the Nex could not stand to see, because a narcissist just hates to see you happy and successful.

As far as the narcissist goes, the problem is that you cause them the biggest ever humongous narcissistic injury when you finally walk away from them because in their opinion no one is ever allowed to discard them. They are the ones that get to do that when they decide to, and not you. They are the ones that have complete and utter control, not you. If you dare to walk away from them, the injury you cause is one of, 'How dare you walk away from me!', and, 'Who do you think you are?!' 'No one walks away from me because I am God'. Because you have caused them this massive narcissistic injury they will set out to destroy you and to bring you down. They will launch the biggest and dirtiest smear campaign that they possibly can against you. And all because they feel that they now need to punish you for what you have done to them.

I hope that this chapter has given you an insight into why a narcissist behaves the way that they do. By using my own examples, I am hoping that you will see some of your own too. Or at least be able to relate to them in some way. That they will answer some of the questions that have been whirling through your head. But most of all so that you will know that you are not crazy, that you are not the abuser and that you, yes 'you', are the real victim here.

Chapter Eight
Why a Narcissist Cannot Change
and Will Not Change

A narcissist cannot and will not ever change because they 'always' must have complete and utter total control! More importantly, it is because a narcissists very narcissism will prevent them from accepting what they are so they cannot and will not ever change.

Maria Consiglio states, 'The thing to understand is, for a person to change, they need to be able to understand another person's pain. They need to have empathy. Malignant narcissists have neither self-reflection nor empathy. A narcissist will never see things your way or even try to understand your perspective. They will never become better people for you, they are not built that way. And if the person is sociopathic, or psychopathic, then they do not have a conscience either, which means they do not suffer from any guilt or remorse. If they 'change', it is only a temporary manipulation for them to get something they want or need, from you, but it is not permanent. Healing involves you acknowledging the reality of the situation and moving on, knowing this could never be a healthy loving relationship you want, or were hoping for'.

A post on Quora says that the reason why there 'is no cure' for a narcissist is because the problem lies in emotional abuse/trauma/neglect as a child because it stunted their emotional development as a child. Dr Malkin claims that although there is no cure it is possible for a narcissist to improve but one needs to be extremely cautious if deciding to venture down this road. Another difficulty for narcissists is self-awareness. The catch twenty-two here is because one of the problems with a narcissist is their inability to accept that blame could lie with them and not with another person. This is because their defence mechanisms are so entrenched. The post goes on to say that what contributed to the narcissism in the first place was because self-awareness was too painful for them.

You will find that a narcissist will generally be self-employed, unemployed, go from job to job, be a leader, have superficial friends, and many broken relationships behind them, unless they are a covert narcissist. These will still have a string of broken promises to their name, just not as many as an overt narcissist.

HG Tudor states that 'Narcissism is a coping mechanism' and that a narcissist will not be emotionally responsive in a healthy way.

Looking again specifically at the covert narcissist, of which the Nex most certainly is one of these, if we look closer at a definition of a covert you are describing someone who craves attention, admiration and importance. Someone who lacks empathy towards others. They manage to get into your life in a different way to an overt narcissist. There actions are more insidious. You literally will not see them coming! Of course, you are still love-bombed, there is no escaping that, even with a covert narcissist.

Maria Consiglio states that, 'Covert Narcissists for example think they are really good people. They buy into their 'humble demeanour'. There is a delusional aspect to narcissism, there must be for them to believe they are perfect or superior. They rationalize all the bad things they do. They find a way to blame you, or make it your fault, or believe you deserve it. That is how they could live with themselves. Especially covert narcissists, they can't imagine being looked at as anything other than wonderful people'.

Reading that statement, along with many others did provide me with so much validation throughout my healing process and during the writing of this book. They made sense of everything that I had experienced and what I had gone through, and further anchored my belief that the Nex is a narcissist.

When we have briefly explored empathy earlier, you may think that 'surely they do feel something?' 'They simply must do'. But no, they do not. A narcissist feels no empathy whatsoever. They know how to mimic it from observation but never actually really and truly feel it. They may recognise that you are upset, angry or frustrated but the narcissist does not personally feel any empathy towards you. If they see you crying, they will not comfort you, unless of course they saw it as a way to draw fuel from you. Whenever I cried, more with frustration and hurt at his unreasonable and abusive behaviour towards me, the Nex usually used to just pretend that it was not happening. If he did acknowledge it, then he would pass a snide comment like, 'I don't know what you're crying for', or 'Those tears aren't going to help you'. I overheard the Nex informing his latest victim that it did nothing for him when she cried, and that it did not mean anything to him as he just switches off from it. They are exceptionally good though at turning on the crocodile tears when it suits them. The Nex used to do this if he saw that he was not getting a rise out of me, or if after one of the end of the relationship routines, I would agree with him and say that I would not stand in his way, then the false tears would flow. It is of course a classic narcissistic manipulation technique, designed to deflect their behaviour towards you and to gain your sympathy. Another classic example was after he went for my daughter. I think he was so scared that she was going to call the police that he played on her empathy traits by turning on the false tears and doling out fake apologies. And just like a bathroom scenario post-split that I will go on to describe later in the book, on came those crocodile tears again and he emphasised this by using his friends' cancer diagnosis to manipulate me.

Likewise, if you have a happy event, the narcissist will not share your joy with you. You can forget it. Their jealousy of your success, their sense of superiority will prevent it. In fact, they will resent your achievement to the point where they will try and sabotage it, just like the Nex did with my graduation. As I have said before, birthdays and Christmas are usually fair game to them too.

If you are looking for words of comfort, then forget it. Often when I would drive home from work which was for the main part, motorway driving, if I rang him to have a moan about the traffic or that we were at a standstill I was calling him to: 1. Vent my frustration and tell him I would be late, and 2. To seek support and sympathy from him.

'You are joking aren't you' I hear you say! 'Did you not realise that he is a narcissist and does not do empathy?' Oh boy, not back then I did not unfortunately. At that time in my life, I had no knowledge on narcissism and narcissists. I did not realise that this is what he was and that I was literally 'Flogging a Dead Horse' if I expected either of the above two to happen. Once learning about their behaviour this was just another flashbulb moment of realisation as to why I did not get the sympathy I was always looking for and hoping for on those drives home.

So, back to those calls home to him. What I always received instead was a barrage of verbal abuse about why I was calling him followed quickly by him stating that he could not do anything about it, blah blah blah. He would ask, 'What do you expect me to do about it?' I did not expect him to do anything other than placate and soothe me. To tell me, 'Never mind, you will be home soon'. Or 'Don't worry about tea, I will sort it out'. Or even, 'What a bummer, don't worry, just get home safe'. Ah no, I was delusional every single time that I called him, for living in hope that he may just one time show me some empathy on just one of those occasions. If I dared to ask him to simply put the oven on so it could be warming in preparation for my return, he would not just say, 'Sure, no problem'. Instead, he would say, 'I'm busy', or 'Are you telling me that I have to stop what I am doing just to put the oven on for you?!' The best part about it was he was never busy when I arrived home. Not in the sense you or I would describe as busy. Rather, he was sat in front of the TV and did not want to get up or move, or rather still, like the true narcissist he was, he simply did not want to do something that I had asked him to do. How dare I ask the great almighty to help me with something! How shocking of me! Nine times out of ten he would just tell me to phone one of the kids who were upstairs and ask them to do it instead!

My new business adventure with the restaurant; after the initial help he gave with the shop-fitting, he proceeded to always pass negative comments about the venture. He was quite literally sat waiting for it all to fall apart so he could rub his hands in glee and say, 'I told you so'.

My new job was met with little enthusiasm and encouragement. Why? Because it was a successful move for me and because he could see that it made me happy and that I was enjoying it. In fact, he blamed my job after we had split up and said that I had changed since starting it. I had not, rather I was subjected to the sustained silent punishment devaluation phase two months before I started my new job which then continued throughout it until we split up the following year.

My illness, what illness?!

My children, they are yours not mine!

My pets, how dare I give them any love and affection!

To a narcissist, how you feel simply does not matter nor does it ever feature into the equation as far as they are concerned.

Quite simply, if the narcissist were to give 'it' or more to the point you, any attention then this would deplete their precious fuel supply. So, instead, they will respond nastily or indifferent, because they know that this will upset you and give them more fuel instead. My use of the term 'it' above is not done lightly. This is because the narcissist sees you as nothing more than an object, like the fridge, you are nothing more than an appliance there to serve them.

I have mentioned my examples before. My beloved late father's death and his response to my rebuff of his fake comfort attempt, the silent treatment that I endured following it. His parcels in my office.

Dr Amie Evacu, PhD, states that 'A relationship with a narcissist will end in tears of one kind or another'.

Tears of rage, disappointment, heartbreak, despair, fear, misery, exhaustion or distress.

A narcissist deliberately sets out to get the continuous attention that they crave, and they must feel 'One-Up' all the time and they achieve this with their Fuel. Therefore, they will never change. The drive will never leave them. Fuel governs absolutely everything they say or do.

When we recap on their precious fuel and their consumption of it, we must remember that you will be devalued if you are not supplying the narcissist with positive fuel or not supplying enough of it for them. Remember that for them to gain fuel an emotional response must be generated. Or you may even be just supplying the wrong type of fuel that your narcissist requires. Or maybe even it is because you are simply not quite strong enough for them. I know when I have explained this to friends in the past you can see the look of puzzlement on their faces. What you are telling them just seems so abnormal in behaviour to even contemplate. I know when I first started reading about it I felt exactly the same way and it took me a while and further research to fully understand and accept what the term fuel, or narcissistic supply, meant and how and why it was so important to a narcissists very existence. It also made me realise that all the research and studies that have gone into narcissism are also correct when they say a narcissist cannot and will not change. You must never forget that their insatiable need and consumption of their fuel, or narcissistic supply, is never done on a conscious level, but rather they just feel a whole lot better when you adore and praise them, or when you are sad and upset because of their abuse of you.

Quite literally, if all is good in a narcissist's world then you can rightly assume that they are receiving adequate fuel, the right 'texture' fuel, the right strength fuel, and everything else is okay about the fuel in all its forms and glory. Of course, with this you will experience a return to the idealisation phase. But woe betide if that fuel level drops for whatever reason, loses its quality or loses any of its potency or worse still you have caused them a narcissistic injury, then devaluation will begin once again. On that hamster wheel you go, it just keeps on turning and turning. You are now subject to another ride on that narcissistic rollercoaster.

You may have even been supplying the narcissist with a good dose of positive fuel because you yourself are enjoying the idealisation phase, and most likely are relieved that it has returned but the narcissist is a fickle creature as you now know. They have once again become bored of your positive fuel because it is losing its potency. You may even be pissing them off without even realising it and the fact that you are being nice to the narcissist is now regarded as an irritation to them. You could quite literally be the world's biggest doormat, but it will just not matter. The old inner demons and insecurities are at risk of surfacing within the narc. Your positive fuel 'is not quite hitting the spot anymore.' So, just like when you have eaten too much of your favourite chocolate and you are now growing tired of its flavour, becoming bored with it, and you want to fulfil your 'taste satisfaction' on a different kind of chocolate bar, you can thus expect an episode of an orchestrated argument or fight to come from out of nowhere with your narcissist so that he will then start to receive the negative fuel that will pour out of you which will then satisfy his thirst for this better potent fuel once more. If you look at this another way, as the saying goes, 'Familiarity breeds Contempt'. In other words, the longer they are with you the less potent your positive fuel is, because they have been repeatedly exposed to it. Hence your negative fuel is now more promising and potent. And so, the cycle just continues, on and on. It will never end because a narcissist will never stop craving that fuel. They only briefly dip you back into the idealisation phase to keep you hooked, to confuse you and to exert more power and control over you. You will never get off that hamster wheel, and that rollercoaster ride, unless you jump off yourself. Then and only then will it finally be 'Game over' for you.

Picture an image of a smiling face surrounded by arrows pointing at it with 'me' spelt at the top and 'myself' spelt at the bottom; this image depicts that 'This is a Narcissist'. This is because everything and anything is 'always' all about them.

Deep down the narcissist feels empty and inferior. They must hide this though at all costs. They must feed off others to make themselves feel good. And so, this perfectly describes their supply of fuel. Their insatiable need for it, the absorption of it and ultimately their supply of it. It is a perpetual hunt for supply, a perpetual need for the sating and the satisfaction that it brings.

A person who is described as a pathological narcissist has a fragile identity and poor self-esteem, but they have a distracted view of themselves as being important, superior, better, worthy, etc.

Not all narcissists though have this sense of grandiosity about them. Likewise, some can be directly aggressive, passive-aggressive or even needy.

HG Tudor states 'It is not accurate to say that all narcissists operate from the same playbook or rulebook, but they do all have the same similarities.'

He goes on further to state 'It is the similarity in behaviour that makes us narcissists, not that we are narcissists, so we behave similarly'.

According to HG Tudor, a narcissist's need for control and punishment are automatic and instinctive. This is to preserve their self-defence mechanism, which if attacked, could cause their mask to slip and to 'reveal the real them'. This is unimaginable to a narcissist. It is their worst nightmare and simply cannot and must not ever happen.

Their narcissism will blame anyone and everyone else instead. He or she will view themselves as the victim instead.

Also, their narcissism will view even the most innocent of events or even responses as you (the real victim) trying to control them. This will of course anger the narcissist and they will unleash this anger on you. That is why at times their outbursts do seem to come from completely out of nowhere. I have lost count of the number of times the Nex would throw that one at me, 'Stop trying to control me!', or 'Why do you always have to try and control me?!'

For a mid-range narcissist, like the Nex, their lack of remorse, or guilt, will blind them to really seeing that it 'is' their fault. They will think that they have done nothing wrong. In fact, they will view you as the unreasonable one, and that they are just responding to that. They have succeeded in projecting the blame on to you. They have succeeded in deflecting the blame away from them.

I have mentioned about the narcissists use of passive-aggressive behaviour. A mid-range narcissist is the most passive-aggressive of all the cadres. He or she is the most likeliest to spit at you 'I wish you were dead' during a rampage, whereas a lesser will just punch you in the face and a greater will just glare at you with an evil expression on their face. The Nex extensively used passive-aggressive behaviour against me throughout our relationship. He also demonstrated it perfectly after we had split up when on one occasion he screamed at me 'Why can't you just hurry up and die?!' and on another occasion, 'Why can't you just stop breathing?!' and finally yet another time, 'Why couldn't you just go quietly?!'

The use of passive-aggressiveness is primarily to fulfil their selfish needs and/or to exact punishment against you.

It can be defined as anger and hostility combined with a learned helplessness in disguise which is expressed in a covert way to 'even the score' against you.

Of course, the use of passive-aggressive behaviour is not limited to a narcissist, but what determines that it is indeed a narcissist using it, is the fact that they cannot hide their sense of entitlement, or their conceit towards you, and even their sense of superiority over you.

For a narcissist, the use of passive-aggressive behaviour is a way of demonstrating that they have not achieved getting their own way with something. I do not mean that they consciously decide to be passive-aggressive, rather it is the instinctive reaction that they and what they have perceived to be a slight against them. They will be sarcastic with you. They will be critical of you. Pick on a weakness of yours. Show open disdain towards you. Display stubbornness. Undermine you. Silently punish you.

The two most classic ones though are:

1. The silent treatment
2. Blaming you.

With both, you may be completely unaware that this is what is happening. For instance, rather than the full-blown use of the silent treatment and not communicating with you at all they will instead be sullen with you, using one-word answers. This is a deliberate ploy to make you feel insecure. A classic example of blame is 'It is your fault that I forgot to do that because you did not remind me'. This is so that they can avoid responsibility by manipulating the facts and of course as we all know full well by now it is also because a narcissist is never at fault. I unknowingly endured passive-aggressive behaviour from the Nex when he was silently punishing me for the last seventeen months of our relationship, as well as on many other occasions throughout our relationship.

Wikipedia states that 'passive-aggressive behaviour is a type of behaviour that is characterized by indirect resistance to the demands of others and an avoidance of direct confrontation.'

The very use of gaslighting, triangulation, smear campaign, hoovering, and especially the silent treatment, are patterns of passive-aggressive behaviour.

When the victim is experiencing this kind of behaviour from the narcissist, the victim will sense that something is not right and that something is 'off', and if you are that victim, you will just not be able to put your finger on it. If you ask them, 'what is wrong' their reply will be 'nothing'. This feeling could last hours and even days until the narcissist unleashes their anger against you. My final one eventually lasted seventeen months for me.

A classic example of the use of this type of behaviour is the one I gave earlier when I described the golf and my dad incident. He had not only agreed to play golf with him but had also instigated this invite to my late father himself. He never really wanted to play golf at all, he was merely future proofing, so he used an excuse at the last minute to not have to do it. He also blamed me for it and said if I had not raised the topic then it would have gone ahead and happened, he would have played golf with my father. His narcissistic personality meant that there was absolutely no filter in place for him to think about how this affected myself or my father. No longer playing golf with my father meant it was my punishment for questioning him and my father was collateral damage.

According to a blog written by Melanie Evans when you think passive-aggressive in relation to a narcissist you must also think 'Stealth' and 'Deception'. How can a person punish another but make it look like they are not? How can they twist things to such a degree so that it looks like the victim is at fault for even imagining their 'off' sensation?

As for the use of the infamous silent treatment. This can be described as the most passive-aggressive of all traits that the narcissist 'will' use against you. It is a form of severe punishment that the narcissist is meting out against you. Experts state that the use of the silent treatment is one of the most painful traumas that we could ever experience. It could even be classed as emotional violence. Once the silent treatment is over, the narcissist simply hits the reset button as if nothing has happened. They are fully aware that they have managed down your expectations. The narcissist simply just 'resets' the relationship and picks up where he left off with no explanations, no reasons and no sorry from him needed. This most perfectly explains the consistent and continual silent treatments that I endured from the Nex, over and over and over. But it also explains why nothing was ever resolved, no argument was concluded, and no outcome or solution was ever sought or found. It was never talked about or discussed once the silent treatment was over.

If you are lucky enough to evade a silent treatment, then they will stonewall you instead. With this, they will dismiss the conversation and absolutely refuse to continue it with you. If you try to continue it, they will threaten you that the relationship is over. The use of stonewalling is purely to invalidate your feelings. If you are as unlucky as I was, then you will suffer both the stonewalling and the silent treatment, one straight after the other.

Still looking at the mid-range narcissist, as I have touched on before, the use of the silent treatment is their preferred method of cruelty to use against their victim. As I have also stated previously, this method was by far the Nex's all-time favourite trait to use against me.

The mid-range narc does genuinely believe that they are truly a good person. That they are nice, kind and decent. If anyone 'crossed' them, then that is the other person's fault, never theirs. How could it possibly or even remotely be their fault when they are such a nice, kind, decent human being?

As so eloquently put by HG Tudor, 'A silent treatment is the calling card of the passive-aggressive mid-range narcissist.'

Of course, without any doubt, the use of the silent treatment against you 'is' emotional abuse. It 'is' psychological abuse. It 'is' used to control you and to 'put you in your place.'

As indicated by these four signs:

1. It is frequent in its occurrence and lasting longer each time it is deployed.
2. It is coming from a place of punishment rather than a cooling off period.
3. It only ends when you, the victim, apologises, pleads or gives in to the narcissist's demands.
4. You, the victim, change your behaviour to avoid one.

I suffered all four of these.

Therefore, to the narcissist, they are right, and you are wrong, always. It really is a black and white as that to them.

The use of mental abuse is something the narcissist cannot prevent from using against you.

The frequent yelling, insults, name calling, bouts of anger, throwing things, accusations, jealousy, spying on you, stalking you, isolating you, making decisions for you, financial control, blaming you for everything, never apologising, threatening self-harm, threatening you, your family or friends, threatening your pets or even your possessions.

I have counted fourteen out of the twenty listed above that I experienced in my relationship with the Nex.

The narcissist will always be the one to pick that fight right out of the blue with you for no reason whatsoever and of course it will always be your fault that started it. This behaviour will not and cannot ever change with a narcissist.

The primary reasons they will have enacted a fight with you is because:

1. They need fuel.
2. Power and control.
3. You have caused them a perceived narcissistic injury even though you will not really have.

You will of course be blamed for starting the argument. Of course, it is your fault. If like in my case, you will also get 'The end of the relationship' routine, the stonewalling then quickly followed by the good old silent treatment.

Remember, a narcissist must always be in control. They do not recognise boundaries. Have 'no' empathy. 'Are' entitled. And let us not forget the most important fact of all, fuel to them 'is' absolutely everything, 'The be all and end all'. The insatiable acquisition of it 'is' what drives them in absolutely everything they say and do.

If we briefly recap on the three-fork phase of idealisation, devaluation and discard:

The initial seduction or love-bombing/idealisation at the start is to gather positive fuel. The devaluation is to produce negative fuel. Of course, you will be experiencing the occasional return to the idealisation phase intermittently for them to garner more positive fuel and to lift the victim up, ready for the next big fall once again. Then the discard, real or not, which will no doubt incorporate a Hoover at some point, and right back to the start again. Round and round it goes. The endless cycle that the narcissist plays with you. The hamster wheel of life with a narcissist. The rollercoaster ride that you must continually endure.

This cycle is purely in play to provide the continuous supply of the narcissists fuel from all the emotional reactions that each phase brings to the narcissist. It also allows the emotions to be contrasted, thus producing a better quality of fuel and a more potent fuel for them.

Fuel equals power equals control equals fuel.

Fuel is needed to create power which in turn provides the devices by which they can remain in control and subsequently obtain more fuel. The perfect narcissistic cycle.

If the narcissist's intimate partner is what is known as a 'co-dependant' then this really is the jackpot in narcissistic supply as it provides a steady stream of fuel for the narcissist.

You can even be forgiven for holding out hope that your narcissist could change and may change. This is a natural empathic belief that a victim of a narc holds. As an empathic individual you will always try to see the good in people. You could even be of a gullible nature and be someone who believes what they are told and if the narcissist is succeeding in making you believe that everything is your fault you will further stay with them out of guilt and also want to try and make everything alright.

I did not leave for these very reasons and because I had been conditioned to believe them. Also, because I was trauma bonded to the Nex. I also tried to justify that it was not fair to uproot my children once again, and of course, once married, I believed in the marriage vows that I had made.

It will not be easy for everyone to just walk away once they have discovered that their partner is a narcissist. The choice to stay or go is a very personal decision for someone to make. They must just understand what they are dealing with and develop coping mechanisms to survive.

A@awakeningwomensupport state, 'Invisible abuse is the most harmful kind of abuse because covert narcissists are so good at making you look like the 'crazy' and 'unstable' one for reacting to their abuse and no one else sees it'.

A quote by E S states, 'A narcissist will not change, they just blame everything on everybody else and move on to someone who is unaware of their manipulation'.

Above all else, remember that a narcissist cannot change. 'Ever!'

A narcissist will not change. 'Ever!'

What you do with that information and knowledge, and how you do go forward, is a personal decision and a choice that you and you alone must make, and it is very much down to you only.

When I say that the Nex never loved me and never loved his past victims, I do also know that he will go on to never loving anybody in the future either, but he will always go on to tell those poor future victims that they are the love of his life every single time.

I did hear the Nex one time, telling his latest victim that he destroys every relationship that he has, that he had now destroyed theirs and that maybe 'Karen' (me) was right with everything I had said about him. Wow! A moment of clarity or quiet self-reflection? Nope, because a narcissist does not do this, it was rather purely his attempt at a grand hoover and a pity play as the relationship had briefly hit the rocks.

The thing to realise when dealing with a narcissist is the fact that once you recognise what they are they quite literally morph before your very eyes into this pathetic, sad little creature in front of you.

For me, I have accepted what I went through, what I experienced, and I am starting to accept my 'lost years'. For the Nex, I just feel sorry for him. For what he is and for what he is missing out on with a normal, real loving relationship. Living life as a narcissist is not a fulfilling one and is not a way to feel contentment and even happiness. A narcissist's life is a false one, no aspect of their life is truly real. It is completely dominated by the false mask that is in place. So, very few people get to see the real them. Any emotions of love are not felt so they cannot and do not experience it. They are devoid of empathy so personally, I cannot imagine living a life not being able to empathize with another human being, or the plight of someone suffering, or even an animal suffering. I could not ever imagine living a life full of grandiosity and self-entitlement. I know that I am nothing more than normal. Nothing on this earth makes me special or feel like I am able to expect more from life than anyone else. Therefore, I just cannot comprehend how another human being, a narcissist, can ever feel like that. I do understand now the mechanisms of it, and that it is caused by their very narcissism, but this still does not mean that I can understand or accept that it does exist, even though I now know that it does, because I have lived through it, but simply because it is so alien to me and to what I, and the majority of other people view as normal.

I now cannot look back on my relationship with the Nex with any happy or fond memories because I now know that they were not real. That in fact they were fake moments orchestrated by the Nex because I had been briefly dipped into an idealisation phase purely because he was pleased and sated. Instead, I view the past fifteen years of my life as nothing more than a mistake that I have since learnt from, years that I can never get back, but going forward I can now use to help others with the writing of this book, and through support groups.

I certainly do not regret the end of the relationship but what I do regret is that it ever even existed because of those lost years. Precious time lost that could have been spent with family, especially my parent's, lost because I sacrificed everything for a false promised life with him. That is what you do when you genuinely love someone. You are prepared to make those kinds of sacrifices, unless of course you are a narcissist.

I will go as so far as to make the bold statement that I do not think narcissists should ever be allowed to have children. Certainly not full-blown ones. If I was ever asked this question, I would give a resounding no as my answer.

Why?

For the very reason that the narcissist cannot and will not change and having children would not alter this fact.

A narcissist will not love and care for their child the way a child should be, would be and deserves to be loved and cared for. A narcissist's child would be nothing more than an appendage of them. The child would be used to gather their narcissistic parent's supply/fuel. This poor child would be set unrealistic

196

goals that they would need to achieve to satisfy the narcissist, and this would prove to be an impossible task for that poor child. The child would and will grow up psychologically damaged and may even be violently physically abused by the narcissistic parent. So again, my resounding answer to a narcissist being a parent would be categorically 'no!' I am sure that there are grown up children of narcissists out there that would agree with me and are even still receiving therapy or counselling because of what they had to endure or went through in their childhood.

Some may say that I am being unduly harsh with the above sweeping statement and by denying a narcissist the chance to be a parent, that I am in fact being cruel and judgemental. I would argue that I am not. I have read the harrowing stories from some of these adult children and seen the damage that it has inflicted.

So, to conclude this chapter, as I discovered with all my research, a narcissist will not change because to them, nothing is wrong with them, and they are perfect. Their narcissism prevents them from ever thinking otherwise and for this very reason alone, a narcissist cannot change.

Below is what I feel is a perfect quote to finish this chapter off with and this is,

'Narcissist Dating in Five Easy Steps'

1. Seduce, charm and study
2. Alternate kind and cruel
3. Mock, abuse and discredit
4. Devalue and discard
5. Repeat

Author unknown

This sums up to perfection why a narcissist cannot and will not ever change.

Chapter Nine
The Post Narcissist Phase and
the Smear Campaign

Oh boy! The stage where you finally get to let go of your toxic, abusive narcissistic relationship. Hallelujah!

The Serenity Prayer:

'God grant me the serenity to accept the things I cannot change, courage to change the things I can, and wisdom to know the difference.'

I love this prayer and always have.

It was first used in sermons in the early 1930s. It can be found in different versions, but I like the best known one which is the one I have cited above. Wikipedia shows that it became more widely known after being brought to the attention of 'Alcoholics Anonymous' in 1941 by a member who saw it written in a New York Obituary. AA's Co-Founder and other staff members liked it so much that they had it printed and handed around and it has been a part of 'Alcoholics Anonymous' ever since.

I thought it rather fitting as not only does it sum up this chapter, but it also fits right in with what I have mentioned before about the victim being 'addicted' to their narcissist.

If you are lucky enough to be in what can be classed as a normal relationship that has reached the end, the splitting of assets will just be a formality that is concluded relatively painlessly.

Not so I am afraid, when a narcissist is involved. They will first and foremost see themselves as the victim. Their goal will be to be proven right and to walk away having destroyed you first in the process.

If you are unfortunate enough to be divorcing a narcissist (like me), then you can truly expect the fight of your life! Made all the worse if you were the one to walk away first. The narcissist will leave absolutely nothing standing in their path. They will engage you in a court battle purely to exert control and power over you. By dragging you through the courts, they will feel a source of power and control.

'A narcissist would rather be your enemy than a nobody in your eyes,' so goes a quote that I read once which made perfect sense.

I have got so much to say of my own experiences with the Nex and the legal battles that ensued but to start with I want to give you a glimpse of what you can expect by way of irrational behaviour from the narcissist, especially at the start, before your court battle will ensue.

To get a really good idea as to why you can expect such atrocious behaviour from your narcissist I will be relating it directly to the narcissistic traits that we have already looked at. This will enable you to understand my examples with the Nex that I will be giving.

Simply put, if your ex-partner were not a narcissist you would not be experiencing the behaviour that I will be demonstrating, it really is as simple as that.

First thing to keep in the forefront of your mind is the typical narcissistic trait that, 'It is their way or the highway.' They will not ever want to meet you halfway. They are the game player here. They will know that the longer the break-up takes the easier it will be for them to manipulate you. It will be their way or not at all.

Be sure beyond any doubt that the narcissist 'will' embark on the mother of all smear campaigns against you! They will throw whatever 'mud' they can at you in the hope that at least some of that 'mud' will stick.

Why would they do this to you?

Because of their lack of empathy. Because you have left them. Because you have unmasked them. Because you have caused the mother of all narcissistic injuries to them that you could. Because now you must pay. Because these actions 'must' be avenged. And finally, because you must be destroyed.

Why?

Because of their desire to win at all costs. Because of their need for revenge. But most important reason of all though is so that they can 'Save face.' The less that their false persona or mask slips will mean that others will not see the 'real them.' This would be an absolute red line to a narcissist. An absolute and total massive no. A catastrophic event. If you have sussed them out, 'outed' them, called them on what you believe they are, then your smear will be harsh, it will be severe, and it will be done so as to destroy you and ultimately leave their mask intact.

The aim of the smear campaign is to not only 'Muddy the waters', hurt your reputation, and ultimately gain support and sympathy for themselves, it is also to continue to derive fuel from you by relishing in the thought of the damage that they are causing you, but they are also obtaining fuel from their supporters because they are now playing the role of the victim. And of course, we must not forget what power they are deriving from the very thought that they are going to ultimately destroy you. What power this action will bring them, what a result for them, what a 'win'!

Maria Consiglio says,

'Narcissists continue to abuse even when they are no longer with you. This time they attack your reputation. Under the guise of being concerned they say you are crazy, out of control, unstable and any number of things. Portraying you in a negative light. You finally find the courage to leave, and you have to deal with their smear campaign. This is how they continue to abuse you and not look like the villains'.

I can and will agree with all of that because I was called crazy and out of control along with a list of other lies.

If you are dealing with a covert narcissist, then they will have been extremely good over the duration of the relationship to not let others witness their mistreatment of you. They will have portrayed the image of a loving partner to the outside world. A covert narcissist will have let most people only see the nice side of them, so that they are liked by them. Only their victim usually gets to see the evil that lurks beneath. When a victim does finally reach out and speak up, their audience will have already been primed by the narcissist to believe that the narcissist is the victim and not their victim. The smearing had already begun long before the relationship had ended.

Once your relationship with the narcissist is truly over, it will be as though you never existed. They will move on quickly to the next relationship. This knowledge finally explained the comments the Nex used to say to me at the start that I have mentioned before such as, 'If you ever leave me I will just switch off from you.' Now I know that he could say it with such conviction because it was true. This of course does not mean that they will just walk away without a backward glance. No, you will not be as lucky as that. They will ensure that they throw everything that they can at you on the way out. They will quite literally make your life hell. They will 'light that match' and toss it behind them on the way out.

Gena da Silva states, 'Your narcissistic ex knows that he/she needs to get into a new relationship very quickly, to convince everyone that you were the problem, not him/her'. This was also true of my Nex who embarked on a new relationship only after a matter of a few weeks after we had split up.

A comment the Nex most recently said to me was, 'I'm not interested in you, and I never have been.' The irony of this email comment was completely lost on him. It was the closest to a confession that he was a narcissist that I had ever had. Of course, he will not have realised this when he said it though!

Any 'good' times that you had with your narcissist during the idealisation phases will just vanish into thin air. This is what makes their behaviour so dangerous because they will go on to cause you the most harm that they can in the smear campaign and any subsequent divorce proceedings.

To them, you are now no more. It will only be their selfish needs that will matter. 'Winning', will become their ultimate and absolute final goal.

The narcissist will deflect everything that you say right back at you. They will want the whole world, including the courts, to believe that it is all your fault. That you are the crazy one and that they are the victim.

To this day I still not only learn, but also hear the Nex telling everyone that I am crazy. That I have serious mental health issues. That I am deranged. That I seriously need help. He even emailed me a few months after we had split up citing these very points and telling me that I had bipolar disorder and said that he would set up an appointment for me if I liked and that he would even come with me. I literally pissed my pants when I read that! I have since learnt that this is classic gaslighting. His all-time favourite as well, that still does the rounds today is the one that I am 'Out of Control.' I really believe that it has got to the point where he just copies and pastes the same comments over and over, from one email to the next, one text message to the next. It is like these comments have become his Mantra that they get him out of bed in a morning. I even heard him telling his latest victim that I had serious mental health issues and that he had made an appointment for me, but he did not know if I would attend. Such was and is his delusion, his crazy making, his projecting, his deflection on to me, the real victim. And of course, no such appointment did exist.

When dealing with a covert narcissist like the Nex, people will sometimes find it hard to believe what you are telling them about the narcissist when you finally open up. They will find it hard 'to see' because they will not have witnessed the abusive behaviour that you are now describing to them. The narcissist will have ensured to have always worn their mask in the public domain.

I do now sincerely believe that the Nex's smear campaign against me began long before we finally split up.

The Nex had already put his flying monkeys in place.

What was so laughable about the Nex's choice of flying monkeys was the fact that these same people had not escaped the wrath of him in the past. His sister-in-law had always been described by him as 'stuck up' and someone who always looked down her nose at him, though I never saw this, but just three weeks after we had split up I was unceremoniously unfriended on Facebook by her. She informed the Nex that she had done this because she did not see me as part of the family anymore and therefore she would be damned if I were going to see anything about them. Of course, I now know that the smear campaign against me had already been waged with these relatives before we finally split up. Likewise, one of his brothers, who I had always thought was a decent person and who I had always got on with whenever I saw him also became one of the flying monkeys. I even looked after him for a week after their mother died in 2010 but this did not stop him morphing into a duplicate of the Nex quite literally overnight! I would hear them both bitching not only about me, but also my poor children, who had done absolutely nothing wrong to either of them. Seriously, it was so eye opening to me. You think you know people then they show their true colours to you. This is the same brother-in-law that thought it was perfectly acceptable, even funny, to post a comment on a post the Nex had put on Facebook, which my daughter could see as she was still friends with the Nex on there. The post by the Nex had asked how he could get 'rid of a problem', aka me, and the brother-in-law had responded with a comment stating, 'get a gun licence'! My daughter was extremely upset to see this, as of course anyone would have been. This was also the same brother-in-law that the Nex once went on holiday with but who he swore that he would never go away again with as his brother had moaned so much. But then, again, I suspect the almighty smear campaign against me was well and truly in full swing and the brother-in-law may have felt justified based on the lies that he had been fed by the Nex. Only the Nex's sister and her family were unaffected by the smear campaign against me because she herself had suffered a six-month silent treatment from him and she had also witnessed his abusive behaviour towards one of his previous girlfriends as well.

For me, I was constantly validated over and over, because post-split, the narcissistic mask that the Nex had worn so well at times, had well and truly come off now. I was witnessing him in all his narcissistic glory, twenty-four/seven.

When you leave or divorce a narcissist, it will never be easy. I wish I had known this at the beginning because I could have been better prepared. I tried so hard to keep things amicable, even suggesting that I was happy to still food shop and cook for him. I know! What a numpty am I! I saw no point in animosity because I stupidly believed that it was what we both wanted. What I did not fully know then was the fact that I 'was' living with a narcissist and that 'my agreement' to the split had caused him a massive, humongous narcissistic injury. What followed was the fallout from this to which I am still feeling the ripple effects even now as I write this book.

A quote I recently read (author unknown) states, 'If being married to a narcissist is hell, divorcing a Narcissist is hell on steroids!'

I believe that the reason why a narcissist reacts this way to being divorced rather than if it was the other way round is to do with control. Or rather it is their loss of control and therefore they enact the kind of revenge that my Nex meted out to me.

A@awakeningwomensupport state, 'Invisible abuse is the most harmful kind of abuse because covert narcissists are so good at making you look like the 'crazy' and 'unstable' one for reacting to their abuse and no one else sees it'.

I have read some articles that talk about narcissists at the end of a relationship and that they will practice what is known as the 'Scorched Earth' policy which means that they will leave nothing but a burning wreckage of the relationship and even the victims' reputation trailing behind them. The narcissist will spear you because his version of events must be right and needs to be right. Their version of events must be believed by everyone beyond anything else. I think that pretty much sums up my circumstances with the Nex that is for sure!

For the narcissist, it will become all about winning and their truth prevailing, whatever the cost emotionally or financially, along the way. I have an email where the Nex cites that he is going to destroy me and bring me down with him. Another one where he tells me that he is going to make me suffer and that his life now means nothing, and he is not going to worry about it because I will be right down there with him. These emails did not come at the start but rather a few months later. What shouts out the most about this behaviour is the hypocrisy when he tells people that he really wanted the split. His actions and words most certainly do not sit with this kind of behaviour, in fact they tellingly betray it.

Depending on your narcissist and which type they are, you may be lucky enough to find that they just walk away without a backward glance. The longer you have been in the relationship though, the less likely this will be.

Once I had outed my Nex as a narcissist he quickly projected this and then claimed to everybody that in fact I was the narcissist instead. He fed that lie to everyone he possibly could, that I was the abuser and that he was the victim. He is still spinning that lie presently. He still perversely believes that he is the victim. The most recent of all emails I received from him while writing this book was in relation to some of the hedges in the garden that needed to come out. He bleated on about how he had had to remove a section as the wall had fallen over and that the council would sue us for people's injuries. Of course, it had not fallen over! This was just a typical 'over the top' reaction from him. I merely replied to this with factual points ensuring that there was no emotion in my email. He replied with an abusive email so my subsequent reply to this consisted of one sentence, 'Ever the Drama Queen'. Nothing else whatsoever. His abusive reply back left me speechless as it was such a typical narcissistic one, full of grandiosity and sense of entitlement (of course it was!), He basically stated that I still loved him and that I could not let him go, and that he had a beautiful girlfriend now and that I needed to find a man soon! The fact that it was me who had really ended us and that I had filed for the divorce was completely lost on him. I did not get angry by it at all and in fact I am still laughing right now about that email as I could clearly see the narcissism pouring out with every word that he had wrote. But then you know this story already.

Think about the narcissists mask. Their carefully constructed false persona that is presented to the world. They cannot at any cost let the world know the real them. Because others will not have seen their maliciousness towards you, witnessed their lies, or the abuse, the control, the manipulation, the gaslighting, the sheer evil behaviour that you have suffered, their lies will flow freely from them. This does not mean that the narcissist now accepts that they 'are' a narcissist. Rather, they simply hold the distorted view that everything is your fault, everything was your fault and that you, the real victim, are to blame for everything that was wrong in the relationship. After all, it could not possibly have been them. They are perfect, superior, faultless, blameless, and on it goes.

You will find it extremely difficult to say and do nothing in your defence when you are being smeared, believe me as I know from experience, because you feel so aggrieved at all the lies being told about you, but you have to not let yourself react as this is the only way to prevail. If you engage with the narcissist, protest their lies, they will simply up their game so they can ultimately win what they perceive to be a battle against you. All the while they are relishing in the role of playing the victim by engaging their flying monkeys against you.

The Nex told his family so many lies and played the victim for what he said was my abuse against him. I now believe that it did start prior to our split because he knew deep down that I was not happy and that I was tolerating his abusive behaviour towards me less and less. Just two months prior I had come back from Japan after visiting my daughter and he had picked me up from the airport. He got out of the van but made no attempt to greet me despite not having seen me for two weeks. Once we were in the van and heading home I pointedly asked him if he had missed me while I had been away, and he scoffed the answer no at me whilst snorting at the same time for more emphasis. I fell silent. He then quickly covered this by saying that he was only joking and of course he had missed me, but the damage and hurt was already done. My son who was with us heard every word and he just looked at me with what can only be described as pity. He knew what the Nex could be like with his tactless comments and his 'hidden' abuse.

When my daughter left for Japan at the age of twenty to study the language, I endured the 'empty nest syndrome' as she was the last one to leave. I was extremely proud of her but was also heartbroken that I would not see her for over seven months until I was going on holiday there for her twenty first birthday. The Nex just looked on with scorn and informed me that I should just be able to let go and switch off and so as always I just hid my feelings from him. At the time, I put his lack of understanding and empathy down to the fact that he did not have children of his own.

Again, not long before we split up, he had yet again verbally insulted my mother despite knowing that she was under investigation for dementia. Remember me telling you that it was one of his favourite abuse tactics because he knew that it offended and hurt me when he did it? Well, I pointedly told him that I would not tolerate it anymore and that if he did it again we were over. It took him an hour and half to come back at me with a response and when he did, he just popped his head around the lounge door and said, 'About what you said earlier. You know where the door is,' then he just disappeared off into another room. Such was his narcissistic mentality and his sense of entitlement to say whatever he liked.

I also mentioned in a previous chapter that I would tell you more in detail about the punishing virtual silent treatment that I endured for almost seventeen months before we finally split up. Think back to the falling out with the two friends and why the fall out occurred which was in the February or March of 2017. Also, his then refusal to attend couples' therapy. It was the June of this same year that I then got the abuse from him about paying towards the household bills. From that point on, we barely socialised together anymore because he insisted that going forward we would not only split the bills fifty/fifty but also any social activities. Another ridiculous action when you think that for the last thirteen years I had paid for almost all the past socialising that we had done. The Nex also started sitting in another room to watch TV, blaming me (of course he did!) by stating that I wanted to watch different programmes to him. Even if I said to come and watch a movie with me he would make an excuse up about already having started a programme. We had a brief respite with a holiday (that I paid for!) in the September of that same year. We then put the house on the market in the October in response to the loss of one of our cats from an RTA. I remember clearly the day that we were going on the holiday because this cat had only just gone missing but rather than go out and help look for him, or even help me with the packing for the holiday while I looked for the cat, he proceeded to sit for what was ten hours straight just watching the TV instead. I was working from home that day, I packed for the holiday and kept going out searching for the missing cat all while another of the rescue cats had collapsed and needed urgent veterinary care. He left me to attend the vets alone and only pitched up when the realisation that this cat may die dawned on him and he did not want his holiday spoiling. There are so many other minor events carried out that year where I simply failed to join up all the dots. It was only after the split the following June 2018 and when he had asked me if I would compromise and be friends with his two friends again that it all came crashing down together for me! I finally put all the pieces together. I finally realised that I had been silently punished and devalued consistently and continuously for almost seventeen months!

During this period when my beloved cat went missing, and the Nex could not be bothered to go out and look for him, I will never know whether that had a direct link to the cat's death or not, but for me, it probably really was the beginning of the end because I just could not help but blame him for the cats death, and try as I might, I just could not shake off this feeling I had against him. So much so, that the following November, two months later, after yet another devaluation from him, I seriously considered ending the marriage and finally having the courage to walk away. In the following January, a further two months on when another period of abuse and devaluation occurred, my daughter finally said to me, 'You have got to do it, Mum, you have got to just walk away, because I cannot see it ever changing'. I knew deep down that she was right, and I think that the Nex also knew the end was finally coming, because a narcissist can sense when you are pulling away from them.

Trust me when I now say that this abusive behaviour towards me during a devaluation was a 'Walk in the park' compared to the absolute nightmare that was to follow post-split.

When I filed for divorce in the October of 2018, four months after we had split up, I cited unreasonable behaviour and I also cited him as being a narcissistic sociopath so I could explain logic behind the reasons that I had had to put on the divorce papers. This was also when I had started to have an understanding on narcissism. I also strongly believed that he displayed sociopathic traits too. I informed the Nex that I had had to use true accounts as reasons and that it was just what was required by law. He clearly did not listen to this or just chose to ignore it because when the papers finally arrived for him (I was away with work thankfully) he went ballistic. (Of course, he did!). I proceeded to get the most vile and abusive emails from him in response to the papers. How could I say such nasty and untruthful things about him! How could I lie about the reasons I had given! What a hateful woman I was! That his brother and sister-in-law (the flying monkeys) also thought that I was hateful, and they had told him that he should not sign the papers until I had changed the reasons. I was very polite, told him that it was not done to 'get at him', and that I had pre-warned him of what to expect. I even sent him screenshots of the government website that explained about the only reasons they would accept and that saying 'They didn't make you a cup of tea in the mornings' simply was not enough. The next morning, I got an email from the Nex to say that he had now signed the papers and sent them back. His email also said that he was now a broken man (classic narcissistic expression!). I later went on to learn that he had written to the judge with the return of these divorce papers and agreed with some of the reasons that I had listed!

I mean WTF?!

At this same time that the Nex did his usual knee jerk irrational over the top reaction to the divorce papers, he also relocated everything into his bedroom. By this I mean that while I was away with work he moved a sofa, a TV and his entire office contents into this room so that when I returned home, a lock was now in place on the bedroom door, and I could not access my clothes or any other of my belongings that were still in there. He briefly allowed me in to retrieve them. He then went on to tell everyone that he was a prisoner in his own home. He literally got off on telling everyone this outrageous lie because it played into his false attempt at playing the victim. He had placed himself there. He still used the kitchen, the bathroom and the utility room at his leisure though! Furthermore, I now know that he also had a hidden agenda for relocating to his bedroom and this was because he had started seeing his latest victim the previous month and wanted to be able to contact her and speak to her without me knowing.

A narcissist will slander you to all and sundry. To anyone that will listen. Their family, their friends, they will even engage them in their lies. The Nex tried to get my daughter on-board with his lies by stating that her father had left me because of my behaviour. She corrected him and informed him of the truth, that her father, by his own admission to her was at fault, and that our break-up was entirely his fault and the reasons why.

She may as well have been talking to the plant pot! Like a true narcissist, he only wanted to believe his version of the events and as I have said before, a narc's lies will become their truths, and this certainly was the case here. The Nex just could not accept that it was not my fault but in fact was my ex-husband's fault. It simply did not sit well with his lie and his beliefs. I had been with my first husband since I was nineteen years old, and he was my only serious relationship before the Nex. We remained amicable after our break-up and today, still are. Instead, the Nex would often hurl abuse at me that my ex had left me because of how abusive I am, and how bad I am and so on. That my ex would agree with the Nex that everything was my fault. He did not and would not accept the true version of events.

Of course, in the beginning you try and defend yourself to the hilt, such is your indignation at their lies and their smear campaign against you. At first, I produced evidence after evidence to prove the facts, but I still felt that his version of events, his lies, were the ones being believed. You do literally get to the point where you beat yourself up right up until you reach that point where you realise that you must just let it go. For your own health and sanity, for your own peace of mind.

When I tell you that a Narcissist can carry a grudge and embark on a smear campaign to their grave, I am being deadly serious, excuse the pun!

At times, you will feel like you are on a battleground or in a battle arena. Their lies can have some real damaging effects on you. The loss of your job, children, even your liberty. It is extremely important to keep a record and notes of what is said for your truth. If possible, make recordings of conversations that will be changed in their version and account of them.

Post-split the Nex used to goad me into a reaction then promptly shove his phone in my face and say, 'I'm videoing you now to show everyone how crazy you are.' Seriously I am not making that up! This is a classic example of reactive abuse. It really is exactly what it says it is. You, the victim, have finally reacted to the torrent of abuse, the lies, blame-shifting and the gaslighting that your narc has meted out against you. Your reaction is not normally 'you' but is driven by their behaviour that has 'tipped you over the edge'. Of course, the viewer will not have seen what led up to the response from the victim. The narcissist is clever enough to ensure that this is not captured on the video. This was exactly what the Nex's videos did, they did not show his deliberate goading of me. I have a prime example to share with you in the 'No Contact' chapter.

This is of course a favourite trick of the covert narcissist, just like the Nex is.

A narcissists' sense of entitlement will see them hacking your phone, your laptop, iPad, emails, social media accounts, listening in on your conversations, eavesdropping, etc. This is born out of their desire to control you and their sense of entitlement that they can control you. And of course, for fuel.

My Nex, obviously, did all the above to me. He also stole my postal mail and then lauded it over me in emails by trying to goad me into a reaction. He then went on to have the audacity to claim that I had been stealing his mail and opening it! A classic narcissist projecting right back at me. He also accused me of stealing his passport when he was going away to Fuerteventura that Christmas, which was the most ludicrous thing ever. When I asked him why he thought I would want his passport, he accused me of trying to jeopardise his holiday which was the most ridiculous thing ever because that would have in turn spoilt my own Christmas with my family. This very fact though was completely lost on him when I pointed it out.

If the narcissist discards you, he will most likely not be discarding you permanently at this stage. He may try several hoovers over the following months and even years, dependant on his current supply. Of course, these hoovers may not be positive ones at all but rather malign hoovers simply because the narc remembers what a good fuel supply you used to be.

I received several malign hoovers from my Nex post-split but did not know that this was what they were at that time. It was not until I read an article by HG Tudor on hoovers that I commented on his article and asked the question as to whether my emails from the Nex could be considered as hoovers. He replied! I have to say that I genuinely had 'fan fever' when he did! I seriously respect all his work, even if he is a greater narcissist. His insight is unreal and compelling to read about. Well, his response was to say yes and that in fact the emails were called malign hoovers. On further reading about these, I also learnt that their primary purpose was to extract fuel from you. Imagine the narcissist sat at his keyboard having sent you the email that contains the malign hoover. Of course, they do not realise that this is what they have just sent you but rather they just know that what they have said in the email or text message will hurt or offend you. Now picture their teeny tiny dicks quivering at the thought of this perceived pain that they are causing you. They will quite literally be peeing their pants in glee!

You must realise that a malign hoover is not designed to draw you back into the relationship but rather is to gain fuel, and to punish you as well. If you know that this malign hoover is a response to something that you have done or said, or even won (court case) then take comfort in the knowledge that you must have wounded them and allow yourself a pat on the back and a little laugh in private!

Examples of malign hoovers are, 'I'm gonna get you for this', 'We'll see who will win', 'You fucking bitch', 'You're out of control!', and 'You'll be sorry'. The point I am trying to make about their hoover attempts is that a narcissist will use all other methods that they can to try and hoover you and get a reaction from you. They will try this by both direct and indirect methods, even engaging other family members and friends of yours in the process. The Nex used my daughter, a friend and even my ex-sister-in-law (my brother's ex-wife) to spread his poison by sending them malign hoover messages. He even made threats to spread malicious lies about one of my friends such was his evil and maliciousness nature!

The only attempt at a positive hoover that the Nex made directly to me rather than electronically and after we had been split up a few months, and more importantly in the early days of the divorce proceedings, was to say to me that even though he was not in love with me anymore, he did still love me! Another WTF moment for me, I can tell you. When I asked him to explain exactly what he meant, he stated that he wanted to 'Feel in love' again. Cue his need for the love-bombing phase, the need for admiration and adoration and the need for a new victim who would be his shiny new toy. By this point, I recognised this and had to supress the laugh that was bubbling up in my throat! This was also when he had recently embarked on a relationship with his latest victim too.

A slight digression there so back to the point in hand. Which is if you are the one to discard the narcissist then woe betide you!

This will be the biggest narcissistic injury that you could ever inflict on them.

How dare you!

You, the victim, are not meant to 'ever' get rid of the narcissist!

The narc will turn nasty and vicious for sure. He or she will want to punish you any which way that they can.

The smear campaign will come thick and fast. You will be dragged through court. They will fight you for everything. They will fight you on everything; custody of the children, property, house, business, pensions, spousal support, even if they do not need it. They really will try and make your life hell so that they can regain power and control. The narcissist will put out such a pity play and pretend to be the victim and you are the abuser in a way that you have never seen or experienced before. They will lie about absolutely everything and anything.

I have given you an example already how the Nex lied on the official court Form-E. He also lied in further subsequent court documents and deliberately misled the court at the FDR hearing with his torrent of lies.

It is important to note that after the FDR court hearing that we had had, he really upped the ante against me. Only eight weeks prior to this my son had been home to look after my cats for me while I was away with my daughter. Note we were still living under the same roof at this point. The Nex had ceased having anything to do with the cats some five months prior, hence my son coming that September to look after them and again this was planned for eight weeks later in the November. At no point, after our split had either of my children got involved and they still spoke to the Nex when they saw him. That is up until that November when the Nex decided that for him all pretence was now off and he did not care if my son now saw the real him, or what evil really lurked beneath his false persona. To cut a long story short he got the police out on my son, told them he felt intimidated by my son's presence in the house and the upshot was my son had to subsequently leave. Please let it be noted that my son has such a quiet temperament that it was absurd for the Nex to state he felt intimidated by him, and the police even said as such to my son. He did not really feel intimidated at all. He was just so pissed off after the FDR hearing, and that I was on holiday again, that he hit out in the only way a narcissist can with my poor son bearing the brunt of it. Yep, there goes another glimpse of the true, real, nasty and evil man that was and is the Nex.

On another occasion post-split, he suspected that there was a hole in the Catio but instead of notifying me so that I could keep the cats in until the hole was found he did not, and subsequently one of the cats did get out! Fortunately, my son and I found him after four hours of searching. The Nex just could not see what he had done wrong and went one step further and took great offence at the suggestion that he had done it deliberately. Of course, he did and of course, he had done it deliberately. Remember what I have previously said that they will use anything against you to hurt and to punish you and he knew full well that if one of the cats got out and got hurt then this would devastate me. Think of the fuel this would have fed him.

Another incident involving the same cat post-split was when the Nex left the bathroom window open, and the cat got out again. It was first thing in the morning, and the Nex trotted downstairs for the first time that day in his dressing gown, post shower, asking on his descent down the stairs whether I had let the cat escape when I took the rubbish out. Straight away I knew something had happened because for all he knew at that point the cat could have been downstairs in the lounge with me. Such was his stupid mentality that I would not suspect something was amiss by this ridiculous question. More important is to note the immediate attempt to blame-shift and project on to me. I knew instantly what must have happened! He had left the bathroom window open after his shower then not closed the bathroom door when he left. He of course denied it and kept blaming me for inadvertently letting the cat out with the rubbish which was so preposterous because I had fed the cat after the rubbish had gone out! Such was his narcissism that even though he knew he was to blame by leaving the bathroom window open he could not and would not just accept the fact that it was his fault and more notably just admit to it. So, in true narcissistic style he projected, he deflected, and he shifted the blame squarely on to me.

As someone once stated on Quora, 'Narcissists are vile nasty creatures!'

If like me, you have recognised and outed them to their face as a narcissist they will then try and destroy you just to maintain their false image and façade.

Another quote on Quora that I think is so accurate is, 'Narcissists try to destroy your life with lies because their life can be destroyed with the truth'.

The more 'dirt' you have on them the more vicious and eviller they will be. They will fight you tooth and nail to try to bring you down. They will draw anyone that they can from both sides to persuade them that they are the victim, and you are the abuser. I know I keep repeating this, but it is better to be prepared for this at the start. And if you have already been smeared then hopefully this book and this chapter will explain why, and what to do about it. The narcissist will try to get anyone who will listen to their lies and maybe even believe these lies, to hate you as much as they do, and they will damage you in whatever and whichever way that they can.

Such is the narcissists campaign of hate against you that you will be tempted to back down for your own peace of mind, but you must not. You must stand up to the narcissist and show them that that you cannot and will not be bullied and intimidated any longer. At the end of the day, a narcissist is another 'school ground' bully, albeit far more dangerous, and the only way to deal with a bully is to stand up to them.

By going 'No Contact', which we look at in the next chapter, this is a way of standing up to the narcissist because you will no longer tolerate or respond to their bullshit.

There is absolutely no boundary on earth that a narcissist will not cross to lessen his or her own narcissistic injury that has been caused by a separation or a divorce.

As well as lying in court proceedings they will also deliberately drag the proceedings out. They will fail to give full disclosure in any financial proceedings, instead it will come in dribs and drabs. If they do perceive a 'win' at court they will use this to show that 'they were right'. They have won. To the narcissist this is a symbolic trophy which in turn is seen as you still providing them with their precious fuel. By going to court in the first place the narcissist does not have to take responsibility if it does not go their way.

For the Nex, the outcome at the FDR hearing was not the one he was hoping for, and he knew that his lies would manifest at the final hearing where evidence can be presented (it is not at FDR) if it continued to this, so he 'jumped' before this point. He then dragged out the making of a consent order that 'he' had wanted and requested, and deliberately racked up my solicitor's bill on the way. He even had the audacity after he had signed it to claim that he had only signed it under duress and that both myself and my solicitor had bullied him into signing it! My solicitor was quick to point out that it had indeed been the Nex's request for the making of the order and that no one had stood over the Nex forcing him to sign it! Again, such is the ridiculous mentality of the delusional narcissist and their attempt to always play the role of the victim. Unbeknown to me, he then went one step further after the signed document had been sent to the courts to then write to them and further claim that he was coerced into signing it. This delayed the order by six months and nearly cost us the sale of the house and when I challenged the Nex about it he claimed he had merely written to the courts about the dining room table! Such were and are his pathological lies.

With any court proceedings even though it appears that they are ceding control, with this very action the narcissist can still maintain an appearance of control.

Even when they are presented with the truth, a narcissist will still lie. This is because a narc will only believe their 'own truth' even when it is clearly and blatantly a lie. Hence the Nex 'perjuring' himself by signing his Form-E as a sworn truthful document that was littered with lies. He also admitted at the first court hearing that he had falsified his business accounts but immediately blamed his mortgage advisor for doing it! He then later went on by email to state that it was all my fault that he had said this in court and that I had bullied him into telling the judge this! Well of course he did! After all he was Mr Blameless! He was Mr Narcissist!

The Nex deliberately racked up my solicitor's bill just because he could. This is how nasty, vindictive and malicious they can be against you. He argued with my solicitor even when no argument or discussion was called for. When I had to send emails to him direct to discuss the division of household bills, these were merely straight forward emails, but the Nex always managed to turn them into a major drama, and I would get long, abusive email responses from him. I did learn to see right through them in the end. I ceased to let them intimidate me, or harass me, and furthermore, I knew full well that he would be feeding his flying monkeys' a complete pile of crap, full of lies, stating that everything was my fault. I learnt to let none of this bother me any longer because I knew the truth, I had the emails to prove the truth, and most important of all, my family and friends knew the truth, and this was all that mattered to me. This was all the validation that I needed.

Once upon a time, his behaviour used to manipulate and control me, it also used to worry and even frighten me, but now I just saw it for what it really was. I finally saw him for the pathetic narcissist that he was. Now I had learnt to just let it make me laugh out loud and they do say that laughter is the best medicine.

Another example of the narcissist's sense of entitlement and how it continued post-split with the Nex is his comments to me after his birthday, a few months post-split. He truly expected a birthday card from my parent's and did not hide his indignation at the lack of one. Likewise, the Christmas that followed soon after, it was six months post-split by then and he genuinely expected me to buy him a present and stated as such! Of course, he was not expected to have bought me one back. I have told you already about the worst one by far which was his expectation to have attended my beloved late father's funeral. He said after it that he would never forgive me for not letting him go.

Clearly this was the least of my worries! He had the audacity to justify his indignation by stating to me that my father had been his best friend! This was so far removed from the truth. He barely saw my father, maybe once or twice a year, never picked up the phone to just chat with him, and when he did see my dad, the Nex just future-proofed by saying that he would repair things for my father and help with jobs around his house but then never did. And especially not when my dad really could have done with this help after his heart surgery in 2016. What this merely highlights and what we all know, and for those yet to find out, is the fact that a narcissist is basically full of shit, was full of shit and will always be full of shit!

In fact, at the very beginning of my relationship with the Nex my father called him a bullshitter which did not go down well with the Nex I can tell you. The Nex proceeded to use his art of love-bombing on my father and won him over in the end, but my dad was always a good judge of character. I just wish I had listened to him right at the very start!

Another example of lack of empathy was demonstrated again by the Nex when his favourite cat died a few weeks post-split. I was away for a few days with my daughter as we were looking at university accommodation for her. Once we received the news we cut our stay short and returned home. We subsequently organised a private cremation for the cat and the Nex came with us to pick up her ashes. On the car journey back, the Nex was messaging and joking with a friend in the back of the car! I was astounded but at this point did not join up all the dots as I had not yet learnt enough about narcissists and their lack of empathy.

The Nex also thought it was perfectly okay to continue to eat my food and drink that I had bought for myself. This continued long after the split and despite the split having occurred eighteen months prior by this point, and despite the animosity that was now prevalent between us, he still did it. Not only did he continue to eat my food and drink my drink, but he also used my toilet rolls, washing tablets, toiletry items, etc. He really was clueless to his outlandish behaviour and of course it was his innate sense of entitlement that led to this pattern of behaviour. I did not rise to it or say anything because to do so would have provided him with fuel and I could not be sure that as well as his sense of entitlement, the added supply of fuel was also the reason for his actions. Another comical example of the Nex's sense of entitlement was to still load up the dishwasher with his used pots thus not only using my dishwasher tablet and having me set it going, then emptying it after, I was thus washing and putting his pots away for him. Still carrying out my role of housekeeper.

The Nex went away for a long weekend just a few weeks after we had split up and automatically expected to be able to use my car to drive to his destination which was a good five-hundred miles round trip. When I explained that I wanted to sell it as it only had a few hundred miles on it, I got the biggest pity play you can ever imagine! I was spoiling his holiday, I was doing it deliberately, he wanted to go and reminisce about his childhood, and I was stopping this. The fact that he had a motorbike he could go on or even catch a train was irrelevant. The fact that I wanted to sell the car was irrelevant. The fact that I was not keen on over five hundred miles being put on the car was irrelevant. The fact that we had split up and were no longer together was irrelevant to him! Such was the Nex's sense of entitlement. Of course, I gave in. I let him use the car. I did not receive a thanks for it though. Well of course I did not! He expected it and as far as he was concerned, he was entitled to it. It would not even surprise me if I were to discover that he had in fact used the car for his first meeting with his latest victim!

The Nex also continued to play his mind games with me in abundance once we had split up. He continuously blocked my car in on the driveway deliberately so I could not use it. I did not say anything to him and eventually I just moved the car away from the house. He put objects on my toiletries in the shower so I would have to move them to get to mine. I again just ignored it and bought a hanging rack instead. I knew what he was up to. So absurd and childish was his behaviour. All to try and get a reaction out of me. He even used items of cookware that I had bought myself post-split then did not clean them! Interestingly it was not until after the court FDR hearing and the outcome he did not want, that he really upped his childish games. It became a pattern that if he were angry at something he would mete out a mind game against me. Turning on all the lights in the house and then going out was another of his favourite tricks. I know what I am describing is petty, but it gives you an example of just how ridiculous their behaviour can be towards you.

Another one was playing a CD of a favourite female artist of mine called Ava Cassidy that he had never liked. He used to state that it made him want to stick his fingers down his throat as it is what I would call easy listening music. Suddenly one of this artist's CDs would be regularly blasted out at full pelt reverberating all over the house. This could also have been a mirroring attempt by him of his latest victim if she happened to like the artist too. Who knows? Anything is possible when you are dealing with a narcissist. Most recently he had acquired a cushion which I presume came from his latest victim with some of this artists lyrics on so like the true narcissist that he is, he deliberately left the cushion outside of his bedroom in an attempt to triangulate me. What made this even more laughable is that the cushion was at risk of one of the cats 'marking' it by peeing on it because of him leaving it on the floor outside his bedroom door! This merely demonstrated that his 'pleasure' from the gift was much less than his need to try and triangulate me.

The Nex also put my distinct 'Exorcist' ringtone onto his mobile phone after we had split up. I had used this as my ringtone since mobile phones had been invented, no lie! I mean him now using it. WTF was that all about?! Creepy or what! Seriously, I am sure a comedy sketch could be born out of his ridiculous mind game behaviour towards me! Except it is and was far from funny at the time. He did change it again of which another relevant incident will be explained later.

The hacking of my phone and so on is also a typical narcissistic trait. The narc justifies this appalling behaviour to themselves due to their extreme sense of entitlement.

If your narc has always used violence against you, this is further justified by them because of their sense of entitlement because in their warped opinion you disobeyed them.

Essentially when using a smear campaign against you what the narcissist is achieving with the use of this smear campaign is to put their victim on the defensive while at the same time masking their aggressive behaviour. They are hoping for a double whammy in that their poor victim will be so tied up trying to bat the smear campaign away and prove their innocence while the narcissist just continues their path of destruction unblemished.

Anne Bona states 'Prolonged exposure to a Narcissist can... Lead to insanity'.

The author of 'Object of my Affection', Rokelle Lerner, states 'Since narcissists anticipate that abandonment is going to happen, they posture themselves so that they are in charge of the exit.'

She goes on further to say, 'In relationships, narcissists will provoke those around them to leave by being cruel, neglectful or abusive. Or they will regularly threaten abandonment to make sure their partner stays adequately anxious and attentive to their needs.'

I can confidently apply both statements to the Nex.

I have already told you about his use of 'The end of the relationship routine' which was meted out after almost every single argument that we had. I use the term 'argument' loosely because as you now know from what I have told you, he instigated the start of every single one and also managed and dictated their outcome.

Interestingly, in relation to her first quote, the Nex used to say to me in the first few years of our relationship, 'Promise me you'll never leave me'. I now realise that this was a narcissistic 'Pity Play' so that I would feel sorry for him and provide him with even more attention. I have also come to realise that just maybe subconsciously the Nex also knew that eventually everyone did end up leaving him because of his abusive behaviour towards them, but he just did not know or acknowledge this.

Because the narcissist needs other people's validation that their version of lies is the truth they deliberately will create manipulative, slanderous, and totally outrageous stories about their victim to try and convince everyone else that the narcs version is the real truth. The fact that you have challenged their fantastical image of themselves, they will do anything and everything that they can to maintain the fantasy that they are always good, all while perceiving that their poor victim is the evil one. Once you, the victim realise that this is what is happening you can start to decipher their lies, wade through them, deflect them and maybe even come out the other side of them relatively unscathed. Even if you do not, you can find solace in the knowledge that you know they are lies, that you 'understand' the lies and that you can finally rise above them.

Remember those videos of you where they have captured you 'finally losing the plot'? These will be rolled out on a regular basis for everyone the narc wants on board to prove that you are the 'bad guy', the crazy one. With the narcissist leaving out the first part of the scene of the video where they have goaded you into a response with their vile abuse, so you were just literally defending yourself in what is captured on the video, they have now managed to frame you in what is really an act of self-defence that has now become you being the vile abuser. All the while the narcissist is thinking, 'How dare you question me!', 'You deserve everything that is coming to you!'

More examples of post-split mind games that the Nex played was despite claiming that 'our' house was 'his' house was to never ever clean it! Not that he ever did during the relationship, but this became ever more prevalent after it. He did at one point agree to clean the bathroom that he had never used before, both of us taking it in turns, but this only lasted for a few months. He then proceeded to deliberately leave the shower cubicle smeared in soap, shampoo and whatever else he could find knowing that I would then be the one to have to clean it. Piss stains on the floor near the toilet and even leaving his shit stains in the toilet pan! Gross I know! All purely designed though to extract fuel from me with the thought that I was then cleaning it all up, cleaning up after him. Remember that at this stage I was 'No Contact' with him, so his previous steady supply of fuel levels was constantly depleted. I simply would just laugh at the childish absurdity and grossness of it all and have satisfaction knowing that it did not wind me up one bit, rather that I was merely now seeing and experiencing the real him, I was seeing the narcissist that he was in all of his blazing glory.

I mentioned triangulation in the index of terminology but have so far only just touched on this in a few earlier scenarios. Generally, its use in a narcissistic abusive relationship is to destabilise the victim by the narcissist bringing another person into the relationship or interaction of it for the sole purpose of belittling the victim. That can be through having multiple affairs or just using a third person to hurt the first.

In a post relationship split with a narcissist, they will use triangulation as a means of controlling and manipulating communication between two parties. The narc will gossip, smear, and slander their victim by spreading false information about. They will even go as so far as to unleash a character assassination against their victim and their lies will be much more damaging and severe. Or like the Nex did, leave objects that had clearly been purchased by his latest victim where I could see them. Another trick the Nex used to triangulate not just me, but also his latest victim, was to tell her that I could not and would not let him go, and that I still loved him. This was done deliberately to make her feel insecure, and of course because his narcissistic sense of grandiosity was as such that he could not accept that someone would not and did not want him anymore. This poor woman then felt the need to send the Nex cards through the post to our matrimonial home where we both still resided until it had sold, with childish writing all over the back of the envelope. Saying things like, 'I love you', 'I miss you', 'I can't wait to see you' and so on. Things that an adult would normally only write inside a card to someone and not plaster all over the outside. These messages were written in such a way that the message she was sending was directly to me to say, 'hands off, he's mine'. This was completely the Nex's fault for triangulating the poor woman and having her believe that I still wanted him.

He used triangulation another time, when he had been with his latest victim almost a year, and he put a photo of them both cuddling each other as his Facebook profile picture. As he was still friends on Facebook with my daughter at this time he knew that she would see the photo and tell me about it. What was most noticeable about this is that he deliberately did it the day after I went on holiday with my daughter to Mauritius. In his warped mind, he had so obviously thought that it would bother me and that in doing this he would spoil my holiday, but it did not at all.

On another occasion, not long after my beloved father had died, the Nex had a stranger visit the house. I say stranger because it was someone I had never met before. When the Nex answered the door, he addressed this man by the name Alfie, which just so happened to be my late father's name. My daughter was convinced that this was done deliberately to upset me. The same man returned later that evening, and as I never heard him leave the house, I then spent a worried sleepless night thinking we had a complete male stranger in the house. Again, my daughter believed that this was also done deliberately and that the Nex had sneaked the man out of the house just to make it appear like he had stayed over. The Nex went on to deny all knowledge that this man had even called at the house in the first place, such was his stupidity and narcissism by attempting to gaslight me and make me believe that it had not happened. Fortunately for me not only had I called my daughter but also a friend was with me when the man first called at the house in the first place. Not surprisingly this man was never seen at the house again. A narcissist is also a very duplicitous liar!

I now believe that just a few months before our split, and because the Nex sensed the end was coming, he had me get him ready for his next victim, his next supply. Why? Because I helped him to lose his weight by cooking homemade soup every week and cooking healthy meals for him in the evenings. I also went with him on his shopping trips to buy new clothes, something he had never done in the past. I do not mean that this was a conscious act on his part but rather that he knew I was growing less tolerant of his behaviour towards me so maybe he did think on occasion consciously 'Is she going to leave me?' Whatever, I am almost sure that post-split he did indeed 'dine out' on an endless supply of Fuel when he looked back over this period and thought 'Silly bitch didn't even know what she was doing!'.

Post-split, and when he had found out about this book, he was stupid enough to state that only a narcissist could write about narcissists and narcissism. He was so clueless as to the personality of a narcissist despite projecting and calling me one, that he just did not realise that their very narcissism prevents a narcissist from being able to write about themselves and self-identify because they do not see themselves as one. He rather, thought that by writing this book, I was only able to do it because I was the narcissist and not him. To date, HG Tudor is the only one I know that can explain and talk about narcissism because of his therapy sessions, and because he is a greater narcissist who have more insight.

Another favourite of the narcissist is to twist their words, for instance, 'I only want what's best for you, I'm really not trying to control you'. Here they are trying to confuse you and throw you off guard.

Yet another firm favourite of the narcissists is to also use projection in their smear campaign against you. The reasoning behind this is because the narc is simply trying to attribute their own abusive behaviour and lies on to their victim purely for it to shift the blame and attention away from the narcissist.

To further validate their false persona and mask of this 'perfect' human being, they will tell as many lies as possible just so that they can present a different story to the truth and thus continue to hide their true real self and preserve their false image. The more they tell their lies and spread their slander against you, the more chance of them being believed so in their delusional narcissistic mind, they start to believe their lie as the truth.

If you are ever approached and challenged about 'the lies' that you are spreading about the narcissist just ask them, 'And what exactly did I (the victim) do next?' You can bet a million dollars that for them the story ended before that point!

A quote I once read said, 'A person who has nothing to lose will help you lose everything you ever worked for'.

Welcome to my world.

Maria Consiglio states, 'Narcissists reveal themselves by projecting their bad qualities onto you. They accuse you of the very things they are guilty of. They may even turn everything around and accuse you of being the narcissist. Narcissists cannot handle the reality of who they are, so they project it on to the people around them. They hate that part of themselves so the best way to get rid of the characteristics they despise is to say it is the other person who is engaging in those bad behaviours'.

AfterNarcissisticAbuse.com states, 'The Narcissist makes their partner feel like they are the one with the problem while projecting an innocent saintly persona to everyone around them. They will make their partner look bad and completely destroy their reputation in order to protect their false sense of self. The narcissist has already attained the trust and belief of everyone around them and anyone close to their partner that they are likely to turn to for help. The partner feels like they are suffering alone, no-one around them can see what the narcissist is really up to'.

@_Weareher states, 'Abusers are just as good at grooming allies as they are at grooming victims.'

Tobymac(hashtag)Speaklife states, 'If you don't like someone, dislike them alone. Don't recruit others to join your cause.'

Jekyll Doesn't Hide states, 'They never tell the full story… Just the part that makes you look bad.'

I did in fact report the abusive emails to the police, especially the ones where he made indirect threats to a couple of female friends of mine. The police logged these but took no further action. Likewise, when I had reported to them that he was stalking me, stealing my mail and hacking my accounts and phone, they chose to take no action whatsoever. When I had cause to inform another officer of another incident a few months later, he finally asked for the evidence to back up what I was reporting, and I duly sent it all to him. This evidence included screenshots of my phone being logged into places that I had not been, the most telling one obviously being the Fuerteventura one. I even provided the police officer with email proof of the Nex owning up to having mail of mine, but the cop's response was, 'Even if we did decide to do something about it, it's not in the public interest to pursue it'. All this did for me was prove why some women do not report incidents of narcissistic abuse, because they go unheard, unchecked, and most important of all, unchallenged because it is classed as non-violent domestic abuse, and in the opinion of the police this does not warrant investigating or prosecuting. I believe also that my local police force is governed by leftist woke attitudes and it sits far better with them to believe that a man could be the victim and the woman the abuser. Let us hope that lessons will be learnt here in future. This police lack of interest is also despite the recent new laws on coercive control and behaviour, of which the actions of a narcissist do sit well and truly inside of. Despite these new laws that are now in place, the police still do nothing, so the likes of the Nex and millions of other narcissists out there, just 'get away' with it, time and time again. Because there are specific guidelines as to what constitutes this kind of behaviour, for example, stalking, financial control and controlling how someone dresses, to name just a few, it is all the other forms of abuse associated with narcissism that are missed. These span physical, emotional and psychological abuse but the police are just not interested if it is not in the textbook or guidelines. We have all read of the tragic deaths where women have reported the abuse to the police, and it has gone ignored and this has led directly to the loss of a poor woman's life. The outcome of domestic abuse involving a narcissist will only improve when the police and the courts finally start to take it seriously.

As the victim it is only right that you get to tell your story.

A quote that I particularly like from @narcissistic-abuse-is-real goes,

'I owe you nothing in keeping your name clean when all you did was dirty my soul.'

Please do not let their use of a smear campaign prevent you from having the courage to finally walk away from your abusive narcissistic relationship. You, the victim, deserve to be free of their vile abusive behaviour. You, the victim, deserve a chance of happiness and contentment. Any 'mud' that they do sling at you can simply be 'wiped off'. The 'mud' that has stuck is not relevant. What you know to be the truth, and what your friends and family and other supporters know to be the truth is all that really matters.

Another quote I like by an unknown author is,

'Sooner or later a man who wears two faces forgets which one is real'.

@spiritual.goal say, 'I seriously wonder how many highly intuitive, intelligent and totally sane women have been labelled as crazy because they got too close to figuring out someone else's bullshit'.

Here is my favourite final quote to end this chapter on that really reverberates by Steve Maraboli;

'I get it.

Things change.

Relationships end.

But you can tell a lot about a person by the way they leave.'

Chapter Ten
No Contact Versus Grey Rock and Why Both Are Important

I am going to start this chapter with a quote that I have read which I thought was a perfect opening. The quote is by 'sold my soul to a narcissist',

'After walking away or going no contact, missing the abuser is the ultimate punishment. But it is not them you miss, it is the person they made you believe they were. The promises they never delivered. What you miss is something that never existed'.

How appropriate is this? How accurate is it?

I would say very.

You have already fought the battle between your head and your heart and have now accepted that your relationship with your narcissist was fake, was a lie, was not real. You may have already instigated 'No Contact'. You may be really struggling with instigating 'No Contact' for the very reasons the quote suggests. But going 'No Contact' really is the 'Go to' tool that the victim should and must use when dealing with the end of a relationship with a narcissist.

You will be so familiar by now with both turn of phrases, not just from what you have read in this book so far but no doubt also from what you have already maybe learnt prior to reading this book.

From a practical point of view achieving 'No Contact' is relatively easy, especially if no children are involved.

You must:

1. Block all calls, texts, emails, even change your number if you can.
2. Block them on all social media platforms, including their family and friends.

3. Move away to somewhere they will not find you. Crucial if dealing with a dangerous, Malignant or even violent lesser narcissist.
4. Avoid places the narcissist is likely to frequent.
5. Change 'all' your passwords to prevent hacking.
6. Remove your contact details from online sources.
7. If needed, apply for a non-molestation order or even a restraining order.
8. No meet ups with them
9. No 'bumping' into them
10. Take your pets with you. A narcissist may use your pet as a tool to 'get at you'.

I have given you the two scenarios I experienced with the Nex and my cats.

Another was during this same period where the Nex used to take this same cat into his bedroom with him and lock the door behind, thus preventing the cat from leaving. If I had been out, this cat and one of the others always greeted me at the door on my return. When he did not I always worried that he had got out of the Catio again, so I would call him and rattle biscuits for him. The Nex used to hear me doing this but would refuse to let the cat out, preferring to leave me worrying as to whether he had escaped again or was just locked in the Nex's room. When I finally caught him red handed grabbing the cat off the stairs to take up with him, he refused to put him back down. In the end he did but not before launching a tirade of abuse at me. This behaviour resulted in my solicitor having to write to him and asking him to refrain from doing it as this cat had a heart condition and locking him in his room just exacerbated this. So instead, to still be able to play his nasty mind games and narcissistic tricks he then started to leave his door open and ajar to entice the cat into his bedroom once again. This is in direct contrast to the lies he had told everyone that I was the abuser, and he was in fear of his life, thus having to always lock his bedroom door after him! I know. Another example of 'You really could not make it up!'

Yet another example of his cruel behaviour involved a tank of tropical fish that the Nex had acquired for himself a few years before we had split up. He tended to neglect these poor fish on a regular basis and in the last two years that I know of, did not once clean their tank out. Around another eighteen months later and well into our split, the heating element for the tank broke down. By now there was only two fish left in the tank that had not died. I gave it five days before I realised that the Nex did not care for the welfare of these poor remaining fish one little bit and in fact was more than happy to just let them die slowly. I on the other hand could not. So, I organised collection of the fish via Facebook and caught them and let them go to their new home. It took him a few months before he realised or cared that the fish had gone!

For me, the most difficult part has not been able to achieve full 'No Contact' for the simple fact that we had to still live in the matrimonial home until it was sold. Well, I say we did, but that is not strictly true. He could have moved out but purely chose not to. 'Of course, he did!' I hear you all shout. And yes, pun aside, it really was a pantomime at times such was his ridiculous and childish outlandish behaviour and mind games towards me. He made my solicitor put a clause in the consent order 'he' wanted drawn up that stated if the Nex left the property I would solely be responsible for the bills. What a waste of time that was! He never had any intention of leaving the marital home (of course he did not!), he was just future proofing again, like the typical narcissist that he is. He of course went on to blame me and said he was not leaving because of an alleged comment I had made about furniture (it never happened), and so I even offered to carry any furniture out of the house for him when he left but as I have already said, he merely replied that he was not going anywhere and of course he was not as he never did have any intention of leaving in the first place.

See, I told you it was a pantomime!

The continuous use of his mind games that he played around the house with my car, other items, the cats, the bathroom and so on. The hacking of my phone and accounts. Spying on me. I caught him one day on his knees in his bedroom, phone in hand peering into the lounge below where I was sitting! I do not know if he was videoing me or using his camera to zoom in on what I was doing on my laptop, but I quickly shut the curtains and never opened them again after that! I have no doubt at all that at some point there was probably a tracker on my car!

Another favourite of his was to switch on every single light in the house so we resembled Blackpool illuminations or something on the Vegas strip. Then he would return to his bedroom or even leave the house with all the lights still on and the house still ablaze in 'neon' glory. Such was the stupidity of his narcissistic behaviour. I of course, never said anything but simply turned all the lights off. He just obtained a slight hit of fuel from knowing I was doing this but no way near as much as if I had challenged him about it. As I have mentioned before, another trick of his was to play extremely loud music for up to two hours at a time. Again, I ignored it, I did not react and just put my headphones on and even on occasion sang along to the tunes! Again, only a trickle of fuel being provided to him because I did not challenge him about his behaviour.

A few weeks after we had split up and while I was still in the throes of the trauma bonding, I seriously wondered if I should stay with him or not, but I suspected that he was already on date sites, and I finally had my suspicions confirmed. He had recently bought himself a 'new' sports car after he had used mine for a holiday and had left his keys in the bedroom. I still had access to the main bedroom at this point as all my clothes were still in it. Of course, I could not resist a sneak peek at the car. The car was not new so required a manual satnav. As I was already suspicious that he was on date sites to which he denied emphatically, I checked his journeys and sure enough the proof was right there in all its glory! He of course continued to deny it and claimed that the journeys had been to pick up new wheels for the car. Bear in mind that they would not have fitted in the vehicle to bring home! All I cared about was the fact that I was not crazy like he had tried to convince me I was for believing he was seeing someone. Trust me when I say that I did not care that he was, in fact I felt so relieved because I wrongly believed that it meant he would finally leave me alone. He went on to retell this story to everyone he could that I had 'stolen' his keys from him or better still, 'broken' into his car. Of course, he would I know you are thinking, because you are hopefully now getting to know the mind of a narcissist! He did not really care at what I had done but rather was so incensed that he had been found out with his lies and I had called him out on them. This is a prime example of how crazy they make you feel and how they make you doubt yourself and your beliefs with their use of lies and gaslighting. I knew that he was on date sites, he knew that he was on date sites, but he still protested his innocence by making out like I was crazy for thinking it and even went so far as to state, 'How dare you think that of me!' and 'How bad are you to believe that I could do something like that!'

This is a classic example of a narcissist over dramatizing by stating that I had broken into his car. While we were still together when one of his devaluation phases began, he would say that we had not been getting on for months or even years which was ridiculous and over exaggerated as just literally prior to that nothing had been wrong, and the idealisation phase was in play.

He further went on to accuse me of the most ridiculous things after our split, but I simply ignored him. I cannot divulge these but save to say that they were always made 'after' he had been found out on a lie or a deception, like stealing my mail and keeping it. I also suspected that as well as my phone being hacked, the house was also possibly bugged. This really was not borne out of paranoia but rather from comments he would continue to make that could only have come from direct observation or him hearing it, especially when he was not even in the house. I did try to deliberately catch him out with various methods, but to no avail, so I stopped calling friends in the house and took the calls outside instead.

I know you must be thinking 'Why didn't you just leave?' but I could not. My job was territorial and home-based, my family and friends lived a two-hour drive away and I would not be able to get rented accommodation in either area with five cats in tow. It was far easier for him to leave and as I have just said, he stated to my solicitor that he was going to leave, even having it written into the court order, but of course he never did. Yet another prime example of a narcissist merely future proofing, but this time it was done maliciously and of course as part of his mind games and game playing against me, the one person that he was determined to destroy. Leaving the house in his warped mind was viewed as a loss and not a win. Plus, remaining in the property meant enacting his mind games came easily for him.

Such was the Nex's crazy making in the first year of our split that at times I did really think I was going mad. Then I learnt more about narcissism and finally I could see the mind games for what they really were. The continuous baiting, even the continued attempt of gaslighting, even though we were no longer together. Finally, in the May of 2019, some eleven months after we split up I went completely 'No Contact'. No speaking, no face to face. Any email he sent me was diverted to his solicitor. When I first notified him that I was not going to have direct contact with him again, after yet another mind game attempt, he emailed me and said 'Sorry, I didn't want it to come to us not speaking'. Well of course he did not! Where was he now going to get his continuous free flowing fuel from?!

230

This was a classic mid-range narcissistic trait. They are renowned for trying to prevent their victim going 'No Contact' and will use false apologies to try and achieve this.

When they see that you mean it, they will then raise the bar and up their level of poison against you in the smear campaign. They will not resort to violence but rather they will sulk, continue to play mind games, and use other methods of abuse against you.

The Nex proceeded to send malign text messages to my friends, send malign emails to me, text messages to my daughter. Play mind games around the home. Anything he could to get a rise out of me. He knew that all these messages would get back to me and he was hoping that I would then respond direct to him about them, but I did not. I forwarded all of them to his solicitor, notified the police and kept a log which they had asked me to do.

Throughout all this the narcissist will continue to play the role of the victim, just as my Nex did.

To anyone who will listen to them the narcissist will paint you as the devil. They must, because of their insatiable need for fuel. By getting sympathy and a listening ear, he or she is getting a supply of their precious fuel. And of course, it is because of their other essential need to protect the false façade and image, so they will deflect all the blame on to you.

By going 'No Contact', you will have to show no emotion whatsoever, no matter what the narcissist says or how they attempt to 'push your buttons'.

The key is to always show indifference and detachment.

Going 'No Contact' is purely a selfish act that you must make. To protect your own sanity. To free yourself from their toxic and abusive behaviour. You need to have time to breathe, to heal, to deal with any potential onslaught coming your way.

Like me, you may have attempted to keep things amicable, even going along with some of their manipulation attempts merely to keep the peace. Trust me when I say that it is just not worth it. While you are playing 'Mr Nice Guy or Gal', the narcissist is already plotting your downfall. The smear campaign against you will already be well and truly under way. By you being nice to them, it gives them the opportunity to 'set you up' for a fall. To capture that manic video moment of you reacting to their abuse. Trust me when I say that I really do speak from experience. By now, you have probably realised that you are dealing with a narcissist, and you are currently reading all that you can on the topic, but this will not prevent the onslaught that 'is' coming your way. What this will do instead, is arm you with a psychological defence system. Ready for the next step. Ready and hopefully prepared for when it comes.

What I learnt to do once I had established the 'No Contact' principle, because I could not implement it in its entirety while we were still living under the same roof, is, I learnt how to manage it successfully. How to avoid the mind games, how to divert them and how to deflect them away. How to lessen his supply of fuel by diverting all written contact to his solicitor. Of course, as far as fuel is concerned, he was still receiving it in trickles from the very fact that I had read the emails before sending them on to his solicitor, but this fuel was diluted sufficiently enough in its potency for him to not get his usual 'hit'. According to HG Tudor, this kind of fuel is known as thought fuel.

Of course, I was not always successful because I was guilty of occasionally breaking my own conviction of 'No Contact' and Grey Rock because after years of being conditioned into responding a certain way to the narcissist it is extremely difficult to just break that pattern and habit. So, there will be times when you will respond to them in a way that you know you are not supposed to, and you will break your own rules. The thing to do is not beat yourself up about it and punish yourself, but rather just accept it, and let it reinforce the fact that you do need to try and stick to your 'No Contact' or Grey Rock rules. The more you practice them the more you will be able to adhere to them. Just do not feel guilty because the longer you have been with your narcissist the harder it is.

The alternative strategy is to use the Grey Rock Method or Technique as I have mentioned above.

By using this, you will have learnt to display no emotion towards the narcissist. Answer them in monotonic syllables. You have not gone the full 'No Contact' because for whatever reason (usually children) you cannot. So, using the Grey Rock Method is a way of managing the narcissist because you do still have to deal with them.

If you use the Grey Rock Method, then ensure that you are fully prepared. Emotionally, financially, physically and of course, spiritually.

Interestingly, HG Tudor does not advocate using this method as he states that it does not work. He goes on to say that narcissists actually relish Grey Rock, and how it gives them what they want. He states that the victim is conned into thinking that it is working but in fact they are making life far harder for themselves.

The overall idea is to deal with them as passively and unemotionally as you can then walk away with your head held high.

For those of you already using the 'No Contact' method or about to use it the key principles to adhere to are:

1. Find healthy distractions
2. Think positive thoughts
3. Allow for moments of weakness
4. Know that it really will get easier
5. Keep strong and move on

If you are lucky enough to already be apart from your narcissistic ex so you do not have to physically see or interact with them, then all the above are so much easier to maintain.

For the initial couple of weeks, your Nex may not even know that you have deliberately gone 'No Contact' with them. This is good because it will allow you the time and distance to 'get your strength up'.

Of course, they will eventually realise this, and their hoover attempts will begin, both positive ones and malign ones, depending on the circumstances of your break-up.

What you must now do is stay strong. Do not respond or react in any way because that is exactly what they want you to do.

If there are no children involved, once property divided, and so on, there 'is' no need for you to have any further contact with the narcissist whatsoever.

For some of you who are new to narcissism, and if you have received a sudden and cruel discard for no apparent reason at all, the temptation to contact the narcissist will be extremely overwhelming. You will want answers, explanations, reasons and so on. That is human nature. It is also the effects of the trauma bonding that you are experiencing.

You must realise that with a narcissist you will 'never' get the closure that you are seeking. Your questions will 'not' be answered. All that your text messages, voicemails and emails will do is provide your narcissist with fuel. They will not respond. Not at first. If you do experience a hoover by the narcissist further down the line, you must ignore it and not respond at any point. To do so will resume contact and you will be 'fair game' to the narcissist once again.

An article by Chris Seiter states that there are seven signs that will show you that your application of 'No Contact' is working. These are:

1. Your ex tries to get hold of you
2. You are spending more time on you yourself and loving it
3. Others start finding you more attractive
4. Your ex starts paying attention to social media more
5. Your ex is more responsive after 'No Contact'
6. Your ex begins sending you gifts
7. Your ex asks about you but not to your face

These are good points to acknowledge but I think that they mainly apply to a non-narcissistic ex. Yes, your Narcissist may do some of the above but having learnt about narcissism by then you will know that your Nex will not be interested in you per se, but only in what fuel he can try and extract from you again.

What you are trying to achieve by using the 'No Contact' route is you are vanishing completely from the narcissist's life while at the same time you are making them disappear from yours.

I do understand just how difficult it could be for someone going 'No Contact' when they still have strong feelings for their Nex. When they are maybe not even aware that they have escaped the clutches of a 'Narcissist'. That person is still remembering the idealisation phase, the love-bombing they were subjected to. Most important of all they are probably still trauma bonded to their narcissist. These people will need an iron will, good supportive friends and family, and a network that can educate them on exactly what they are dealing with.

The use of 'No Contact' when dealing with a narcissist is the most powerful tool in a victim's armoury that the victim can use against the narc. This is because you will be denying the narcissist their regular supply of fuel from you. The only type of fuel the narcissist can obtain is that thought fuel. Clearly a hell of a lot less potent than any other type of fuel.

With a covert narcissist, like my Nex, they will attempt to use pity play on you. The covert narc can literally cry on cue to take the focus, to achieve contact and to especially get their own way. The Nex really could literally even find real tears for more effect. When you realise what they are doing, you do resist the urge to respond whereas in the past you probably did not. I got to the point where I found his attempts just comical.

The main thing to recognise and remember about a narcissist is that everything they do, and I mean absolutely every single little thing, is for a reaction. When you have gone 'No Contact', you have suddenly cut off their main fuel supply and this is unacceptable. How dare you! You must be punished! How will they get a reaction from you now? How will that reaction be able to release their flow of fuel if they cannot contact you?

Therefore, they will go all out to try and contact you, by whatever means presents itself to them. Bombard you with calls, texts and emails. If you do not live together, they will pitch up outside your house or your work. Therefore, it can be so difficult to maintain your 'No Contact' strategy. This is when the Nex emailed and texted family and friends instead.

Sharie Stines, Psy D states that 'Leaving a narcissist is similar to breaking a heroin addiction.'

This is because you experience cravings for the narcissist, due to the depletion of the hormone Oxytocin. This is by far the hardest part and the weakest moment where you could break your 'No Contact' rule. This is when you must be the strongest you have ever been in your life. If you are not, then you will be presenting the narcissist with an opportunity to hoover you back into the relationship or equally as bad if not worse, present him with an opportunity to unleash his venom on you.

The author of 'The Emotional Hell of Going No Contact with a Narcissist' states that it is one of the hardest and most painful things that she has ever done in her life.

The 'Aftermath' as she terms it, talks about her brain not catching up immediately to the fact that her narcissistic relationship was finally over. She talks about feeling broken and alone. She relates to the anger she felt at the chaos her narcissist had left behind, not wanting to believe that the relationship had not been 'real'. She asserts the general belief that there is no closure with a narcissist. She states that 'they either discard you, rage at you for discarding them, or plead with you nonstop to try to get you to come back to them because they do not like taking no for an answer'.

The cascade of emotions that you will go through after your break-up with a narcissist range from denial, anxiety, obsession, loneliness, isolation, suspicion, doubt, shame, grief, despair, fear and anger. For me, I certainly experienced anger and suspicion, and even grief, but I think that because I delved so deeply into narcissism and narcissists, I spared myself from feeling any of the others. That and having such a good support network in place with my family and friends.

In fact, the more I learnt the more I felt empowered, so my feelings changed very quickly to relief, thankfulness, gratitude and finally acceptance. I think this is what gave me the strength to finally go full 'No Contact' with the Nex. As difficult as that was with still living under the same roof. It also gave me control. The ability to control my own life going forward. Unfortunately, I hit a slight dip in the road where email contact did occur briefly, but I quickly resorted to the Grey Rock Method to deal with this at the time, before going back to 'No Contact'.

As I have stated before, if for whatever reason you cannot go full 'No Contact' then at least set yourself clear boundaries and ensure the narcissist knows that these boundaries are firmly in place and that you will not tolerate any being crossed.

As mentioned prior you can adopt the other technique if full or partial 'No Contact' is not achievable so instead use the Grey Rock Method.

Using the Grey Rock Method is not only invaluable in intimate relationships with narcissists but may also be the only option available to you, especially when co-parenting. Likewise, in non-intimate relationships. For example, the narcissist in your life could be a work colleague, a parent, a friend, or even a child. By initiating the Grey Rock Method, you are setting a very firm boundary to ensure that you, the victim, remains grounded when dealing with your narcissist. Using it ensures that you will ignore all attempts by the narc to bait you. You are essentially removing any of the chaos and drama that they thrive on. Any fuel that they are hoping to glean from you is nothing more than a trickle.

Another term for the Grey Rock Method is 'Detached Contact'.

I recently read a quote from @thenarcissistgames' that I thought was very fitting for this chapter and that is,

'Narcissists check in with you to make sure they still have access to your supply'.

A perfect quote to sum up what I have been talking about with the narcissists' use of hoovers and why they use them. And another perfect reason for going 'No Contact'.

And finally, the perfect quote to sum up Grey Rock, as told by @the.little.shaman (Healing Podcast) on narcissist.sociopath.awareness2,

'The Grey Rock method is not about repressing your emotions. It is about controlling your reactions'.

Of course, it may just be that you are not quite ready, emotionally to 'let go' of your narcissist, especially if the discard was fast and sudden. You may need time to acknowledge what is happening. To come to terms with it all. This is okay. There are no 'right or wrong' rules here. But therefore, it is so important that you do educate yourself about narcissism because knowledge really is power.

You may find that like I, you will need to 'dip your toe' in and out of both of these methods, 'No Contact' and Grey Rock Method, along the way, because some form of contact is unavoidable, but as long as you stay true to yourself, remain steadfast, and keep that narcissist 'under control' you will find a way that works for you.

Chapter Eleven
Red-flags – What to Look for, and How to Avoid Them in the Future

Red flags. What exactly do we mean by this terminology?

What exactly is a red flag?

The dictionary describes the red flag as something to be used as a warning of danger.

It is used to indicate that danger is present and that you should stop. A red flag is acting as a danger signal, a warning.

In narcissism, a red flag is an indication that something is seriously amiss with your partner, or within the relationship. You will 'see' warning signs but may dismiss them or even attribute them to something more rational and even less harmful. They are neither. They are a warning sign that you should heed and need to heed. Learning about these red-flags and recognising what counts as a red-flag will be invaluable to you if you are ever unfortunate enough to find yourself entangled with a narcissist.

Maria Consiglio @understandingthenarc states, 'A Red-Flag for narcissism is that they lack empathy'. She goes on to say that this is a big one and the most important characteristic that distinguishes them from other people. The reason being is that a narcissist is incapable of putting themselves in other people's shoes.

At the start of the relationship, during the love-bombing phase, there will be many red-flags to look out for. But of course, these will be masked, they will be subtle and designed to display another false meaning. The biggest red flag by far is if the narcissist tells you that they 'Love you' after only two or three weeks. Big tick there for me then. The Nex told me after only three weeks. I did not find this odd at the time and in fact I was flattered by it and believed that because we had chatted for almost two months prior, and so developed a real connection, it was not odd. This was a ploy all along. A well-rehearsed technique designed to swallow me in right at the very beginning. I just did not see it. I had come out of a previous twenty-year relationship, so I was very naïve to the dating game, and especially online dating.

Remember the card given to me after our very first meeting? Another great big red flag that was waved in my face. In my defence, I did always find it slightly strange, but I was so flattered by this action that this led to me missing the red flag that it was. Obviously once I had learnt about narcissism then the realisation that this was in fact a red flag certainly hit home.

The 'test' I had received when we were first communicating online. The Nex's disappearance and no contact for a month then poof he was back again. Yet another almighty red-flag.

The insistence on visiting me for that overnight stay, another red flag.

On his second visit to my hometown after this, just over two weeks after meeting, he again made a 'spur of the moment' visit to see me mid-week. Yep, you guessed it, another red flag. During this occasion we went to the local shopping mall for late night shopping as I still needed to buy my children's main Christmas presents. It was around the middle of December and was midweek. I selected two child electric guitars for them, one pink and one blue, costing £99 each. The Nex made comments about the cost of these items and why did I feel the need to buy them for my children. Had I not already bought them enough? I was irked by this comment, that is why I remember it so well, but just put it down to the fact that he did not have children so simply did not understand. Oh no! That was yet another great big fat red-flag that he was flying right there in my face but I neither saw it, recognised it or realised it.

Another red flag that I missed was again in the incredibly early days of the relationship when the Nex insisted that I start divorce proceedings against my ex. Because the ex and I were amicable we had not rushed into divorce, not because we would get back together, but rather because we had not given it any thought, but the Nex was adamant that I file for it immediately. He said it was not fair on him. Now, with hindsight, I see that this was an example of control, which of course is a major red flag.

On another occasion a few months into the relationship, he had again come up to my hometown. By this time, we were seeing each other every weekend and alternating between mine and his. I happened to tell him that I was going to be having a work dinner with my best friend (female) and a work colleague (male) one day the following week as it was the male colleague's 40th birthday and we had both in fact gone to school with this man, so we had known him for years! The fact was, along with this man who I also happened to work with, and along with my best friend who also worked at the same place as both of us, we were merely going to go to the café across the road from where we all worked for lunch to acknowledge his 40th birthday. Nothing sinister or clandestine about it at all. In fact, it was all so very innocent, part of a normal working day. Well, the Nex immediately got up and said he was leaving. He said that there was 'no point' in our relationship if I was going to have lunch with another man. He marched to the door as he was saying this and proceeded to make his way out to his car. I was gobsmacked! WTF?! What had just happened? I tried to explain that this man was nothing more than a work colleague and old school friend, but the Nex was having none of it. The upshot was, I had to tell the Nex that I would cancel the work lunch and forget all about it which is what I did. That was another great big fat major red flag that I missed bigtime. What was so hypocritical at that time was the fact that the Nex had a female 'best friend' who he saw on a regular basis and saw absolutely nothing wrong with that at all! This itself was yet another red flag that was waving and screaming double standards at me.

The initial love-bombing phase when he repeatedly told me how wonderful I was and so on, yet another red-flag that I missed.

I missed so many red flags at the start and they did not end there neither. In fact, looking back over the relationship they were constantly waving at me throughout it but of course I did not know that these are what they were.

If we look at classic red-flags of narcissistic abuse and warning signs to look out for:

1. The narcissist has a sense of superiority about them
2. They have a sense of entitlement
3. Back handed compliments
4. They will shower you with attention, gifts, say 'I Love You' early on
5. The relationship moves very quickly
6. They appear to have two sets of rules
7. Their stories do not add up.
8. They do not talk much about their past, especially relationships
9. A lack of empathy

10. Poor or no boundaries
11. Extremely sensitive to criticism of any kind
12. A 'My way or the Highway' attitude
13. Initial charm
14. The need for admiration and adoration
15. The use of the silent treatment
16. The use of ghosting, gaslighting, projecting, blame-shifting, stonewalling, baiting, triangulating, futureproofing, crazy making

The last two, numbers 15 and 16 come later in the relationship and of course when devaluation has begun. The rest may be apparent much sooner, but you simply make excuses up for them to yourself, or even the narcissist makes up the excuses for their behaviour. Either way, it is extremely easy to miss all the above as red flags. I sure as hell missed them, especially when 'all' sixteen were frequently waved at me during the fourteen years of the relationship.

With hindsight, I should have spotted something really because once you are deeper into the relationship these red-flags will not be so subtle, but you probably still will not recognise them as red-flags, just like I did not, rather you will just know that something is amiss but not know exactly what. You will feel that something is not 'normal' with your relationship, just like I did but you simply just cannot put your finger on what it is.

Further red flags that can depict a narcissistic relationship are,

They never apologize, according to them they have lots of crazy ex's, isolating you, being mean and cruel when arguing, they have anger issues, lying to you, being dismissive of your wants and needs and finally, over the top jealousness.

Relationship 'Green-Flags' which indicate a normal relationship are,

They show an interest in your hobbies, you have open communication, they value honesty, you resolve and make up after any conflict or argument, they talk fondly of others to you, you laugh together and there is no pressure in the relationship.

As devaluation may or may not have already begun, if you do dare to challenge the narcissist about a lie, or particular behaviour, you will not get a straight answer from them but rather it will become all about you and your perceived faults. If you push them harder than a full-blown argument will arise so you back down and back off because this is your first taste of what devaluation is and you are blindsided by it and confused because only the day before, or even an hour or minute earlier, the Idealisation phase was firmly in place, and you could do no wrong in the narcissist's eyes. You were painted white as HG Tudor would say, and now you have become black simply because you have questioned or challenged the narcissist. Or maybe even they just need a bigger hit of fuel.

A great big fat red-flag while this is underway is the fact that your argument will not end in a normal way. There will be no resolution for you. No compromise. No solution. You will still be reeling from all of it, maybe even believing the narcissist that it is all your fault, and so you back down and begin to learn how to walk on those eggshells instead, still not recognising those red flags. Having the presence of eggshells in a relationship 'is' a red flag in itself.

For me, on the rare occasions that I did not get 'The end of the relationship' routine I would instead get, 'I don't think I love you anymore'. It hurt every time obviously because that was exactly what he wanted, so sometimes I would just say 'Okay, I understand, so let us put the house on the market and go our separate ways'. I mean how else are you supposed to react to that kind of comment?! Someone telling you that they did not think that they loved you anymore. You cannot beg or try and change their mind on something like that. You simply walk away, respect intact, and try and move on. But the Nex would instead then throw an even bigger strop and tantrum, and eventually when I asked if he had meant it he would say that he did not really mean it and tell me that he did still love me and excused himself for saying it by stating, 'I only said it to punish you'. Or 'I just said it in my defence'. Yet another major red flag that I missed every single time when he said and did this. Of course, I now know that what he was really doing was telling me the truth, he really did not love me. You do get this with a narcissist, occasionally, that very rarely they will pass a comment that is an honest and truthful one, but you miss it every time. Except I did not miss the one he made when he said that he had never had any interest in me. I saw that one loud and clear once I had learnt all that I did about narcissists.

Another red flag is when you start to feel like your relationship is all one sided. Like you are the one doing all the giving and the narcissist is the one doing all the taking. Especially if you have started to make sacrifices to keep them happy but this still does not feel like enough. Like that whatever you do is never right, not good enough. You begin to feel inadequate, and even unlovable. What you are not realising is that slowly you are being manipulated. Traits that were once endearing to the narcissist no longer are. Confidences you once confided in them are rolled out and used against you.

When my friend reminded me about my move across country to live with the Nex, I had never thought of the events surrounding it as a red-flag but now I can see that it most certainly was a red-flag. The fact that it was more sensible and more practical for the Nex to move to my hometown. My children's father was there, all our family and friends were there. My parents and a friend lived less than five minutes from me, so childcare was never a problem. I had a career where I had worked for seventeen years, albeit at that point I was working part time because of the children. I had a lovely four bedroomed property remarkably close to the children's schools, in one of the nicest parts of the city. Whereas the Nex had no children, lived half an hour from his family in a different city, had a smaller property that ended up needing an extension on it when we moved, but most important of all was self-employed. Therefore, he could take his work anywhere. But no. When suggested that maybe he could move up to be with me because it was the easiest option for everyone and the least destructive, his response was a firm non-debatable no. It was never properly discussed. His work was there and that was it, end of conversation. If I wanted to be with him, then I was the one who had to move, despite this being the hardest and most disruptive choice out of the both of us. 'This was' a red-flag and I missed it. To make the sacrifices that I did with the move demonstrated my love for him but on the flip side it was one he would never have made himself because the love was never there in the first place.

Remember that all these red flags could be coming very slowly, just like the 'Frog in the boiling pan' scenario. Therefore, it can be so easy to miss the signs, explain the Narcissists behaviour away and most important of all, not recognise that these 'are' all red flags that are waving at you and that you are missing.

As stated by 'World Narcissistic Abuse Awareness',

'Narcissistic Abuse does not usually include forms of physical abuse with physical signs like bruises. The signs of narcissistic abuse are invisible, which makes it harder to identify. The abuse is more ambiguous and difficult to prove, but it is no less damaging because it is a form of spiritual rape. Over time, the abuse chips away at the target's self-confidence and self-esteem. The target is not even aware it is happening until the damage has been done. The abuse is always about control'.

Another early red flag that I completely missed with the Nex was the one where he kept saying to me 'You won't ever leave me will you?' This was because of his further insecurity with the loss of all his previous relationships. I think that subconsciously he knew that he was at fault for the loss of them due to his narcissistic behaviour but consciously his very narcissism prevented him from realising this. So instead, I had that question over and over for the first couple of years of the relationship.

Yet another red flag that will come both at the start of the relationship and at points throughout it is the narcissist's use of futureproofing or faking. If it is the start of the relationship or the first few months, they will talk about your future together. Possibly marriage, children, where to live and so on which appears normal behaviour, just as it can be in a normal relationship. The difference here is it will come much sooner, especially if you appear to be backing away. In the early days of the relationship, they may even promise to buy you a car once you are living together, just as I heard the Nex tell his latest victim once, which of course brought a chuckle to my throat and really made me laugh out loud! He also promised her that he would move to where she lived despite only seeing her once a month and despite on another occasion him informing me that the relationship was nothing to him and he had no intention of moving anywhere for anyone! Seriously, once you are an 'expert' in narcissism you see right through them and intuitively know which narcissistic tool they are using and when they are deploying it. In this case with the Nex, it was the futureproofing one. Once you are in the relationship or marriage their use of futureproofing will certainly continue because a narcissist cannot stop themselves from using it. For me, the Nex promised me that special weekend away that never materialised. The holidays he never booked. Then it was the honeymoon we never had. At first it was just mentioned as a future event, but then the Nex put a timeframe on it when he said, 'For our tenth wedding anniversary'. They may even tell you that you will not have to work, such can be the narcissists outlandish futureproofing promises. Of course, none of them ever materialise.

HG Tudor describes future-proofing as future-faking. He states that, 'It is the imposition of control and acquisition of fuel in the 'now' using a 'future event'.' What he means by this is the simple fact that the narcissist never had any intention on delivering what they claimed they would do but instead conned you into believing that they would. HG describes it further as an easy manipulation. That it is nothing to do with the narcissist changing their mind but simply instead, it is the narcissist controlling you by promising you something later that will never be delivered.

Once you are ensconced in the relationship the red-flags will come thick and fast in the form of lies, deceit, gaslighting, blame-shifting, projection, mirroring, silent treatment, stonewalling, ghosting, sulking, hypocrisy, double standards, crazy making, selfishness, verbal, emotional and physical abuse.

Of course, some of the above can and will be played out in a perfectly normal functioning relationship but the big difference is how an argument ends, how a debate is resolved. In a narcissistic relationship, they never are played out normally because you will instead suffer abuse or the use of stonewalling and the silent treatment for the narcissist to gain control and power over you once again. The argument is not resolved but rather it is just buried along with all the rest. This is a major red flag that can and will be missed over and over.

I knew that I was being treated to the silent treatment every single time it occurred, which trust me was often, I just did not know that this was a trait of narcissistic behaviour and abuse. More importantly I did not recognise it as emotional abuse, which it clearly is. Yet another massive red flag that I missed continuously. Also, because the Nex never actually physically punched me in the face, but rather his bouts of violence towards me were more subtle, more insidious in the form of pushes, poking, grabbing hold of me by the scruff of the neck and waving his fist in my face, throwing objects and items at me, I stupidly did not recognise these as still physical abuse. What is even more ridiculous here that I missed it, is the fact that I have always abhorred violence towards women and had stated previously that if any man ever punched me in the face then that would be it, relationship over. But because the violence I suffered was far more subtle, insidious and over a more sporadic, sustained period, I did not connect the dots. I could not view this as 'Physical Abuse' in the sense that I had always believed it to be. The severe punch in my back that woke me up in pain that night, that left a bruise on my skin, was played down by the Nex who claimed it was only a prod to stop me from snoring. Something ironically, I have never done before nor after! Such was his use of gaslighting against me.

Basically, I was living with red-flags on a regular basis but just did not realise it or recognise them to be red-flags. To be honest I did not even know what red-flags were. I had no reason to. Just like I never knew what narcissism meant or what a narcissist was.

Kim Seed, in her article, 'Stop Focusing on Narcissist Types and Start Investigating These Toxic red-flags', points out there are five early warning signs with narcissism,

1. The nagging feeling that something is not right
2. Constant anxiety
3. Disregard for boundaries
4. Subtle manipulation
5. Arrogance and self-centeredness

If we look at the first one, yes I can hold my hand up to that. The incident with my work colleague, the 'I Like You' card, the children's Xmas presents, the never-ending silent treatments, I ignored these, pushed them to the back of my mind and explained them away as something else. As Kim Saheed states, 'Our bodies are meant to work to survive. If something (or someone) is threatening that survival, we'll feel that nagging sensation in our gut'. She emphasises that we should 'Listen Up!'

In the second one, this is that constant need to walk on eggshells that we have looked at previously. Again, for me, I walked on these from the very beginning. I learnt to really think about what I would say to the Nex, pictured every conceivable scenario in my head, before I finally found what I thought was the right way to say something to him, such was my fear that he would take it the wrong way. He usually ultimately still did though, such was his narcissism and in his mind 'Who the hell was I to even dare to ask such a question to him!', or 'How dare you ask me to do that!' so I usually did not ask, or I found what I thought was a non-offensive way of asking, but it never was. He still always found fault. His knee jerk reaction to anything was always a resounding 'no!' Until he had then thought about it, then sometimes he would come back and say, 'Now I've thought about it I've changed my mind', but not before the initial outburst first though.

Number three, again, Kim Saheed states that, 'Opposing values isn't inherently a red flag. Most healthy couples have a fair number of differences between them. However, disregarding your physical, emotional, or even financial boundaries represents a serious red-flag. Our boundaries are what separate us from other people. They provide us with implicit safety and protection'. One of the boundaries that the Nex crossed in the beginning was the one in relation to my children's Christmas presents, I just did not realise this. He did continue to cross this boundary over and over in relation to my parenting skills, time and time again.

Number four, the use of subtle manipulation. When I had to cancel the birthday lunch with my work colleague, the Nex had used manipulation against me by stating that we were over if I went for that lunch. Of course, it was hidden with comments about how he would feel. Typically, a narcissist has a real problem accepting another person's viewpoint that is different to theirs. But the result was that he achieved what he had wanted and that was the lunch being cancelled. I will state though that at times the manipulation was not so subtle and was blatantly stated out loud. Like the threat of the end of the relationship, over and over.

Finally, number five. You will find that a narcissist will talk a lot about themselves. Especially at the start. The Nex boasted that his building business had turned over 50–60k a year in the past, but this was a great big fat lie. When I used to visit before we lived together, I would often go food shopping for him and buy him his cigarettes because he would claim poverty and state that he was waiting for payment on a job which clearly conflicted with his boast about earning so much. He claimed to be a good chef and loved cooking, but I soon found out this was another 'white lie'. Sometimes, the narcissist will also put other people down to you in favour of themselves. The most difficult thing about recognising what is arrogance and what is not, is the fact that most narcissists have this innate air of confidence about themselves, so it is difficult to know when it is genuine and when it is not. For me, it was all complete and utter bullshit that the Nex was drip feeding me. When I sat and thought about it while I was writing this book, I came to realise that he had never really had anything per se apart from his mortgaged house, because it was always the woman who was financially secure or had wealthy parents. With me, once I moved in with him I paid off his mortgage and left change in the bank for him.

All five of these are of course red flags that will come in the beginning and continue to keep on coming throughout your relationship with the narcissist.

A massive red flag that I also missed involved my ex and the Nex.

At the very beginning, the Nex was amenable to meeting my ex, my children's father, but my ex did not feel ready to at the start. Fair enough, there was no rush. So, a few weeks later when he then said he did feel ready, the Nex decided that he had changed his mind. The Nex did not want to meet my ex. I now think that he probably never had wanted to, but merely future-proofed at the start. I also now believe that because he was angry that the ex-had first declined his offer, the Nex was now punishing both me and the ex for it. Both are plausible reasons knowing what I do know now about narcissists and their sense of entitlement. Well, I moved to be with the Nex eight months later and visited my hometown every two weeks so my ex could have his children. On some occasions, this was not possible so instead I would meet my ex halfway. Well, if the Nex insisted on coming with me to the meet point then it was a total nightmare scenario as the Nex also insisted that he must not at any point 'see' the ex and that 'seeing' the ex must be avoided at all costs. We used to meet at a motorway service station and if I got there first I would have to park far away from the entrance then take the children inside and meet the ex there. I then would have to leave before they did. If the ex got there first, then he had to wait inside for me to arrive. At no point ever, was it possible that the children could just switch cars in the car park. This ridiculous scenario played out for ten whole years! It was not until my son graduated from University in 2015 that my ex and Nex finally did get to meet each other, and this was only because it was unavoidable.

On another occasion after this meeting of them both in 2015, and interestingly it happened during my 'silent' punishment in 2017, my ex travelled down to where we were living to see his daughter, who was home on a visit from Japan. For the very first time ever, he came to the house to pick her up, and as it was such a nice summer's day, I was out in the garden. My daughter answered the door and invited my ex in as she was not quite ready. He came out into the garden to me, and we discussed my daughter's imminent travel plans back to Japan. I was slightly nervous as to how the Nex would react when he saw my ex in the garden, but I just reassured myself that he would be fine as he had met the ex now and I had been separated from my ex for fourteen years by this point, and my ex had been remarried a few years himself. The Nex arrived home and did appear fine with it, he shook hands with the ex and had a short conversation with him. To say I was relieved was an understatement. Not for long though because as soon as my ex and daughter had left his fury surfaced.

How dare I invite my ex here! How dare I invite him into our home! I did not spare a thought to the Nex's feelings with my actions. He was heartbroken at my betrayal. And so, on it went. I tried to tell him that my daughter had answered the door, that I had no idea until the ex had pitched up outside in the garden, but the Nex would not listen to me at all. It was all my fault. I was a horrible and nasty person because I had put him in a 'situation'. He finally ended up screaming at me that I had well and truly 'Broken his heart' and of course then ensued the infamous usual 'End of relationship' scenario and subsequent silent treatment. In the end even my daughter apologised to him and explained that it was all her fault and not mine, but he would not listen. Being the narcissist, I now know that he is, he had in fact suffered a perceived narcissistic injury and I was entirely to blame for it. I of course, had to apologise, see it from his point of view and so on. He then proceeded to bring this incident up time and time again, even after we had spilt up and use it against me. In fact, after we had split up he went so far as to state that this incident was the beginning of the end for him. He could not ever forgive me for it. His narcissistic injury was that severe. Of course, this 'incident' would never have played out in a normal relationship.

This is yet another major red flag to look out for. In a normal relationship, once an argument or fall out is resolved, both parties move on from it and it is generally never mentioned again. Not with a narcissist. As you have learnt by now they are the kings and queens of sulking and grudge holding. You can bet your life that every argument that follows, not only will the last one be revisited, but 'all' the previous ones before that will be too, and they will be thrown at you one after the other after the other. EVERY SINGLE TIME!

All these incidents of mine that I recount to you were and are red flags. Behaviour patterns that were not only abnormal but were also indicative of narcissistic behaviour. I did not know this then and did not learn this and realise this until I had educated myself on narcissism and what it entailed.

Yet another incident that was a great big fat red-flag as it highlighted the Nex's sense of entitlement and lack of boundaries was the final Christmas of 2017 before we split up. Realise that this now also fell during the silent punishment period that I was inadvertently and unknowingly in. I had already endured the usual Christmas silent treatment routine from him and on this occasion it was again from the 23rd up until Christmas Day. The Nex had had the audacity to accuse me of stealing some money from him. Yes, I was called a thief and so on, and I ended up sleeping in the spare room because his venom towards me was so vile. He did not like this because he was concerned about how it would look to my parents'. He did eventually realise where the money had gone (he had spent it) but of course there was no apology forthcoming to me whatsoever.

Well fast forward to Boxing Day when the Nex's family would always come to us every year. As usual, the Nex did nothing to help with the food preparations and I was running behind so I asked him nicely if he could ensure that when his family arrived they went into the lounge rather than gather around the Bar that we had in the kitchen. By this point, my beloved late father and son were helping me get the food ready and dished up and placed in the dining area. What a complete waste of time it was asking him for this one reasonable request! Oh no, instead of directing everyone into the lounge the Nex took great pleasure in gathering everyone into the kitchen, around the bar when he could clearly see that I was flustered with the belated preparations. Such was his blatant cruelty towards me and by this time he was not even bothering to hide it or disguise it from me. I knew he wanted a reaction from me, but I just remained silent and got on with what I was doing. Even then, just six months before we finally split up, I did not recognise that this was a massive narcissistic red flag he was waving at me. I just knew that it was yet another cruel and hurtful, unacceptable pattern of behaviour that the Nex had displayed. But then it was also during my long silent punishment devaluation period too.

'Inner Integration' say that the biggest red flag of the narcissist is the flattery they use on you at the very start of the relationship. If this book can help you identify the pitfalls to avoid, then it will also prevent you from embarking on a narcissistic relationship.

When we look at the difference between flattery and compliments, it is important to recognise the difference. The dictionary defines flattery as, 'Excessive praise', even insincere and it almost always has an ulterior motive. Whereas a compliment is defined as, 'A polite expression of praise or admiration'.

Flattery is a shallow praise that is usually given when the giver expects something back in return. When a compliment is given it is a form of respect, designed to boost one's morale but most important is given whilst not expecting anything back in return. Flattery is not genuine, it is calculated and given with an expectation of something in return. Flattery rather than a compliment is what a narcissist will use.

Recognising the difference could be the very difference that could help you avoid becoming entangled with a narcissist.

A narcissist will use flattery because they want something from you whereas a 'normal' person will compliment you as an expression of admiration towards you. It is a natural emotion.

When you are ensnared by a narcissist in the beginning, you are in the throes of the love-bombing phase, where you will receive constant flattery as the narcissist is trying to secure your love and trust. In return, you will be complimentary towards them and thus they will have started to receive their precious supply of fuel, further enhanced from your admiration and attention towards them.

'Inner Integration' go on to state that the narcissist will get you addicted to the pleasure and gratification that their flattery is bringing you. The feel-good chemicals whirling in your brain. The narc will also go on to learn all your insecurities and flatter them too. This in turn ensures you transfer your sense of approval from inside yourself to the narcissist. This is the first stage of Abuse. This 'flattery' will soon turn into little digs then into full blown criticisms. A prime example with the Nex was him constantly telling me how good I was with words at the start and so he would let me 'fight' any 'battle' for him. This was soon used against me though and became a criticism that the Nex would often roll out against me, especially after we had split up. He would say that I was not a nice person and that I loved to 'fight' everyone which could not have been further from the truth. My wish to write a book soon became a ridicule for him to imply that I was a sayer and not a doer. 'Are they saying something nice to you or about you, or do they have an ulterior motive like they're trying to stroke your ego to get you to give them something, or do something for them?' (Inner Integration).

Therefore, it is so important to recognise the difference between what is flattery and what is criticism.

Another red flag to be aware of is the narcissists lack of use of the phrase 'Thank you'.

I was very rarely thanked for any of the holidays that I totally paid for and took the Nex on. Nor any of the weekends away, days out, shows we went to, gifts I randomly bought him, and so on. I can probably count on one hand how many times he may have said it. This was also a red flag to his sense of entitlement.

In the November, five months post-split with the Nex, when things had become hostile after the divorce had been filed, he had started using my bathroom (his was downstairs) and as the lock was faulty I had a locksmith put a proper key lock on the door. I had already had a couple of incidents where the Nex had just walked in when I was in the shower despite the faulty door lock being on. Well, this immediately triggered two events. One that he told the locksmith that it was his house and that he had to stop what he was doing. The Nex had not realised that I had heard this and when I challenged him he quickly denied it and said, 'Of course it is your house as well, I would never say that it wasn't'. He even reiterated this in an email to me later. This did not stop him from going on to lie to everyone later though, including the courts, by claiming yet again that he owned our house outright. The second event it triggered because I had caught him out lying to the locksmith was for him to come to me once the locksmith had left and turn his crocodile tears on and tell me that one of his friends had been diagnosed with Cancer. He had used a classic narcissistic trait of deflection and it had worked because I immediately felt sorry for him, and the locksmith incident was never mentioned again. This was another red flag that yet again, I had missed.

Think about the three-phase cycle that we have talked about in this book. Especially the idealisation and devaluation ones. The narcissist wants adoration and praise and admiration, so you provide it in response to their flattery towards you. When you stop giving them this, or it reduces, the devaluation starts, and the narcissist instead now wants to punish you so they will now criticize you. And so, the cycle is in play. The incidents I have already referred to where he would often state that I never praised him when I really did, and so to rectify this I would then praise him publicly but still to no avail. It still did not stop the constant accusations of not praising him enough though.

In the last few years of our relationship, the Nex forgot our Wedding Anniversary three times, two in quick succession. Obviously, an excuse was given each time, blaming something else for his memory loss. Well, the third time he forgot, I had bought him the usual card and gifts and left them downstairs for him in the morning. I was already in the kitchen when he came down and saw them. Still the penny did not drop until it eventually did. No word of a lie, his response was worthy of an Oscar! He knew he had forgotten our anniversary yet again, and I knew he had forgot it yet again, but he proceeded to state that it was not our Wedding Anniversary until later that day, 4 pm to be precise, as this was when we had married. Therefore, in his opinion, he had not forgot, he was not at fault, and he was not going to open my card and present to him until after 4 pm that day. And he did not! He went to work, pleased as punch with himself that he had managed to 'exonerate' himself from any perceived 'wrong-doing'. I on the other hand was left to feel like absolute shit and at fault for remembering our anniversary and was then suitably punished for this by being made to wait until that evening before he opened his present and card from me. He justified his behaviour by stating that when he returned he would have my card and gift from him, and we could then both open them together. Just think of how much Fuel he 'dined out' on that day knowing that he had both punished me and hurt me because I had remembered while he had forgot. The extra hit that this event would have provided for him.

AfterNarcissisticAbuse.com states,

With narcissistic abuse the only person who realizes there is a problem 'is' the person closest to the stealth narcissist, who is forced to suffer extreme psychological abuse (very subtle emotional blackmail, mental abuse, and psychological manipulation).' Narcissists twist literally every little detail back round onto the victim. This abuse is so well hidden within communication dynamics that the partner often does not pick up on it and is left scratching their head wondering 'is it me?'

The point I am trying to make here is to recognise what is normal behaviour and what is not. The examples I have given you with my own stories are not normal behaviour. You must recognise what are red-flags and understand examples of red-flags. If your gut is shouting at you that something does not feel right with the relationship, that it 'is not right', then listen to it because your gut instinct is never wrong.

All those other accumulative red flags that I also missed. Lack of concern for my illness, the annual pre-Christmas devaluation, the annual poverty claims around my birthday, hardly ever paying when we went out, the list quite

253

frankly goes on, to the point where you do end up questioning your own judgement as to why you never saw it. Our annual BBQ that we had held in the last few years, filled mainly with all his family and friends, where he would quite literally 'come alive' during it and morph into this animated individual. Strutting his stuff like the lord of the manner, relishing in all the attention he was receiving. I always just assumed it was the excitement of the day but looking back now with my narc glasses on, I see that it was because he was flying high on all the fuel he was receiving from the attention and from the praise.

@understandingthenarc/MariaConsiglio under the heading red-flag for narcissism state that,

'Your needs, wants or whatever is important to you will never be considered. Narcissistic individuals cannot see past themselves. Everything revolves around how it is will affect them. They either cannot see your needs, or they just do not care, either way they put no energy into it. That is why many victims of narcissistic abuse feel like they are fading away, and they do not know who they are anymore. When your life becomes all about someone else, it is quite easy to lose yourself in the midst of all of it'.

They go on to state under the heading; Red-Flag for Narcissism – They are Always the Victim,

'No matter what they do, no matter how much damage they cause, no matter how many lives they destroy, the narcissist will always see themselves as the victim. Do not ever expect them to take responsibility or own anything they do. The pathology leads them to believe they never make mistakes. So, anything that goes wrong no matter how false or untrue, is your fault, or at least it is never their fault. This is a relationship where you always lose. And any bad things they do to you will never be acknowledged. This is a relationship where you are conditioned to only acknowledge the needs of the narcissist. When you are never seen, heard or considered, your spirit feels like it is dying a little everyday'.

I will finish this chapter with one more quote by Caroline Strawson which states,

'The moment you start Googling someone's behaviour in an effort to understand it, is probably the biggest red-flag you will ever need'.

Explore narcissism, and find out what a narcissist is, but most importantly explore what red flags are. Especially in relation to relationships. They could save you many weeks, months or even years of heartache. That knowledge might even go on to save your life!

Chapter Twelve
Life Beyond the Narcissist and
How to Move On

Maria Consiglio states,

'Narcissists do not want honest relationships, they want cheer leaders. They want people who always give them the right. They want blind loyalty. They want unconditional acceptance, no matter what they do. As long as you do not question anything they do, or give them the wrong on anything, they might just leave you alone. But watch out, if you disagree with them, or go against them in any way. In their eyes, this is the deepest betrayal. And it never goes unpunished. Narcissists are spiteful and vindictive'.

I thought this quote was very appropriate at this point in the book and begins to describe a narcissist perfectly.

It certainly describes what I endured post-split from the Nex.

Of course, there is so much more to a narcissist then what this quote depicts though, by far more, as by now you are no doubt starting to realise having nearly reached the end of this book. The narcissist is such a complex individual. Narcissism and narcissist are currently two buzz words of the present day, as more and more people are starting to learn about narcissism, to understand it, and even realise that this is what their relationship was or God forbid, still is. Unfortunately, though the term narcissist is also being used all too frequently and too flagrantly and thus has the potential to cause damage by diluting the effects of narcissism on a victim of a real full-blown bona fide narcissist.

Another helpful quote from Maria Consiglio states,

- 'The most important thing in life for a narcissist is gaining narcissistic supply (fuel). This is what they live for.

- You will never get validation or a genuine apology from them.
- They hate to experience shame and will project that shame onto you.
- They truly start to believe they are the victims.
- They have no self-awareness, so they do not know or care how they affect the people around them.
- They hate to be vulnerable. And they hate weakness because they cannot tolerate it in themselves.
- They project who they are onto you, or people around them.
- They are unable to love in any healthy way or manner'.

For all you survivors out there, and for all you victims that are still in the throes of the evil that is narcissism, remember and digest the above eight points. Read them over and over if any doubt starts to creep into your thoughts. If at any point, you have a weak moment and want to return to your Narcissist. You will just be walking back into the fire.

A question that was once asked by a member of 'narcissist-survivor' was, 'How many of you stayed in abusive relationships because you were not getting abused physically, and did not know that emotional, mental, sexual, financial, psychological or verbal abuse were equally if not more damaging?'. The response was overwhelming!

It is only natural to want revenge when the relationship is over, especially when you have discovered that it was a narcissistic relationship that you were in. To come to realise that the entirety of the relationship was false, a lie, that your narcissist never actually loved you as you discover that they are incapable of feeling this emotion. You feel duped, even conned and you may well have been conned. Not just your emotions, your heart, but also your finances, your home, your car, your entire life. And of course, not forgetting all those wasted years.

It is extremely important that you do not act on this emotion for revenge. Why? Because you will not win, 'ever'. The narcissist will merely 'Up their game' against you. In fact, they could even go all out to destroy you and stop you from unveiling the true monster that lurks beneath their false mask.

The narcissist will take every opportunity that is presented to them to keep you 'chained' to them. For them to gather their precious fuel from you, to hurt you and to destroy you. If you seek revenge, you are also validating their false claim that 'you' are the abuser and that they are the victim. That you really are the crazy one and not them.

Remember the story that I told you about in an earlier chapter that related to the Nex and a previous girlfriend of his who had kept coming around to his house and who he ended up throwing a bucket of water on? I found it such an incredulous tale that I was never really sure as to whether it actually happened or not but since learning about narcissists, and recognising that he is one, and since starting this book, I realised that this story could in fact be possibly true. And if so, then no doubt that he had discarded this poor girl so suddenly and abruptly that she had just kept on showing up looking for answers. Something she would never have got from the Nex as he simply just moved on to his next victim and like he used to tell me, he had just 'Switched off from her'.

HG Tudor states, 'The worst thing you can ever do to a narcissist is to ignore him by going 'No Contact''. Therefore, this is exactly what you must do!

Also, the biggest injury you can cause a narcissist post relationship is for them to see you happy. Whether that is in another relationship, job, home, new friends and even a new relationship. They cannot stand it that you are happy without them. It is incomprehensible to a narcissist that you can move on and survive without them, such is their sense of grandiosity.

If while you are reading this book and have reached this final chapter and are still in contact with your ex-narcissist, and you do not have children with them, you must now block them on every apparatus that you have. Block their number on your phone, your email accounts, your social media accounts, and you must do this now without another moment's delay!

If you can, do not let them know where you are now living. I know this could be difficult where children are involved and 'No Contact' is virtually impossible, so if you can, meet them somewhere neutral and away from your home. If 'No Contact' is not possible, then use the Grey Rock Method with them instead.

Leaving a narcissist and what is a narcissistic relationship could be the most dangerous part for you, especially if the narc senses that he or she is losing control. They will 'up' their level of abuse against you to try and exert more control and power over you or try to regain it. They may even stalk you, monitor your comings and goings, like the Nex did, or hack your accounts and your phone, just like the Nex did as well. In a very worst-case scenario, the narcissist may even kill you. We have already looked at the statistics of this and every day we seem to be reading more and more about abusive relationships and the violence that is meted out to partners, often resulting in their death.

The harsh reality about your narcissist is the fact that you were only ever a means to an end for them.

The narcissist never regrets when a relationship is over, and I mean 'never'. They will be angry and vengeful that their best source of supply has gone but they will not regret losing you, the person. For my Nex, he lost his financial security, his housekeeper, his 'easy life', his dogsbody, his cleaner, his cook, his proverbial 'punch bag', but most of all, his constant steady continuous flow of narcissistic supply/fuel. I passionately believe that this is the only reason we lasted fourteen years, and not because he 'loved me', because as you will have learnt by now, a narcissist is incapable of love. He was just too lazy to seek it elsewhere because I provided him with everything his narcissism required.

A quote that I have read (author unknown) that sums this up perfectly is, 'No one can throw a bigger tantrum than a narcissist who is losing control of someone else's mind'.

The Nex said to me on several occasions after we had split up, 'Why couldn't you just go quietly?' and, 'Why are you still breathing?' After fourteen years together I can be forgiven that I may have been afforded a little more respect than this; not with a narcissist.

HG Tudor again states that the key to gaining freedom from a narcissist, whether you are still with them or not, is to understand them. He goes on to say, 'One of the central principles to understand with our kind is the fact that our perspective is vastly different to yours. You gauge our responses, our actions, and our words through the lens of 'your' world view'.

In other words what HG Tudor is asking us to understand, and in fact do, is to think like they do and see what they see. Once we do and we can, then we will understand what is happening. We will then recognise what the narcissist is doing to us and why they are doing it and we will no longer engage in their pathetic mind games of 'one-up manship'.

I agree whole heartedly with this statement. I had learnt the hard way.

Why?

Because for the first eight to ten months I did inadvertently engage in the Nex's mind games. I responded to his abusive emails (Malign Hoovers) and so before I knew it we would have fifty of them between us on that one singular occasion! He blamed, I responded. He accused, I responded. Such is your frustration at the lies and false accusations that are flying out at you. Such is your sense of indignation that you feel that you must reply, professing your innocence in the process. What a complete and utter waste of time that is and was! 'that' is exactly what the narcissist is after. What they want from you because when you do respond and protest, out flows their precious fuel from you to them. The more fuel, the more they will provoke you, prod you, annoy you, abuse you, and ultimately have control over you.

The narcissist will use blame-shifting, projection, mirroring, gaslighting, triangulation, flying monkeys, smear campaign and whatever else is in their arsenal to attack you so that your fuel will just keep on flowing post break up.

The trick here is to not respond, not reply, not engage in any way whatsoever.

Trust me when I say that this is the hardest thing for you to do. To ignore all the insults and lies that are coming your way, but you must. Therefore, it is so important to educate yourself on what you are dealing with, and most important of all, who you are dealing with. I cannot describe how it feels when you reach that level of understanding! The weight that falls off your shoulders. The clarity you see. Most of all, the knowledge and understanding of what is happening to you and what has happened to you. Suddenly you have all the answers to all those questions you silently asked yourself during your toxic abusive relationship. For me, I finally understood why my relationship with the Nex was not normal and was never normal. I finally learnt why he behaved the way that he had and the way that he did. Why I endured those endless bouts of the silent treatments. Why the relationship was always taken to the brink over some silly little perceived spat. Why post-split I literally felt like I was fighting for my life.

From that exact point of realisation onwards, you recognise every attempt at a hoover; positive or malign. Every deployment of yet another mind game, every attempt to gaslight you, to blame you, to project or deflect their behaviour on to you. The smears that come your way are thick and fast. Believe me when I state that you must rise above it, and that you will rise above it. You will rise above all of them and everything. You 'must' rise above it all to be able to move forward and to start to heal. This is not about 'winning' for you. This is about surviving, escaping, moving on, healing, recovering from what you have been through. Accepting that it is finally over. You are finally free of the abuse, control and manipulation. You finally have your life back.

The sheer sense of empowerment that this brings for you is indescribable. For the first time in an exceptionally long time, you see 'The wood for the trees'. You see 'The light at the end of the tunnel'. You realise that you 'will' get past this and more importantly that you 'can' get past this. I am not for a single second saying that you will ever forget it, or maybe even get over it, but you will learn to live with it, deal with it, acknowledge what you went through and even why, and finally move on from it. To be free of such a toxic abusive relationship as what a narcissistic one is, is not a win over your narcissist but is a victory to you and for you and you alone. Do not ever forget that. You survived it!

A quote I recently read, author unknown, sums this up perfectly,

'Stalking me won't change how your life is. Telling lies and talking shit about me will not make people doubt me because they already know who I am and that I can be trusted and that I am real. If you continue trying to destroy me, by knocking me down, you will only make me stand up stronger. I will not be a participant in your petty games because I won a long time ago'.

Those nasty smear campaigns. They are a 'three pronged' fork for sure, in that first you are verbally abused and called names by the narcissist. Secondly, they will then do things designed to hurt you, directly or indirectly. Thirdly is the deployment of the smear campaign far and wide, telling all and sundry what a wicked person you are, how you abused them. Quite frankly they will tell just about anyone who will listen to them! There will not be one single ounce of truth in the lies that they tell either. For you, you must be prepared for this fork to come, because believe me it will. You must rise above it, not retaliate like I did, and ignore the lies that are told. You have your story, the truth, and if the right people believe you, then that is all that matters.

Another quote by 'AfterNarcissisticAbuse.com' states,

'When the victim of this abuse eventually begins to develop awareness of the manipulation, it gradually dawns on them that they have already been abused long before they anticipated and the people that they turn to for help have already been made to believe that it is them who has issues – they have already been turned against the victim by the narcissist'.

Once I had 'exposed' the Nex as the narcissist that he was, I saw, I felt, and I experienced his narcissism in all its nasty glory. Nothing was hidden anymore, the mask was well and truly off.

The Nex had sure as hell worked a spectacular smear campaign against me. He turned nearly all his family and friends against me with his lies. I have told you that I used to get emails from him telling me that I had bipolar disorder and that he would make appointments for me to discuss it, and even more bizarrely that he would support me at these appointments! I also told you that most recently I had heard him telling his latest victim that I was crazy, had serious mental health issues and that he had made an appointment about it for me, but he did not know if I would attend or not! Such was and no doubt still are his outrageous lies and confabulations about me. I stopped caring about what he said anymore. I knew the truth, as did my family and friends, and that was all I cared about. Now, when I look back, his crazy making just makes me laugh out loud.

Another quote by '@narcissistic-abuse-is-real' says, 'Blood is thicker than water; Blood mixed with poison is fatal. #flyingmonkeys #toxicfamilies'.

K. Sierra states, 'He was a man of many words, but never a man of his word' and this sums the Nex up perfectly. My Nex sure knew how to future-proof, how to lie expertly, but then all narcissists 'are' pathological liars.

Another good quote goes, 'You can't be with someone who is unable to see the wrong in themselves. They will never be able to see the right in you'.

I have had several conversations with a particularly good friend of mine where we have discussed memories of the relationship. She too was in a similar relationship with a narcissist. I told her that for me, my relationship was all a lie, that all my memories of it are made up of falseness and so I was going to try and forget that the relationship had ever happened, I would learn from it and move on from it, but ultimately seal it in a box in my mind so I would not dwell on it or let it define me. She said that she could not do that, and that she was going to keep those 'happy memories' in place because she had had children with her ex. She could not let go of those memories and I understood this and why.

The very last thing a victim of a narcissistic relationship wants is tough love from their family and friends. The very definition of 'Tough Love' is to enforce certain constraints on someone or require them to take responsibility for their actions. How can you ask a victim of abuse to take responsibility for 'their' actions?

It is difficult enough to explain to someone what you have gone through, or what you are currently experiencing, especially if they only ever saw the 'nice guy' routine from your narcissist. They will have a hard time picturing that same 'nice' person with the ogre and bully you are now describing. They may even think that you are somehow to blame for their behaviour.

You have two choices at this point:

1) Educate them on narcissism, and/or 2) Step away. It is of paramount importance that your family and friends validate what you are telling them. That they understand and more importantly, believe you. You have just come out of a toxic and abusive relationship where you have been invalidated for so long. The very, very last thing you will need is 'Tough love'.

Thankfully, my brother had worked in mental health for many years and was all too familiar with narcissists. He understood exactly what I was now going through and more importantly what I had been through so was a real source of comfort and knowledge to me. I also have a wonderful support network of family and friends who patiently listened to me over and over after I had split up with the Nex. When I was telling them of the latest outrageous stunt that the Nex had meted out against me, they were always there with sage advice.

For me, I think that if you do have self-doubt, you do really need to educate yourself about narcissists and narcissism, because trust me, you will stop having any further self-doubt that is for sure. You will no longer doubt yourself but most important of all you will not blame yourself anymore. That curtain that has been sitting across your view, preventing you from seeing the abuse for what it is and what it was, opens, revealing the true and real horror of what you experienced. I will not pretend for a single second that the sheer enormity of what you have been through does not hit you hard and knocks you firmly off your feet. It does, 'hard!' But, for me, the understanding and realisation that followed was far more important, far more beneficial to my recovery, and most important of all, it validated all what I had gone through, and survived.

A quote by 'Empaths-survival' says,

'People will often ask why you did not leave a toxic relationship knowing that he/she was abusing you. Narcissists tend to covertly abuse victims. They know when to abuse and how. Some days they will be overly affectionate and some other days they will gaslight, manipulate, cheat and lie. This creates a fog in the victim's mind. The victim doesn't leave because he/she is trauma bonded'.

It is important for not only victims to acknowledge and accept this, but also for their family and friends to as well. A victim must 'never' be made to feel guilty for not walking away from the abuse sooner.

Another saying that I have read is, 'You won't realise until the end, they have been lying to you from the beginning. You were in love with a complete illusion, a lie, a fraud. Welcome to the world of the narcissistic manipulationship'.

Maria Consiglio, under the heading 'Do relationships with narcissists ever work?' states, 'The thing to understand about this is, when going into a relationship with a narcissist you immediately have different agendas. The narcissist is looking for narcissistic supply, you are looking for love. The narcissist is looking to win and be right, you are looking to communicate. The narcissist is looking for control while you are looking for mutual respect. You are on different pages from the beginning, you want completely different things. The problem is they lie about their agenda, they make you think they want the same things you do. A healthy relationship is one where the two people involved are getting their needs met. This is not even close to happening with a narcissist. You must understand all the dreams they sold you were just illusions. They were mirroring back to you, yourself. They were never that person to begin with. The dynamics of a relationship with a narcissist is created from illusion, not reality'.

For me, the title of this very book, 'I promise I'll make you happy', sums up the above passage. Happiness is what I was looking for and happiness is what the Nex sold me, albeit it was nothing more than a lie, nothing more than a narcissist futureproofing.

The Nex mirrored all my likes and dislikes at the start of the relationship but as the years went by these began to slip. If I suggested that we do something he would say, 'I don't like that', or 'That's not for me', and if I pointed out that he had always told me that he did like it he would respond by saying 'You must have got me mixed up with your ex'. Towards the end of the relationship when he used the usual end of the relationship routine with me, he would roll out another favourite routinely, 'We've not been getting on for years', or, 'We've nothing in common', despite the fact that probably the previous week

264

I had been treated to an Idealisation phase. I think the real truth of the matter is that we never had anything in common, he purely lied in the beginning during the love-bombing phase and mirrored everything that I liked to make me believe that we did have lots in common. As the years passed and his narcissistic mask continued to slip more often and the devaluation phases lasted longer, this all became apparent and started to stand out.

When the Nex hit that bump in the road with his latest victim and I suspected that she had suffered her first silent treatment from him, he was immediately back on the date sites looking for his next victim again, this was despite the Nex having emailed me only a few weeks prior to this to gleefully inform me that he loved his girlfriend more than life itself and could not wait to marry her. She was stepping into my shoes already and unbeknown to her, he was out searching for who he could con next before 'the ink had even dried'. This behaviour, as well as him being on date sites so soon after we had split up just further validated that he is a typical narcissist, always ready to quickly seek out 'his next fix', and further proving that he was most certainly not a victim.

I can honestly say that from maybe 2016 onwards, little by little the Love that I had had for the Nex was slowly and continuously being eroded due to his escalating volatile abusive behaviour towards me. I had reached a point where I had started to resent the abuse, the gaslighting, the stonewalling, the silent treatments, and the sheer abnormality of our relationship. I still did not understand at this point that this narcissistic terminology and behaviour was what I had been and still was experiencing. I started to look at the future and what was to come. When hopefully I would be blessed with grandchildren. How the Nex would no doubt be jealous of them, and if I gave them attention, moan if I spent any time with them or worse still, gave them money. How the silent treatments would 'never' end. How the 'End of the relationship' routine would 'never' cease. How the Nex would 'never' stop manipulating me and controlling me. I still did not have any knowledge on narcissism back in 2016, but I did know that I did not want to live the rest of my life like that. That it was not normal. That I deserved better.

A quote that I read that I think sums this up perfectly for me (author unknown) is,

'I think it all started when I stopped liking him. I still loved him, but I didn't like him anymore… and that's when I knew my mind was preparing my heart for that moment – the one where I would say 'I'm done' and really mean it'.

By this point, I was frequently confiding in my daughter over FaceTime, as she was living in Japan then, about the latest onslaught from the Nex, and she would often ask me when I was finally going to walk away from him. She would say that both her and her brother liked the Nex, but they thought he was a dickhead! She had never learnt the full extent of the abuse I went through until after the split, and when she experienced it first-hand herself. But the trauma bonding is what stopped me leaving, every single time, until that very last time when it did not.

When we think about abuse we must acknowledge that not all abuse is physical. Abuse can be emotional, psychological, sexual, verbal, financial and even consist of neglect. Recognising that you are a victim or were a victim, and that you were victimized is an important step in your recovery.

Recovering and moving forward is essential for your well-being, your health and your peace of mind and is essential to ensure that you can move on. Whether a narcissist is around to see you suffer is inconsequential as long as they know that that you are suffering. I have recently read an article by Bobbi Parish, MA, that says narcissist abuse and trauma survivors are often diagnosed with auto-immune disorders or chronic pain because of the long-term exposure to Cortisol and Adrenaline (fight or flight chemicals) which causes inflammation in our bodies. These chemicals can cause our Immune system to attack itself because it thinks that the inflammation is caused by a disease and so needs to be eradicated. I will probably never know whether my own auto-immune disease that was diagnosed in 2012 was caused by the Nex's treatment of me or whether it was already a pre-existing undiagnosed condition that was then exacerbated by his continual covert abuse and narcissistic behaviour towards me.

I have always in the past considered myself to be a strong person, a person that could handle almost anything. My job 'trained' me to do this with the trauma and chaos that working in an acute environment in a hospital brings. So, I thought I could handle anything that was thrown at me. But, when you become entangled with a narcissist it is only after the relationship is over that you learn that it was your very strength that drew them to you. Then it is this very strength that they then set out to destroy because they view you as threat to them. I had not realised just how much of my strength had been destroyed until I did come out the other side. I know that I am not the same person that I was before I met the Nex. I know that as humans we can and do change as we get older, we get wiser and usually more confident, but I do know for a fact that I will never get back that strong confident woman that I used to be. I am always going to be wary now where any possible future relationship is concerned, looking out for those red-flags and wondering whether a narcissist is lurking. Never being sure if the person is one or not, or if they are just very clever at hiding it like my Nex was. I do not think I will ever lose that 'fear' of being duped and conned again?

Here is another fact for you; Your narcissist 'never' 'had your back!' Not ever. Wrap your head around that thought just for a moment. When you embark on a relationship, you are expecting and hoping that there will be mutual respect, understanding and support from one another. Not with a narcissist. Not in a narcissistic relationship. Not 'ever'.

Quote: 'You can use the worst experiences of your life as the key to your best victories'.

The very fact that the narcissist is no longer in your life, stealing and 'sucking out your soul', means that going forward you can live your life in peace and contentment and hopefully even find and experience happiness again.

A quote by narcissist.sociopath.awareness states,

'When you accept that their love was a lie, you will finally be free'.

The very last thing you will want to do is embark on another relationship that is for sure. Your trust has gone. You are 'damaged'. The abuse you have suffered at the hands of your narcissist has hurt you in a way that you have never been hurt before. Emotional pain is real. You do not see the scars that it leaves but you certainly suffer in the exact same way as you would suffer a physical pain. You must allow yourself time to recover and heal from this. That for me is what was so laughable when the Nex tried to claim that he was the victim, and I was the abuser. Shouted from his lofty perch where his next victim was already sitting beside him.

As I have said before, the Nex had soon moved onto his next victim and relationship after only a matter of weeks. On the one hand, I was so relieved because I naïvely assumed it meant that he would leave me alone but oh boy, how wrong did I get that! He was four-six months into his new relationship when he was actively stalking me. When he monitored my comings and goings via a CCTV, he had set up outside the house, when he cloned my phone, hacked my social media accounts and so on. So, even though they may appear to have moved on to their next victim and their next narcissistic supply, they are still not going to let go of you, their last victim. Another reason why 'No Contact' is so vital to your recovery process. And on the other hand, I felt so sorry for this poor woman who had become his latest victim because she had no idea of the nightmare that was to follow.

I guess for me, the first part of healing was learning all I could about narcissists and narcissism. I had to understand what I had been through, what I was still going through. I had to acknowledge and accept that the entire relationship and marriage had been a lie, that the Nex was incapable of love. That I had been used and abused the entire time of the relationship. That I was never anything more than a convenient 'Meal Ticket' for the Nex. Nothing more than his housekeeper and fuel supply. At times, his behaviour was covert and others, it was overt. The constant walking on eggshells was not normal and is never normal. Being made to endure the silent treatment was not normal and is never normal. This really is a form of emotional and psychological abuse. My gut instinct had been right all along.

Another quote I read that resounded with me is,

'Staying in a relationship just because you love somebody is not worth it. Love is not all you need. Respect is what you need. Reassurance is what you need. Happiness is what you need. Knowing every day, you are their favourite person is what you need. Learn to love yourself instead'.

Maria Consiglio also states,

'It's very important that you understand that narcissistic individuals don't function the same way that we do. That is why they never make sense. Their primary goal is to gain supply (fuel), while our goal is to be loved. We are never on the same page, from 'The get go' we have different agendas. They are trying to control you to get supply. And you are trying to get the love back from them that they showed you during the love-bombing stage. That is why you are so confused as to why they do the things they do. 'Why can't we just work it out and have peace'. 'Why don't you listen to me?' 'Why can't we resolve anything?' 'Why is it that no matter what I do it's never good enough?' 'Why do you have to ruin every holiday?' 'Why can't you just stop, just stop!?' They cannot just stop. They must have power over you. They must control you. They must gain fuel supply from you. Therefore, there is no real solution. I do not think the narcissist wants resolution or even cares about resolution, they just want narcissistic supply. Their resolution is them always being right, and you just 'Get back in line where you belong'.

If you have already managed to get out of your abusive toxic narcissistic relationship, then great! Happy days! (That has reminded me of something I must share with you in a minute…). You have just got your life back. If unfortunately, you are still in the relationship, then having learnt all you can now about narcissists and narcissism you must now decide how to proceed. If you stay for whatever reason, then use all that you have learnt to take back control of your own life, to manage the narcissist as best you can. Use the Grey Rock Method whenever you need to. But most important of all think about whether you really want to stay with your narcissist because it will never ever get any better. If anything, it will continue to get worse. I know if young children are involved there are practicalities involved but in the long run getting out of the relationship is what is best for both you and the children. If you are still currently with your narcissist then it is vital that you set boundaries and most important of all to ensure that you live by them. A narcissist is an expert at crossing all those lines! What is absolutely crucial for you though, is to realise that you deserve so much more than your narcissist can ever give you or will ever give you.

A quote by Anne Bona that sums this up perfectly is, 'When you leave a narcissist it usually gets worse before it gets better… But you'll get through it though and you will be okay'.

So, what did the words 'Happy Day's' just remind me of?

During the period of having to live in the house while it was being sold post-split, 'Oh Happy Days' which is my all-time favourite Gospel tune, happened to have just been played on the radio and I was singing along to it in my office. True to form and just like the typical narcissist that the Nex is, I later heard him telling his latest victim that I had been singing that song. Nothing wrong there hey? Except he had turned it around and made it all about him! He belittled my use of it in song and claimed that it related directly to him, to wind him up, and I heard him throw out a veiled threat too. What was so ridiculous is the fact that an innocent song, a favourite one of mine at that that had just been played on the radio, was now being used by him to further his own vile agenda. I was gobsmacked! I also later learnt that he had changed his ringtone after this from my exorcist tune to a crap version of 'Oh Happy

Days'! I have of course, now included it in the Nex playlist at the end of this book! It has also in turn, been turned into a positive, by providing me with more material for my book!

On another occasion, I heard him telling his latest victim that during his cancer treatment he had had no friends contact him whatsoever during it and how lonely this had made him feel. He went on further to state that this was all my fault as I had probably controlled those friends and made them stay away! Unbelievable and hurtful, considering all the support that I had provided to him! But by no means surprising. A group of friends that he had drank with on a Friday night when I had met him five years earlier had stopped socialising with him three years before he had cancer when he had unceremoniously dumped his labourer and best friend the evening before they were due to build the house for his brother in 2008. He put his labourer out of work overnight! Someone who was also allegedly his best friend. The Nex effectively discarded his friend as he had no more use for him. The others were appalled by the Nex's treatment of him as he was also a friend of theirs. Therefore, I suspect that he was no longer welcome on their Friday nights out because they loyally stood by their friend, his labourer. All I know is that those nights out abruptly ended, and he blamed it on another person who had recently joined the group. Some other friends of his did help during his cancer treatment any way that they could and even gave me a lift to and from the hospital, a 60-mile round trip, on one occasion. I am sure that if they knew now that he was 'dissing' them by 'dissing' me they would be extremely disappointed, especially as two of them are the very same two friends that allegedly colluded with him against me in 2017. Remember what I said before that not one person, not even family or friends can escape the venom and spite that spews out of a narcissists' mouth. I am not sure either that at these times that I could hear him 'slagging' me off loudly, he was doing it deliberately as yet another mind game of his because he knew I could hear him. His bedroom was above my office after all. In fact, about a year into the split my daughter and I discovered a perfectly round hole in my office ceiling. We both concluded that he must have drilled this before he vacated the office to use as a spy hole. We quickly bunged it with chewing gum! It may well have been an innocent hole, but I had never noticed it before and when you are dealing with a narcissist, anything is possible.

Another quote that I have read states,

'Narcissists hate the truth. The fastest way to get rid of one is to hit them with the truth every chance you get. They can put up with it for a short period of time but if you bombard them with the truth constantly, they will run. Truth blows their fake world apart and they aren't having any of it'.

Maybe this is what the Nex was referring to when I overheard him tell his latest victim that he gets bored easily. He gladly informed her that he not only gets bored easily but also fed up with someone quickly, so he just switches off and moves on. This was a major red flag for her and was also a narcissist being truthful for once, albeit unconsciously, but it unfortunately appeared to just go straight over her head. What he was really meaning is that when he is rumbled he runs! He also stated to her that he was no good at relationships. This is also the closest subconsciously that the Nex has ever come to admitting that he IS the problem without him realising that this is what he had just done! He went on further to state that if something excited her it did not excite him, and he also confessed that he found it hard to comfort anyone. I was quite literally sat with my jaw on the floor because I was listening to 'Confessions of a Narcissist'! When I had heard him tell her that he just switches off from people and with him already having told her that I was the narcissist and he was the victim, you could be forgiven for assuming that she would have done her homework about narcissism so the alarm bells would have rung, and she would have realised the truth.

So, how does it feel when you finally make your escape?

Well, when you do split with your narcissist you experience all the emotions that are associated with grief. In a way, you are 'grieving' for your relationship that never was. You feel denial, anger, depression, bargaining and finally acceptance. You deny at first what you have been through. You feel anger at what you have been through. You become depressed when you start to learn and understand what you have been through. As you learn and understand you try to 'bargain' with yourself that surely some of it must have been real. Finally, you accept. You accept all what you have learnt. You accept that you have been deceived, conned and lied to. You accept that your narcissistic partner had never loved you, that you were nothing more than a supply tool for them to use and abuse, and to extract fuel from. You accept that the narcissist will not and cannot ever change. You accept that the only way for you now is to move forward without your narcissist. Onwards and upwards!

And so, you have effectively indeed gone through the stages of grief. You have grieved for a relationship that never really existed. Grieved for a love that was never ever there or felt or reciprocated. You may well go through the stages of grief in different ways and a different order to the norm, it really is not a 'one size fits all'.

@elizabethbarre_coaching states, 'We are not only grieving the loss of a relationship when we leave the narcissist, but also the time we have lost living in the toxic cycle of love-bombings, devaluations and discards'.

I am acutely aware from my research that there are far more horrendous and harrowing stories out there then mine. Where some women felt that their only way out was suicide. Others developed PTSD, had children removed by the courts, and all at the hands of their narcissist. So, my book does by no means trivialise a narcissistic abusive relationship, rather what I am trying to do by telling my story, is show you that the relationship is still toxic when you endure the kind of treatment that I did. It can still cause physical, emotional and psychological damage to the victim, especially if it is endured over a long period of time. I am hoping that this book will help other victims who have been in a similar situation to me and maybe even still do question their current relationship and do not understand why it is not normal. Or maybe they just cannot understand what they are going through because there is nothing tangible for them to see. You realise that your partner does not respond in a normal way but if you are unfamiliar with narcissism you will not recognise what you are experiencing. So, by writing this book and telling my story I am truly hoping that it does help, or has helped, or will help other men and women out there.

A quote I read by SocialMeems states,

'You can only let someone throw so many stones at you before you pick them all up, put them together and build a wall to keep them from doing it again'.

Shannon Thomas wrote for the southlakecounselling.org in 2017 that,

'Survivors of psychological abuse often feel disappointed with themselves for not recognising the abuse sooner.' She goes on to say that this is because it takes time for a victim to see the pattern of harm that is being done and because abusers go to great lengths to hide it by creating confusion. She also says that it takes more than one event to form a pattern. Like picking up pebbles from a beach you can carry many before they become too heavy. If you liken the pebbles to abuse episodes, then it will take a long time for the victim to feel the full weight of harm that the abuse has caused. Therefore, if you were or are dealing with a covert narcissist like my Nex, you will not feel the full effects of the harm that they have caused you until possibly after the relationship is over.

This is particularly true as told by Gail Meyers who states,

'A narcissists weapon of choice is often verbal – slander, lies, playing the victim in flipped tales of who was the victim and who was the abuser, gossip, rage, verbal abuse and intentional infliction of emotional pain. It is a systematic dismantling of another person's relationships, reputation, emotional, physical and spiritual health, life and very soul. Therefore, narcissists are so often called 'Emotional Vampires'.'

An important comment someone made on Quora was that once we are liberated with the truth, in other words we know that they are a narcissist, we then control every aspect of the narcissist. In other words, we control how they treat us. We are no longer their victim. They are no longer our problem. Positive thoughts to hold on to for sure.

Another quote I like (author unknown) states,

'When a narcissist lies and you catch them, they lie again. When a narcissist lies again and again and again, this causes great cognitive dissonance in their victim. This dissonance creates tension and tremendous self-doubt. If you have been lied to again and again, over time you may begin to question your sanity'.

As I have stated earlier, I know for sure that my story is a drop in the ocean compared to what some victims will have gone through, and some are still going through. For me, I am lucky that the control and violence was not anywhere near as bad as others, but this still does not lessen the emotional and psychological impact and damage of being in a relationship with a narcissist. For me, it spanned fourteen years and the very fact that the Nex is a covert narcissist, made it even more insidious and harder to detect.

I have to say that deep down my empathic trait does truly hope that the Nex can find real happiness, even though my rational brain tells me that this is impossible for him to do so. When it was good with us it was really good, he could even make me laugh, but then those memories are now tainted because all I can think of is that they were false moments, fake events, created purely for him to extract his precious fuel from me. Nothing more than periods of

Idealisation. When all was right with the narcissist's world. Just like when he took me to see the northern lights for my 50th birthday. This was top of my bucket list. Now I cannot help but think that it was only done in the grand gesture style that it was, to merely gain more fuel from me, and from others that witnessed his presentation of this to me. That there had always been a hidden agenda behind it, I just never saw it. Such is the way you live your life with a narcissist, and after you have come out of a narcissistic toxic relationship. You simply cannot help but dissect it and question every aspect of it. This trip did take place but was nothing more than just purely one of the brief idealisation periods right before the devaluation ones resumed. Literally weeks before we finally went on this trip of a lifetime, I had experienced yet another stonewalling and silent treatment episode from the Nex. Another 'End of the relationship' episode, where I did question myself as to whether the trip would even happen. On the evening of my 50th birthday, after his grand gesture of presentation of my birthday present, it also happened to be my son's 21st the day before, so we all went out for a big family meal with the rest of my family, but the Nex did not offer to pay one single penny towards this meal, he did not even make an attempt to offer, and did not go anywhere near putting his hand in his pocket but just sat back and let someone else pay for his meal for him, which of course was me!

Despite everything, being an 'Empath' as HG Tudor would call me, I still cannot help but wish for happiness and contentment for the Nex however impossible I know this really is.

The one fact that none of us can ignore and that by now you have learnt, is that a narcissist cannot and will not ever change. They are inherently 'evil'. They will vary in the degree of narcissism that you will experience with them and from them, depending on where they are on the spectrum scale, but the fact will always remain that 'any' relationship with a narcissist is not a healthy one. Remember the passage I wrote by Maria Consiglio at the start of the chapter, 'Why a narcissist cannot change and will not ever change'? This sums it up in a nutshell.

I am not going to lie. I will tell you that I do still find it difficult at times to get beyond the fact that my entire relationship with the Nex was not real. That it was fake, and nothing more than a lie. Just when you think that you have got your head around this fact and accepted it, got passed it, there is just one moment, a memory that flashes into your head of a nice time that you had with your Nex, like my northern lights that I have mentioned above, or of something nice that they did for you, that makes you think just for a split second, 'Was it really all fake?', 'Was any of it real at all?', 'Surely that memory was real?'. And then you must remind yourself that no it was not real. Not in the true sense of the word real. The moment or memory that you have just recalled was a fake moment, a memory of a fake occurrence designed by the narcissist purely to extract fuel from you. It happened because the narc was feeling good about themselves. They were merely 'treating' you to an idealisation moment. It was not a genuine moment, it was not borne out of love for you, it was not borne out of respect for you, it was anything but genuine. And this is difficult, even now, for me to accept. I would say that ninety five percent of the time I accept what I have learnt and what I now know, but just five percent is still of memories of events and happenings that pop into my mind that I still find hard to accept were not real. I think it will take a little while longer to reach that one hundred percent goal of full and final acceptance. But this is okay. It takes as long as it needs to take. There is no right or wrong way in recovering from a narcissistic abusive relationship, especially if your narcissist is a covert one. We are all different. We are all human. The main thing to remember it that you 'will' recover, you 'will' heal, and you 'will' move on.

A quote by narcissistrecovery states,

'It's okay that you don't know how to move on. Start with something easier… Like not going back'.

Another one I like by narcissist.sociopath.awareness and Notsalmon.com states,

'Sometimes walking away is the only option. Not because you want to make someone miss you, or realize they took you for granted. But because you finally respect yourself enough to know that you deserve better'.

But the one I like the most by author unknown and goes,

'I walked away because you were too busy finding faults with me while I was too busy overlooking yours…'

I think that the hardest thing to accept and come to terms with once you know without a doubt that they are a narcissist and that your relationship with them is over, is the fact that these 'Beings' never actually cared for you or loved you. To have put all the years, the tears, the effort, and even your whole existence into what you thought was a true and real relationship and then to discover that it was nothing like that at all but rather that it was all an entire lie and a wicked game that the narcissist had played with your heart, your soul and your life, is devastating. There is no escaping that. As I have said already, looking back, the red flags were all around me, I just did not know that this is what they were and that this is what I was dealing with. Hence the vital importance of recognising and identifying those red-flags and most important of all, listening to your gut-instinct.

I do not hate him, but I do hate what he is, and what he has done to me. My entire life was turned upside down when I met him. His fake promises and his lies sold me a dream, a fairy tale, that I stupidly bought in to and as the title of this book says, 'I Promise I'll make You Happy', was what he repeatedly stated to me before I moved to be with him. But it ended up being anything but happy and certainly turned out to be no fairy tale. I cannot get back those wasted years and who knows what different path my life would have taken if I had never met him. I think about the times I could have had with my parents who had just lived round the corner from me, their birthdays and other special occasions that I missed. How I could have done more for them, kept a closer eye on my beloved father, and I can never get that time back now. I know that I cannot dwell on it because it cannot change anything now and all it will do is just chew me up even more inside, so I have to just accept what has happened and put those fourteen wasted years of my life behind me and try to keep moving forward.

It will 'scar' you for life that is for sure, but you can move forward and wear that scar with pride because you survived! It will not break you. You must not let it break you. You can learn from your experience and ensure that you never fall into a narcissists trap again. Trust me when I say that you will come out of this a stronger person. Remember that the worst thing a narcissist can see or hear about is the fact that you have moved on, recovered from their abuse, and are now content and happy. And that they are nothing more than a very distant bad memory. I have come to terms with it, accepted what the relationship was, and now understand what I experienced. When you come to fully understand narcissism, you acknowledge that the narcissist cannot help who they are, what they are and what they do. They must live like that for the rest of their lives. They will never know true love, real happiness or contentment, but most of all peace. Their life will always be a turbulent one. An emotional chaotic one. Whereas you, their latest victim, you will get past it and move on. Always remember that you were chosen by your narcissist for all the qualities that you possess, that drew them to you, and not because it is a bad reflection of you. Your empathic qualities drew them to you, which in the end says a lot about you as a person and how good 'you' are.

I know without a doubt that if I had remained with my Nex two things would have happened: 1. Any potential final discard by him would have come after both of my parents' deaths and he had benefitted from them. 2. He would have carried on living off me and abusing me.

A quote I like that sums this up (author unknown) is,

'Happiness is lying in bed and realizing that you broke a toxic cycle'.

Another one by E S says, 'It doesn't matter how much you do, what you do, or how well you do it. Nothing will ever be enough to keep a narcissist happy'.

The scariest part about love is that we never really know if it is real or not. Or whether it is true or fake. For any future relationships, we will just have to take a gigantic leap of faith but not without looking out for those red flags first!

What a narcissist fails to realise is that life 'is' real. It is not fake or fiction. Life is what happens to ordinary people day after day, good or bad. It is 'not' their world of make believe.

Remember that you did not fall for the narcissist, but rather you fell for the person that they pretended to be. That underneath that false mask lies the true nasty, evil person that is their real self.

When the Nex found out about my book, his first thought was how much money he could get out of it! Unbelievable right?! Not what the contents of it were, just what he could be entitled to. I took great pleasure in telling him that this was a great big fat zero!

If you have already been discarded by a narcissist, then consider yourself extremely lucky There are people out there who will still not know what a narcissist is, or that their partner is a narcissist, and they will wonder what the hell is happening when the guaranteed devaluation and discard starts. Let us hope that they will rid themselves of this 'Entity' quickly and if not they are fully prepared for the battle that will follow once they do get out.

Because I had suffered the silent punishment treatment for the last seventeen months of my relationship, and because I had realised it would only get worse, I think that I was fortunate when we did finally split up as I was saved from an emotional point of view of the distress that some victims do go through. Don't get me wrong, realising that my relationship had been fake was mind blowing to say the least, but the more I learnt, the easier it became to accept what I had been through and what had taken place. Ultimately, it led to me writing this book. I know that some poor victims are discarded so abruptly that it does quite literally come from out of nowhere for them, and the trauma bond that they have with their narcissist is suddenly severed which does leave them reeling. They simply cannot understand what has happened to them, and why would they, if they did not know that they had been in a narcissistic relationship. That the person they had loved, and did love, was a narcissist. So unfortunately, they do struggle to understand and to break free. This book is also written for them.

The examples I have used throughout this book will hopefully help identify what can be construed as Abuse. Will validate those who are not sure of what they have been through or are experiencing. I know that my experiences are only the tip of the iceberg. I could have shared so many more, but I felt that it was equally important to write about narcissism as well.

I do strongly urge all my readers to log on or sign up to Narcsite.com, HG Tudor's web page where you will find so many more articles and access to his books that will enlighten you even more, and in a far more eloquent way then I have, because of course, they are from a narcissists' point of view. My book merely gives you an insight into narcissism and what it feels like to be in a narcissistic relationship in the hope that any victims out there can identify with them. His articles and books titled 'Knowing the Narcissist', certainly helped me from a recovery aspect and from finally realising and acknowledging that I had been a victim of a narcissist.

Most recently, the Nex was finally honest with me on a couple of occasions when he sent me two emails, one stating that he had never really cared about me, and the other email stating that he had never loved me. If I had received these emails from a normal person, a non-narcissist, I would know that they were lies being told just to hurt me. But because a narcissist had sent them to me I knew full well that I was witnessing a glimpse of the truth and that the Nex was finally stating it how it was and how it had always been, so he was finally telling me the truth, albeit he did not realise this.

As told by Jackson McKenzie in 'Psychopath Free',

'From the moment you left or were left by the narcissist, you were given your first true compliment by the narcissist. You are now the narcissists' worst nightmare, the type of person he or she no longer wants and will want to avoid at all costs and because of this, 'Rejection' never felt so good!'.

A quote I have heard recently in a TV programme but to which I do not know who the author is I felt was a perfect way to end this book,

'We all have two wolves inside of us. One is kind and generous and moves towards the light. The other is violent and angry and brings despair. The two wolves are always fighting, but only one will win. That is the one that you feed'.

I guess the morale of this quote is to never give in or give up. Do not let your narcissist win by leaving you angry all the time. By trying to look for why it happened to you or how. By leaving yourself bitter and twisted by it. Once you have educated yourself on narcissism you can look past what has happened to you. Look to what the future now holds for you. The future that is narcissist free. The future that is light and hopeful, where peace and contentment lie, where even you may find happiness once again. You have just won your biggest battle in life by ridding yourself of that narcissist!

But remember the statistics, that in England and Wales, two women are killed each week by a current or ex-partner according to the Office for National Statistics. Please make sure that you do not become one of those statistics. Leave as soon as you can and as safely as you can using all the support and help that is out there for you. For many narcissistic abuse survivors this will be relatively straightforward, and the smear campaign and mind games will be the only things that you will have to endure. For the few others, please be careful but do not let this prevent you from leaving. What lies ahead, a life narcissist free, is worth the risk.

Another quote that rang true for me from 'lessonslearnedinlife.com' is,

'Maturity is when you have the power to destroy someone who did you wrong, but you just breathe, walk away and let life take care of them.'

Another one, author unknown,
'The toxic monster that you saw at the end… Is who they really are.'
And from an Egyptian philosopher who once said,
'As hard as it is to accept, Life is for the living.'

Another quote again author unknown goes,

'They are just angry because the truth you speak contradicts the lie they live'.

While you are moving on, narcissist abuse free, living the rest of your life as 'you' want to, just remember that karma really is a bitch because while you sit back and wait, you will not need to exact any revenge of any kind because those who hurt you will eventually screw up themselves and if you are lucky enough, God will let you watch.

Because my Nex loves to play the victim he tells everyone that he has lost everything and in a way he is right. He has lost his best source of narcissistic Supply, he has lost his dogsbody, his housekeeper, his meal ticket, his punch-bag and his servant. These are what he has lost and what he means when he says that he has 'lost everything'.

A quote by narcquotes goes,

'A narcissist will always have someone they accuse of ruining their life. It is invariably the same person the narcissist is trying to destroy'.

Another one, author unknown which I particularly like is

'A narcissist will stab you in the back and convince everyone that they are the injured one'.

I have always considered myself to be a strong woman. In my line of work, you needed to be. But since all this, since learning what I have, I do occasionally doubt myself until I re-read a quote by Sonya Parker which says that 'a strong man can handle a strong woman. A weak man will say she has an attitude'.

I want to end this book on a light note with a few amusing jokes that I have read. The first one is by 'someecards' and goes,

'What do a narcissist and a sperm have in common? Both have a one in three million chance of becoming a human being!'

The second one, author unknown, which not only do I find amusing but also promising is,

'Every cell in the human body is destroyed and replaced every seven years. How comforting to know that one day I will have a body that was never touched by you'.

And lastly, again author unknown,

'Did you know that Narcissist spelt backwards is asshole?... Hey if they can make up shit, so can we!'

I think that at the end of the day, if you are still in a relationship with a narcissist, the decision on whether to stay with your narcissist or not, if you have realised that this is what they are, is a very personal one to make. There could be a hundred reasons why you do not want to leave or even cannot leave and that is okay. It is after all, unfair to lambaste all narcissists, especially if they are low down on the spectrum, and you can manage their 'outbursts'. It is unfair to suggest that they are not entitled to have a relationship at all. But the full-blown narcissists, especially a malignant one, are not. They do not have a right to destroy someone's life, to use and abuse someone, and to 'steal' months or years of that person's life away from them. They do not have a right to abuse and manipulate someone so they can have control and power over that person. This is not a relationship. If you are unfortunate to come across such an individual or, are even currently in a relationship with one but do not want to leave it, then arm yourself with as much understanding on the subject as you can. Deny them their fuel by not reacting and go Grey Rock on them when they are trying to devalue you. But most important of all, never forget your own worth and value. Never forget that you are an individual worthy of real love and respect. Worthy of a relationship that is free of abuse, drama and conflict. Always remember to just validate yourself.

It is important that you tell your story, and that you share your story with whoever you can. This will not only bring you validation as to what you have been through but most important of all it will make you realise that you are not alone.

As Angelina Beltran@Warrior against narcissistic abuse states,

'I thought I was alone with what I was going through. But the more I opened up about it, the more victims I saw of narcissistic abuse just like me'.

Another quote that I like (author unknown) is,

'Sometimes no matter how nice you are, how kind you are, how caring you are, how loving you are, it just isn't enough for some people'.

I really hope that you have enjoyed this book. I hope that you have found it to be useful, informative and helpful for you. Most important of all, I hope that you can and do move on from your narcissist, that you find peace, contentment and happiness, and that you truly learn to love yourself because you so very much deserve all of this! If you do go on to another relationship by now you know what to look out for, what to avoid, and realise that there are genuinely nice 'guys and gals' out there who do know how to respect and treat their partner right, and conduct a normal healthy relationship. After all, you only get this one life, what you do with it is up to you, but each and every one of us is 'entitled' to a happy one, to be treated fairly, to be shown respect, but most of all, to be treated equally.

For me, writing this book has not only been a journey of recovery but also a healing and cathartic exercise. It has validated everything that I did go through in my relationship with my narcissist. It has shown me that I was not crazy, that what I experienced was real and that my relationship with the Nex was not normal. Most important of all, it has shown me that I not only deserve far more and far better but that I am also more worthy of it.

Anne Lamott states, 'You own everything that happened to you. Tell your stories. If people wanted you to write warmly about them, they should have behaved better'.

I am also finding myself once again, because of the Nex, packing up my entire life as I know it and moving back to my hometown. I have always believed that everything in life happens for a reason. For this, I do believe that my narcissistic relationship happened so that I could fulfil my dream of writing a book but also so that I could change my career pathway and look to set up support groups for other victims of narcissists and offer counselling, advice, support and help, not only to victims but also to other professional bodies that are still very much ignorant as to what damage narcissistic abuse can and does cause.

I have since come to learn also, that the Nex's latest relationship has ended. Predictably though he was back on those date sites within twenty-four hours, and so the cycle just continues with yet another unsuspecting victim out there who is completely unaware that they are soon to be ensnared by a narcissist.

In every corner of the globe, there is someone currently in a narcissistic abusive and toxic relationship. Not knowing what is happening to them but knowing that it is not right and that it is not normal. For all those out there, I say stay strong and stay true to yourself, you have done nothing wrong, you are not to blame for everything. It 'is' abuse that you are suffering from, it 'is' control and manipulation. It 'is' gaslighting. You are 'not' going crazy. You 'do' deserve better, and you 'do' deserve more.

I have used the term 'victim' throughout this book because that is what you are when you are with a narcissist. But going forward, post narcissist, you no longer are. The fact that you have 'escaped', left, or have been discarded, then makes you anything but a victim. For the very simple fact that you are now free of them. You become the victor, the survivor, and the warrior.

A quote that sums this up perfectly is by 'Mr Never Give Up' and goes,

'I love the ones who are in my life and make it amazing and I thank the ones who left my life and made it even more fantastic!'

A quote by Annie Kaszina from 'recoverfrom emotionalabuse.com' says,

'A narcissist will keep showing you how little you matter to them until you finally get the message and walk away'.

As Maria Consiglio has said, 'You will never feel more alone than when you are in a relationship with a narcissist'.

When I look at the Nex now, I do not see the man I originally fell in love with and went on to marry. What I do see is a stranger, a person I never knew, a person I do not even like. A person I wasted fourteen years of my life on. I can now clearly see the person he only ever truly was but hid so well behind his false self, behind his mask. The narcissist that he really and truly is.

As an unknown author once said,

'There will be very painful moments in your life that will change you. Let them make you stronger, smarter and kinder. But don't you go and become someone that you're not. Cry. Scream if you must. Then straighten out that crown and keep moving'.

I have compiled a playlist on Spotify that I am hoping to produce as a CD to go with this book for you all. If I cannot do this for copyright reasons, then I have added this playlist at the end of this book for you to make for yourself. Even if you do not have Spotify or Apple Tunes, it is worth signing up to a free trial, just long enough for you to compile it. The songs will take you through your journey with your narcissist, the lyrics really 'hitting home' and resonating, and the playlist finishes with upbeat, feel-good, survival songs that I hope will have you all singing from the rooftop and dancing around your home too!

I truly hope that they empower you and strengthen you to know that you have survived your narcissistic relationship. That you have managed to walk away with your head held high and you are now on that journey of recovery.

Enjoy them, just as I do, let the music soothe and heal your heart and your soul.

'And suddenly you know… It is time to start something new and trust the magic of new beginnings'. Author unknown.

'Sometimes in the waves of change we find our true direction'. Also, author unknown.

'Warrior'

'This is the story that I have never told

I gotta get this off my chest to let it go

I need to take back the light inside you stole

You're a criminal and you steal like you're a pro

All the pain and the truth I wear like a battle wound

So ashamed, so confused I was broken and bruised

NOW I'M A WARRIOR'.

By Demi Lovato

I thought the opening lines of this song that does feature on the Nex Playlist was perfect to draw this book to a close and now I have told my story and truly hope that all of you can too. Be brave, go forward and never ever look back.

I finally managed to walk away from my narcissistic abusive relationship and so can you.

A fitting end to this book is a quote by Angelina Bettran which I found, that depicts the cover on the back of this book,

'If anyone asked me what is hell? I would answer them "Being involved with a narcissist".'

I will end this book with one final quote by Madalyn Beck,

'Start over, my darling. Be brave enough to find the life you want and be courageous enough to chase it. Then start over and love yourself the way you were always meant to'.

There is only one word to sum that up and that is 'Amen'.

Nex Play List

1. 'Broken Strings' by James Morrison and Nelly Furtado
2. 'Lose You to Love Me' by Selena Gomez
3. 'Somebody That I Used to Know' by Gotye
4. 'Rise Up' by Andra Day
5. 'Jar of Hearts' by Christina Perri
6. 'Praying' by Kesha
7. 'Warrior' by Demi Lovato
8. 'I Can See Clearly Now' by Johnny Nash
9. 'Roar' by Katy Perry
10. 'Hold On' by Wilson Philips
11. 'Free' by Ultra Nate
12. 'I'm Still Standing' by Elton John
13. 'I will Survive' by Gloria Gaynor
14. 'Stronger' by Kelly Clarkson
15. 'This is Me' by Keala Settle
16. 'Firework' by Katy Perry
17. 'The Climb' by Miley Cyrus
18. 'Ain't No Stopping Us Now' by McFadden & Whitehead
19. 'Oh, Happy Day' by The Edward Hawkins Singers
20. 'Unwritten' by Natasha Bedingfield
21. 'It's My Life' by Bon Jovi
22. 'Step by Step' by Whitney Houston
23. 'Come and Get Your Love' by Redbone
24. 'Ain't No mountain High Enough' by Marvin Gaye and Tammi Terrell

Any order you like is good. This was just my preferred order because it takes me through the journey that led me to write this book. I especially love the last two songs to finish with after recently seeing number 21 as a heart-warming European Christmas TV Advert. And of course, it is featured in the first 'Guardians of the Galaxy' movies. I love Groot! Number 22 reminds me that true love, honest love, is possible and is out there somewhere. It also tells me that it is okay to move on, to heal and to hope that you CAN find Love once more, this time a Love that is real!

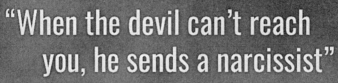

"When the devil can't reach you, he sends a narcissist"
- *Romario*

Cover by Craig Cumberton